BROADCAST WRITING AS A LIBERAL ART

BROADCAST WRITING AS A LIBERAL ART

Seth Finn
University of North Carolina at Chapel Hill

PRENTICE HALL, Englewood Cliffs, New Jersey 07632

Library of Congress Cataloging-in-Publication Data

Finn, Seth.
  Broadcast writing as a liberal art / Seth Finn.
     p.   cm.
  Includes bibliographical references and index.
  ISBN 0-13-084609-0
  1. Broadcasting--Authorship.   I. Title.
  PN1992.7.F56 1991
  808'.066791--dc20
                                                     90-7984
                                                        CIP

Editorial/production supervision and
  interior design: Michael R. Steinberg
Cover design: Lundgren Graphics, Ltd.
Prepress buyer: Debra Kesar
Manufacturing buyer: Mary Ann Gloriande
Acquisitions editor: Steve Dalphin

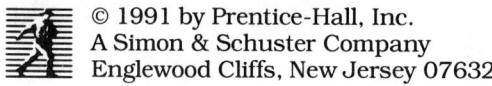 © 1991 by Prentice-Hall, Inc.
A Simon & Schuster Company
Englewood Cliffs, New Jersey 07632

*All rights reserved. No part of this book may be
reproduced, in any form or by any means,
without permission in writing from the publisher.*

Printed in the United States of America

10 9 8 7 6 5 4 3 2 1

ISBN 0-13-084609-0

PRENTICE-HALL INTERNATIONAL (UK) LIMITED, *London*
PRENTICE-HALL OF AUSTRALIA PTY. LIMITED, *Sydney*
PRENTICE-HALL CANADA INC., *Toronto*
PRENTICE-HALL HISPANOAMERICANA, S.A., *Mexico*
PRENTICE-HALL OF INDIA PRIVATE LIMITED, *New Delhi*
PRENTICE-HALL OF JAPAN, INC., *Tokyo*
SIMON & SCHUSTER ASIA PTE. LTD., *Singapore*
EDITORA PRENTICE-HALL DO BRASIL, LTDA., *Rio de Janeiro*

For Olja, Sasha, and Sonja

Contents

PREFACE   xi

1 ELEMENTS OF BROADCAST STYLE   1

The Communication System   3
Unpredictability and Redundancy   9
The Elements of Style   10
English Composition and Broadcast Writing   14
Additional Readings   17

2 BROADCAST SCRIPT FORMATS   19

Control Rooms and Studios   21
Radio Script Formats   22
Television Script Formats   28
Additional Readings   39

3 RADIO COMMERCIALS AND PUBLIC SERVICE ANNOUNCEMENTS — 41

- Exposure and Response 42
- Writing for Radio 45
- Public Service Announcements 46
- Persuasion and Ethics 56
- Scriptwriting Assignment 58
- Additional Readings 58

4 BROADCAST INTERVIEWS — 61

- Real-Time and Edited Interviews 62
- Technical Considerations in Editing 64
- An Interview with Candidate Quayle 65
- Selecting Versus Condensing 70
- Interviews as Pseudo-events 76
- Scriptwriting Assignment 77
- Additional Readings 78

5 RADIO NEWS — 79

- News Value and Information Processing 79
- The 30-Second Reader 82
- Getting the Lead Right 83
- Identifying the Source 85
- Timeliness 86
- An Abbreviated Stylebook 87
- Writing the Broadcast Version 89
- Scriptwriting Assignment 93
- Additional Readings 94

6 TELEVISION NEWS — 95

- News Value of Videotape 96
- Judging Video Information 98
- Matching Sight and Sound 99
- Piecing Together Video and Audio 100
- Cycle of Television News 110
- A Postscript on Documentary Production 114

Scriptwriting Assignment   *119*
Additional Readings   *120*

7 POLITICAL COMMERCIALS   **121**

Hammer-It-Home for Eisenhower   *122*
Deep Sell for Johnson   *123*
Types and Functions of Political Spots   *125*
Mechanics of Campaign Spots   *128*
Conveying Visual Ideas with Storyboards   *132*
Scriptwriting and Storyboard Assignment   *136*
Additional Readings   *137*

8 SITUATION COMEDIES   **139**

Characterization, Setting, and Plot   *140*
Plot and Character: A Sitcom Example   *142*
Sources of Comedy   *149*
Comedy Versus Tragedy   *151*
Scriptwriting Assignment   *152*
Additional Readings   *153*

9 SCREEN ADAPTATIONS   **155**

Selecting Material for Adaptation   *156*
"The Blue Hotel"   *157*
Elements of Adaptation   *160*
Writing the Treatment   *163*
From Story Idea to Treatment   *169*
Scriptwriting Assignment   *170*
Additional Readings   *171*

10 MASTER SCENE SCRIPTS   **173**

Master Scene Format   *174*
Basic Rules   *179*
Adapting Dialogue   *180*
Dramatic Structure   *182*
Problem Stories   *185*
A Note on Broadcast Violence   *187*

Scriptwriting Assignment   *190*
Additional Readings   *190*

11 Epilogue   **193**

Photo Credits   **198**

Index   **200**

Preface

The notion that broadcast writing has a role to play in a liberal arts education is based on a distinction between the liberal and the servile arts that has existed ever since Greek philosophers began debating the qualities of an ideal education. Broadly speaking, the liberal arts are those cultural and civic activities that a free individual must learn in order to participate fully in his or her society. The servile arts are the repetitive, unthinking tasks that are assigned only to slaves. Simply put, the impact of broadcast programming in modern society is too great for free individuals to remain ignorant of the processes that underlie its production, and control of its content is too critical to be regarded a servile task.

Liberal studies—those studies appropriate for the education of free people—have always changed with the times. The Greeks and Romans divided liberal studies into seven arts. The trivium included grammar, logic, and rhetoric. The quadrivium brought together the sciences: arithmetic, geometry, music, and astronomy. In the Middle Ages, St. Thomas Aquinas reconciled Aristotelian philosophy with Christian doctrine by crowning the liberal arts with the study of theology. The Renaissance brought a new emphasis. The study of classical literature became the focus of a liberal education.

The experience of American universities has been equally diverse. In the early 19th century, when the entire catalogue for the University of North Carolina could be printed on a single sheet of paper, surveying, mineralogy, and navigation were included in its plan of liberal studies, but not English literature. Incorporating broadcast writing into the liberal arts curriculum today is one way to empower students to act as knowledgeable consumers of broadcast programming and to instill future professionals with an allegiance to educational ideals and public service. These goals are not new to thoughtful broadcast educators and professionals, but by articulating these social values in the title and the content of this text we can assure that the ends of broadcast writing are not obscured by its means.

ORGANIZATION OF THE TEXT

To a great degree, the writing of this text is modeled after a book published by Hyatt Waggoner the year after I was graduated from Brown University. As an American literature student, I enrolled in an upper-level American poetry course taught by Waggoner, who was then well known as a Faulkner scholar. This was the tenth and last year Waggoner was teaching the course, because, as Waggoner announced to the class, he was about to complete his manuscript, *American Poets: From the Puritans to the Present*. Waggoner's plan seemed eminently reasonable to me then, and it came to mind after I completed my tenth semester teaching an introductory broadcast writing course. By Waggoner's standards, a text was in order. Waggoner's impact may be reflected in one other aspect of this text—my penchant for intensive readings of broadcast scripts, which, like poems, may be rather brief compositions.

This text is divided into 10 chapters devoted to both nonfictional and fictional writing. The first two chapters deal with the elements of broadcast style and five standard broadcast formats. Beginning with Chapter 3, the text presents eight in-depth discussions that correspond to eight scriptwriting assignments. The chapters focus first on journalistic and persuasive writing: radio public service announcements (PSAs), broadcast interviews, radio news, TV news, and TV political spots. Then we move on to dramatic programming: situation comedies, short story adaptations, and master scene scripts.

The assignments for the last two chapters comprise a two-step final project. The students must adapt a short story to the screen, writing first a treatment and then a master scene script. Students without experience in dramatic writing find the assignment daunting but soon learn that it is both manageable and rewarding. Because the short story author has already shouldered the formidable task of creating compelling characters and an intriguing plot, students can employ their creative energies solving the problems of transforming words into images.

The course must move at a challenging pace for students to complete all eight assignments in a 15-week semester, but the assignments are exactly those I require of my own students. The Greek orator Isocrates once argued that "the proper use of language is the surest index of sound understanding." I agree. The broadcast scripts that students write are the most accurate measure of how well they understand the processes by which broadcast programming is produced.

For career-minded students, these assignments have a critical professional dimension as well. Even though this is an introductory text, the first six assignments prepare students for exactly the types of writing assignments they are likely to confront as interns at radio and television stations. The better they master these fundamental broadcast writing assignments the more likely they are to receive sympathetic instruction from professionals on the job. By the same token, broadcast executives in charge of news, public affairs, or creative services departments could well select appropriate assignments from this text to test whether a beginning student is ready to benefit from an internship in their organization.

There are two other aspects of the text worth mentioning. Instructors teaching on a 10-week quarter system may have to adopt a more selective sequence of written assignments. To reserve time for the final project, they may want students to read certain chapters but not complete the assignments, depending on the focus of their department's curriculum. In departments that emphasize journalistic writing, instructors may want their students to opt for a nonfiction final project. To meet this need, I have extended the Television News chapter with a postscript on broadcast documentaries. One section describes procedures for organizing audio materials and writing a radio documentary. Thus, it provides the outline for an alternative final project—a short radio documentary script based on original interviews recorded by the student. In a 15-week semester course, it is tempting to let students choose one option or the other. But by doing so, you effectively cut in half the class time available for helping them prepare for either choice.

Finally, let me note that one purpose of a liberal education is to show how knowledge is interrelated. Every chapter in this book is aimed at developing new connections, not pruning them. Each chapter marks just the beginning of an exploration. No chapter is complete. Thus, at the end of each chapter, I have provided an annotated list of further readings, sound recordings and videotapes. They can be used to enrich classroom discussions, provide additional examples, or satisfy personal curiosity. Like the chapters themselves, though, these lists remain incomplete. As I revise this text, I look forward to your suggestions for new materials and connections or even a competing vision of broadcast writing as a liberal art.

ACKNOWLEDGMENTS

When I used to produce a nightly television news program, it was common practice to thank the technical staff in the control room and colleagues in the newsroom who had made special contributions to the program's success. In writing a textbook, however, sources of support and inspiration are so widespread that it is difficult to know where to begin. Like Tristam Shandy, I am tempted to begin at my conception, thanking my parents and Dr. Spar who oversaw my Caesarean birth.

My editorial instincts tell me, however, to keep the list short, because it is better to offend a few friends than bore potential readers. My friends will forgive me. Thus, here are my minimal acknowledgments. To John Bittner and Hap Kindem, who, as chairs of my department, gave me the time, resources, and encouragement to write this book. To my colleagues, Anne Johnston, David Haynes, and John Freeman, whose expertise shaped the sections on political ads, storyboarding, and writing dramatic treatments. In addition, I must acknowledge numerous graduate assistants, who shared the burden of teaching and critiquing, but also the delight of witnessing unexpectedly good student writing. Student scripts were contributed by James Bolen, David Venable, and Sudi Dannenberg. Special appreciation also to Gary Mauney for graciously permitting me to reprint a speech that he knew I would pick to pieces.

Beyond the university, I wish to acknowledge Charles Kuralt, Nina Totenberg, Bob Elliot, Glenn Mitchell, and Linda Yee, writers and reporters whom I admire, who freely granted permission to publish substantial portions of their work. Special thanks are also due to Saul Shorr and David Price for use of their political spot and Bill Allen of MTM Enterprises who modified corporate practice to permit reprinting of dialogue from the "Newhart" show. Finally, I wish to thank Steve Dalphin and Michael Steinberg at Prentice Hall, Professor Carolyn Matalene of the University of South Carolina, Professor Henry Breitrose of Stanford University, and an anonymous reviewer at Syracuse University, all of whom faithfully supported my personal vision for a broadcast writing textbook that suits a liberal arts curriculum.

Seth Finn

1

Elements of Broadcast Style

All too often, students are attracted to broadcast writing as an area of study because they believe that they will be able to express themselves more imaginatively if they could only escape the rigorous formalisms of the printed word. Nothing could be farther from the truth. The creation of a broadcast program is a complex and costly enterprise, and the production of sights and sounds comes only near the end of a long and arduous process. Long before the director orders, "Roll tape!" or "Action!" someone has articulated an idea that has been defined and developed using a remarkably inexpensive medium: the printed word. What St. John said of Biblical creation is no less true of every broadcast production: "In the beginning was the word."

The failure of students to appreciate the role of written communication in broadcast production is not surprising. After all, they are often attracted to the field as a result of their experiences as audience members. But, while the creators of broadcast programming make every effort to spare their audiences the degree of mental effort associated with print, there is no free lunch. If broadcast programming is effortless to digest, that is because it is so carefully prepared. And that care extends to both the language to be heard by the audience and the technical instructions for the production itself. Thus, every participant in the production process comes to understand the value of a few well-chosen words, whether they report a fact, set a scene, or sell a product.

When students gain entry into a broadcast organization, they soon come to recognize the importance of good writing. But, in beginning courses, they are often impatient with the tedious corrections that their instructors insist on within the classroom environment. This impatience might be dissipated, however, if they better appreciated the fundamental role of language and literature in all mass media. Seeing the big picture will not automatically make them better writers, but it may help them understand the contribution their literary knowledge and skill can make to the broadcast productions they take part in.

One of the best hidden secrets of the broadcast industry is the degree to which it is shaped by individuals who are voracious readers. How can this be? In all probability our misperceptions about the nature of broadcasting and the people who create programming stem from the tendency to draw overly sharp distinctions between broadcasting as a new medium and print as an old one. In the long-run—humankind's 50,000 year history—the 500 years from the first movable-type printing press to the diffusion of television technology is a short clip. Even more important to remember is that print was not a mass medium until the latter half of the 19th century, when universal literacy became a social goal and cheap paper and high-speed printing presses made the newspaper and pulp fiction available to all.

From then on, each generation witnessed the birth of yet another mass medium. After print came film, then radio, and finally television. Because they all burst on the scene in relative short order, it is often more enlightening to look at their similarities rather than their differences, especially from the viewpoint of the audience they are meant to serve.

More than one group of mass communication researchers has come to recognize that the way people use the mass media suggests how the media are truly related. One design is the circumplex illustrated below.

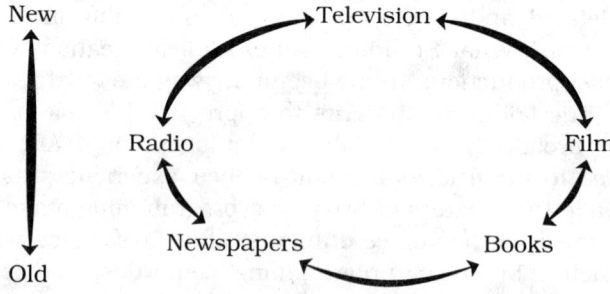

To some extent, the diagram confirms precisely the differences between the mass media that we generally acknowledge. Clearly, we can separate the upper and lower halves of the diagram to emphasize the conflict between modern electronic and traditional print media. But, if radio, television, and film resemble each other much more than they resemble newspapers and books, that is only a difference in form. The broadcast writer must be equally concerned with content.

At the content level, we begin to recognize the inherent flow of ideas within this circumplex. Neighboring media often unabashedly share very similar types of content, providing the audience two different means to acquire the same material. Both newspapers and radio, for instance, devote a considerable portion of their resources to the presentation of timely information: news, sports, weather, and advertising. And, while most radio stations now rely heavily on recorded music as a source of programming for their audiences, modern newspapers meet this same demand for entertainment with a wide assortment of canned (or syndicated) features from crosswords and comics to astrology and advice.

Of course, television has been a voracious consumer of the content of technologically similar media. Game shows, soap operas, and situation comedies are just a few categories of entertainment programming that television took over from radio in the 1950s. On the reality side, news, sports, weather, and talk shows were absorbed. Then it was up to film to fill the remaining holes in the television schedule. After some early hesitation, Hollywood moguls joined television rather than fight it. Their studios turned out action-adventure series and sitcoms. Similarly, the feature-length motion picture was eventually shared among theater distribution channels, over-the-air broadcast, and now cable television.

The most telling content relationship, however, may be characterized by the proverbial question of popular critics: Which was better, the movie of the book? The very question confirms the fact that printed fiction provides an immense reservoir of material for dramatic films and television, while newspaper accounts and nonfiction books continually replenish the stock of new ideas for reality-based programming. That's not to say that the flow only moves in one direction. Print journalists report events and interviews first seen on television, and blockbuster films spawn books or engender new editions of books long forgotten.

But, in the end, creative people in television cannot afford to overlook the rich stream of ideas and stories that first find their way into print. "M*A*S*H" was a book before it was a film before it was a television sitcom. Similarly, reporters and commentators know they will learn little that is new or trend setting if they depend solely on the electronic mass media. Everyone in the broadcast industry appreciates the talents of a skilled writer precisely because they are so dependent on the print media for fresh ideas and new material.

THE COMMUNICATION SYSTEM

One of the results of the rapid development of new forms of mass communication in the twentieth century has been an intense interest in the impact of these new technologies. An early mass media researcher, Harold Laswell, put the question this way: "Who says What to Whom with What effect?" For the writer, however, there is an even more basic question to be asked: "How?" How do people communicate?

Interestingly, one of the best answers came from a mathematician, Claude Shannon, who worked at Bell Laboratories in the 1940s. Shannon, who was concerned with the most efficient means of conveying a message through a telephone cable, came up with a rather astounding conception of what communication was all about. What Shannon realized was that the messages that people communicate are never really sent to one another. What we send with soundwaves, light beams, electricity, graphite on paper, or any other physical means are signals that represent messages. If communication is to take place, then the source and the destination must first agree on a set of signals that are matched to a set of messages they might want to communicate. Thus, "to send a message," the source sends a signal to the destination that tells the destination which among a set of possible messages is to be selected. Shannon's famous diagram of a general communication system is reproduced below.

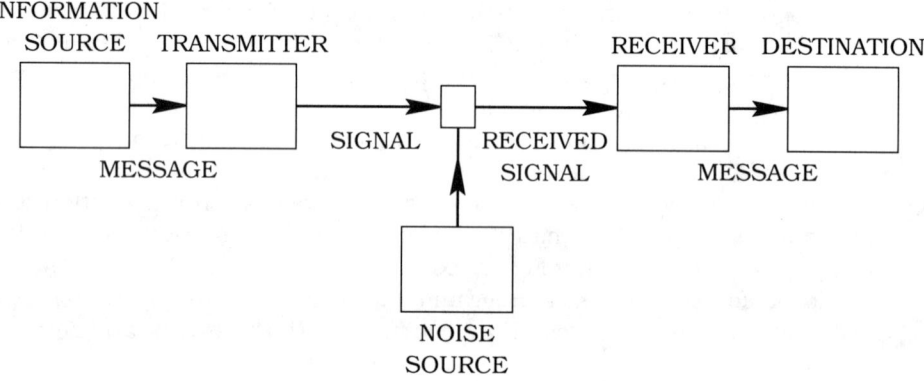

Note how the "message" that appears on the left side of his model must first be encoded as (or be matched to) a prearranged signal. That's what the transmitter does. The signal then travels through a communication channel to a receiver that decodes the signal into (or matches it to) a corresponding message.

In everyday conversation, the communication channel is the air. One person (the source) thinks up a message, encodes it as sound waves, which another person (the destination) decodes by matching the nerve impulses from the eardrum to memories in the brain. The technical nexus of the communication system can be repeated many times over. Thus, in broadcast communication the sound waves strike a microphone, not an eardrum. The microphone recodes sound waves as electrical impulses that are transmitted as electromagnetic waves that are captured by a radio that converts them back into sound waves through a speaker. At that point, the air again becomes the transmission channel. Physical interference—static from a thunderstorm or chatter at a cocktail party—can distort the signal and create errors in decoding. But, ultimately, what Shannon's model reveals to us is that messages stay put at the source and destination.

This admittedly curious notion of the communication process may seem far removed from the skills involved in broadcast writing. But it provides a remarkably important insight. Words are simply signals that conjure up meanings in the minds of the audience. Accordingly, a broadcast writer must have a good sense of the messages already stored in the minds of the audience, if he or she is to assemble a series of signals that will effectively inform or entertain the viewing or listening public.

Thus, it is no small part of the broadcast writer's job to know what the audience knows. For starters, I want you to consider a very straightforward radio commentary that illustrates this point. To heighten its impact, the writer exploits very specific, but widely diffused knowledge in the minds of his audience. The commentator is Glenn Mitchell, whose syndicated features have been broadcast on National Public Radio.

> A note from the newspaper read verbatim: "Parents often object to the violence and bad influence of television. Pamylle Greinke objected to the bad influence of *Jack and the Beanstalk*. 'It is bankrupt in terms of morality,' said Greinke, 29, who lives in Peconic, New York. 'Jack is rewarded for stealing.'"
>
> Greinke therefore rewrote the fairy tale. Her book, *Jacqueline & the Beanstalk* contains no goose, no golden egg, no death of a giant. Instead, Jacqueline is an orphan, who lives with her short-tempered, hard-drinking Uncle Ralph. The girl meets an old woman in her dreams and is told to climb up the beanstalk. At the top, she sees a giantess and her child and falls in love with the toys and clothes she sees. The old woman of her dreams tells her to steal whatever she likes, but Jacqueline refuses. The woman then tells her the purpose of her adventure was to inspire her to work for what she wants. The moral is that Jacqueline and all people have within themselves the ability to achieve their dreams.
>
> Well, swell. But if that's the tack people want to take, why stop there? Yes, yes, there are more important things to get worried about. But if we're going to do a job, we might as well do it right. Coming up next from the Unabridged police blotter—"The Weekend Report."
>
> Authorities booked two youths for the murder of an elderly woman at her remote forest cottage. Detectives say the pair lured the woman, who was almost blind, near her large oven, and pushed her in, where she burned to death. Because the case involved juveniles, their names were not released. Attorneys for the pair, who said they are brother and sister, reportedly will tell the court that their clients will plead self-defense.
>
> Crimes against property department reported a case of breaking and entering, petty theft and vandalism at the home of the Bear family. Minor theft of food seemed to be the extent of the goods taken, although the family reported the bedroom and living room had both been searched. So far police report no leads, although a young blonde girl was reported loitering

6 *Chapter 1 Elements of Broadcast Style*

in the neighborhood about the same time the break-in would have occurred.

Also over the weekend, county game officials arrested a hunter for shooting a wolf without a hunting license. To further complicate the hunter's plight, the wolf is of course on the endangered species list. The hunter's companion, a female minor identified only as Red was released after questioning. The district attorney's office said the case would be handled as a misdemeanor, although animal rights groups have already promised to make the case a public forum to promote more humane methods of animal control.

Vice officers raided a country establishment notorious as the home of a gang of seven unemployed characters of unsavory reputation. Acting on a tip, they found a woman on the premises who performed a number of unknown services for the gang. The woman, single and in her late teens, was not identified by name, but a nickname —"Snow"— has led investigators to turn the case over to narcotics authorities, who had had the establishment staked out for some time.

Finally, metropolitan police had their hands full yesterday afternoon when a large crowd tied up traffic on a busy downtown street to watch a man casually saunter down the boulevard absolutely naked. By the time the police arrived, the crowd was almost unmanageable. The man was arrested and quickly hustled into a squad car, taken to central police headquarters, and booked. Only then did police learn the man was a visiting dignitary...an emperor, who did not, he claimed, realize he was violating any laws. State Department officials quickly secured the man's release.

And what the D-A's office is going to make of Pinocchio is anybody's guess. Leave him alone. I'm Glenn Mitchell.

What this commentary anticipates is the audience's intimate knowledge of six classic fairy tales. In five cases, the titles—"Hansel and Gretel," "Goldilocks and the Three Bears," "Little Red Riding Hood," "Snow White and the Seven Dwarfs," and "The Emperor's New Clothes"—need never be mentioned. Once Mitchell establishes the context of his commentary by summarizing the plot of *Jacqueline & the Beanstalk*, he can conjure up the other fairy tales with a few key words that identify the central features of each story. At the same time, he fashions a series of satirical narratives by adapting the facts of the fairy tales to the form and content of contemporary broadcast news reporting. But before Mitchell can recombine these elements into a humorous commentary, all the necessary components must be in place in the minds of the audience. His sensitivity to what the audience knows permits Mitchell to zip through each of his adaptations in half the time it took to describe *Jacqueline & the Beanstalk*, which, because it was unknown to the audience, required a more extensive explanation.

This emphasis on efficiency and economy in broadcast writing generates parallels with a second major aspect of Shannon's theory of communication. While the American philosopher Charles Peirce and the Swiss linguist Ferdinand de Saussure both devoted immense intellectual effort to explain how human language permits communication through the use of signs and symbols—their works formed the basis for the contemporary study of semiotics—it was Shannon who seized on the dissociation between messages and the signs that represent them to develop a mathematical formula to measure the relative amount of information each message was worth. Shannon was among the first to reason that if messages themselves are not transmitted, but only the signals that represent them, then the amount of information contained in a message is directly related to the probability that the destination could anticipate the specific signal it received.

To understand Shannon's theory fully, we must at least temporarily focus on the technical nexus in his communication system. Remember that communication is possible only if a similar set of messages matched to a corresponding set of signals is lodged in the memory of the source and destination at the outset. To make communication possible, humans have developed signal systems—what we often call codes—that permit one person to indicate to another person what he or she is thinking now. Simple codes are made up of a finite set of signals, each of which represents a shared meaning.

When Paul Revere specified that one lantern in the steeple of Boston's North Church meant that the British were coming by land and that two meant they were coming by sea, he developed a simple binary code like the one that underlies today's electronic computers. More complex codes—such as human language—are supplemented with a set of agreed on rules that permits the source to recombine a limited number of signals into a vast array of possible patterns that correspond, in turn, to an enormous number of compound messages. Some of these recombinant messages, in fact, have never been communicated before. Perhaps equally important, some patterns of signals will never be transmitted, because the recombinant messages that they conjure up are meaningless to either the source, the destination, or both.

Technically, then, as Shannon realized, communication involves the transmission of a finite set of signals that correspond to a finite set of messages. While the meanings of these messages cannot be measured, the amount of information that a message contains is directly related to how many other possible messages the source could have indicated through the signaling system. In the simplest case, we assume that all messages are equally probable.

In Paul Revere's case, if there were a 50-50 chance that the British were coming by land or by sea, then the two possible signals from Boston's North Church would convey an equal amount of information. But if Paul had been 80 percent sure that the British were coming by land, then the two-lantern signal indicating that they were coming by sea (a 20 percent chance) would have provided much more information to Paul than the one lantern signal that only confirmed his very strong expectation. Thus, it is possible to estimate the relative amount of information conveyed by a signal on the basis of the predictability of the message to which it corresponds. Coming by land was 80 percent predictable; coming by sea was 20 percent predictable. In this particular context, the two-lantern signal would have conveyed four times the amount of information that the one-lantern signal did.

Shannon's mathematical formulations are much more sophisticated than the measurement system I've adopted for this example, but both are based on the same theoretical insight into the relationship between how informative a message is and its relative predictability. Obviously, then, a writer is going to have more impact on the audience if the words he or she chooses are on the whole more unpredictable than not. If the audience could have guessed what you were going to say, why say it?

Shannon's attention to coding systems provides additional insights for the broadcast writer. As I have mentioned, more complex codes not only include a set of signals but also a set of agreed on rules specifying how signals can be recombined to indicate unique messages. One code we're all familiar with is the spelling system for written English. Although we rarely think about specific spelling rules, we all recognize that certain combinations of letters are likely in English and others are not. Suppose you were a telegraph operator in the Old West or even playing a game of hangman with a friend. If the letter "q" appeared in a sequence, then you would be a 100 percent certain that the letter "u" would follow. Similarly, you can probably think of numerous words in which the letter "t" precedes an "h," but you might have to search your memory for a moment to name a word in which "h" precedes "t." Shannon calls this characteristic of codes that makes some combinations of signals more predictable than others redundancy. And he goes on to prove in his theory that any message can be coded with sufficient redundancy to assure that it is accurately conveyed to the destination, despite noise in the transmission channel.

While the predictable "u" that follows "q" may seem to be a waste of space on the printed page, imagine once again that you are a telegraph operator on a stormy night. In international Morse code the difference between the words "kick" and "qick" ("quick" without the "u") is a single dash. If static garbles the "q," the "u" helps the telegraph operator correct the error in transmission. Thus, a certain degree of predictability—or redundancy—in the coding system helps assure accuracy in communication.

Shannon ran some experiments, in fact, to see how well a person can predict the next letter in an English sentence given all the letters that precede it. His conclusion was that, on average, written English is about 50 percent redundant, a conclusion that you'll often see in books on communication theory but without reference to its basis as an estimate of the degree of redundancy in English spelling only. Redundancy in English can be estimated subjectively on multiple levels, as we shall see.

Finally, there is one other technical term that Shannon introduces in his theory that is useful to the broadcast writer. The term is equivocation. Even if a signal is accurately received at the destination, there can still be some ambiguity about its correspondence to a particular message. For instance, the meaning of the word "bank" may not be clear to the audience until the context of a river or a financial institution is specified. Even if all noise in the channel is eliminated or overcome by redundant coding, the audience can still misconstrue messages due to equivocation. Humor, of course, is often dependent on equivocation. Where do fish go to borrow money? To the loan shark. (You probably thought they head for the river bank.)

UNPREDICTABILITY AND REDUNDANCY

If you have been paying careful attention to this discussion, you may well be perplexed by a built-in paradox in any communication system. To transmit signals accurately, you must take advantage of redundancies in language and meet the expectations of the destination. But to attract attention and be informative, your message must be unpredictable. With broadcast writing in particular, scripts must be written in a simple style appropriate for aural comprehension but convey a high degree of information in a limited time frame. One way broadcast writers achieve this goal is by fashioning scripts that rely on mental frameworks already available in the minds of their audiences. Even more precisely, writers learn to exploit the human mind's capacity to decode signals simultaneously at multiple levels, even within a single channel. When we process language, we pay attention to syntax as well as semantics. Unpredictability at one level can be balanced by redundancy at another.

Consider, for instance, this excerpt from Edward R. Murrow's famous broadcast as American forces liberated the Nazi concentration camp at Buchenwald at the end of World War II. Earlier we discussed how redundancy in English language spelling might be estimated by guessing missing letters. In this excerpt, I have deleted every fifth word so that we can estimate the redundancy at the lexical level. This sort of testing is called cloze procedure. It is a way of rating the comprehensibility of English prose. The easier it is for test readers to guess the exact missing words, the easier the passage should be to understand because of its greater redundancy. Try to replace the deleted words yourself.

AS I WALKED DOWN _____(1)_____ THE END OF THE _____(2)_____ , THERE WAS APPLAUSE FROM _____(3)_____ MEN TOO WEAK TO _____(4)_____ OUT OF BED. IT _____(5)_____ LIKE THE HAND-CLAPPING OF _____(6)_____ . AS WE WALKED OUT _____(7)_____ THE COURTYARD, A MAN _____(8)_____ DEAD.

What is critical here is a distinction that psycholinguists make between function words and content words. Function words are the prepositions, pronouns, articles, helping verbs, conjunctions, and simple adverbs that provide the surface structure of language, the syntactic glue for organizing thoughts. Not surprisingly, they are the shortest and most frequently used words in English. Content words are the nouns, verbs, adjectives, and adverbs that carry the meaning of the message.

The key element in making a script informative is its content words. When the writer truly conveys new information to the audience, the content words are difficult to predict. On the other hand, good writers try to fashion messages that are almost effortless to decode. Thus, the function words, whose predictability reflects the relative complexity of the syntactic structure of the message, must be easy to guess.

This excerpt is a good example of that. The words relatively easy to guess are the function words (1, 3, and 7): "to," "the," and "into." By contrast, the words that truly grab our attention and generate surprise are the content words (2, 4, 5, 6, and 8): "barracks," "get," "sounded," "babies," and "fell." Interestingly, Murrow has been successful here because he evokes a familiar mental picture of a wartime prison camp but shocks us with unexpected details. Of course, writers can also engage their audiences by presenting familiar content in unexpected formats. Such is the case with an author such as James Joyce or a poet such as E.E. Cummings. But such a strategy—carried to the extreme—puts a burden on the audience that is rarely countenanced in broadcast writing.

While producers are always in search of novel content, they strongly favor traditional forms of linguistic expression. For that reason, many of the rules of broadcast writing reflect downright, old-fashioned notions about what constitutes a clear and unencumbered writing style. Einstein once said that the most difficult thing to understand about the universe is that we understand. When we consider Shannon's notion of communication and the tenuous relationship between shared meanings and the signals used to conjure them up, it is not surprising that the best writers—those from the broadcast media included—must use infinite care to make the audience understand.

THE ELEMENTS OF STYLE

Down deep, broadcast writers appreciate the formal rules of English composition, even if they can give good examples of when each should be ignored. While I need not review the basics, I can direct you to the most useful reference available: *The Elements of Style* by William Strunk, Jr., and E. B. White. Of the two authors, White is the more familiar as an essayist and the author of *Charlotte's Web*. Strunk was his English professor at Cornell University in 1919. Forty years later, White edited and published anew the 53-page textbook Strunk had originally written for his own composition students.

White revised the book in 1972 and again in 1979, six years before his death. While written as a guide for print media, Strunk's advice—directed by his unfailing commitment to the *needs* of a reading audience—is remarkably appropriate for electronic mass media as well. The flavor of the book is well represented by Strunk's explanation of perhaps his most famous rule: "Omit needless words."

Vigorous writing is concise. A sentence should contain no unnecessary words, a paragraph no unnecessary sentences, for the same reason that a drawing should have no unnecessary lines and a machine no unnecessary parts. This requires not that the writer make all his sentences short, or that he avoid all detail and treat his subjects only in outline, but that every word tell.

Strunk and Shannon would have seen eye to eye. They both recognized the tenuous relationship between a coding system and a set of possible messages, appreciating what it meant to convey accurately an unanticipated message using a minimally redundant combination of signals. Interestingly, in the 1960s, computer scientists at Bell Laboratories attempted to integrate many of Strunk's elementary rules into a text analysis program for UNIX, their computer operating system. The utility is called Writer's Workbench and still exists. The style-checking program for your personal computer is in all likelihood derived from the original Bell Labs program.

Among Strunk's elementary rules of composition there are at least three others well worth repeating. Strunk recognized, first, that the writer must adopt an organizing structure for any composition. Choose a suitable design and hold to it, he wrote. The design can be as rigorous as the 14-line rhyming scheme of a Shakespearean sonnet or as loose as a love letter. But the basic point is that good writers, by virtue of adopting a design, always know where they are headed, even if they are not sure how to get there.

In broadcast writing, there are two aspects to the design. Each message requires both (1) forethought about its logical structure and (2) adherence to a technically correct format. In the chapters that follow you will be introduced to a series of broadcast script formats appropriate for various types of fiction and nonfiction productions. You will also find that in the world of broadcasting, where time constraints are ever present, a suitable design helps the writer eliminate extraneous material. The clock is a ruthless dictator. The writer with a clear plan knows what fits in the script and what does not.

Strunk is also famous for alerting his students to the advantages of the active voice. As a rule, the sentence "Columbus discovered America" is much preferred to the passive alternative "America was discovered by Columbus." Strunk argued that the active voice is more direct, more vigorous, and more concise. For the broadcast writer, there's the added advantage that three words do the work of five, which saves precious air time as well.

But, like any rule of composition, we can press the advantage too far. While normally the subject-verb-object order of the active voice results in a more economical use of language, there are times that the object of the verb deserves to be the subject of the sentence. If someone were to shoot the president, even Walter Cronkite, on first report, would use the passive voice: "The president has been shot." Nor would Strunk ridicule the crime victim who shouts, "I've been robbed!" instead of "Someone robbed me!" In these cases, the object acted on is initially more important than the unknown actor. When the Wright brothers made their historic flight at Kitty Hawk, North Carolina, on December 17, 1903, the local newspaper report began: "The problem of aerial navigation without the use of a balloon has been solved at last." The reporter failed to identify the Wright brothers until the fourth paragraph.

Strunk recognized that there is a case to be made for structuring thoughts so that the subject of the discourse is also the subject of the sentence. Sometimes the passive voice is unavoidable. To update Strunk's example, consider the following sentences.

PASSIVE VOICE: The op-art paintings of the 1960s are scarcely appreciated today.

Here, the passive voice is acceptable because the focus is on op-art painting. Sentence topic and sentence subject are the same. But let's say that the preferences of contemporary art critics is the topic. We can write the sentence using either form.

PASSIVE VOICE: The op-art paintings of the 1960s are scarcely appreciated by contemporary critics.

or

ACTIVE VOICE: Contemporary critics scarcely appreciate the op-art paintings of the 1960s.

In this second example, however, the active voice is more direct, more vigorous, and more concise. The passive construction is both awkward and wordy. To avoid it requires constant vigilance. Indeed, the use of the passive voice in initial drafts and impromptu speech may be the all-too-natural representation of how thoughts are associated and linked by topic and subject in our brains. In a like manner, we may be prone to overuse the first person point of view in our spontaneous speech, because it too provides an easy means to unify our thoughts. As we refine our ideas, however, we should try to shed these mental crutches.

Finally, Strunk was a champion of concrete language. "Prefer the specific to the general, the definite to the vague, the concrete to the abstract." Strunk argued that the greatest writers were effective because they dealt in particulars and reported the details that mattered. All too often writers attempt to broaden their audience by appealing to the general case instead of the particular, employing abstract terms rather than concrete examples.

The linguist S. I. Hayakawa illustrated this problem precisely with what he called the "abstraction ladder." Consider the case of the farmer's cow, Bessie. As we move up the ladder noun by noun, the farmer's cow is identified as Bessie (a unique animal), a Guernsey, a cow, livestock, farm assets, assets, and, finally, wealth. At each higher level of abstraction, Bessie's relationship to the farmer is put into a broader perspective, but the characteristics that uniquely identify her must be left out. While we can clearly envision a picture of Bessie, the Guernsey cow, there is only the faintest trace of her image as we try to conjure up a picture of the farmer's wealth. An important lesson here is one that Strunk explicitly recognized. Details and particulars have the power to call up pictures in the audience's mind, an observation that's particularly important when writing for radio.

These few examples should convince you to read *The Elements of Style* as a regular exercise. It never fails to reward you, because Strunk's advice for improving clarity in written expression so often makes equal sense for the spoken word. For instance, he argued that it was better to express a negative in a positive form. Hence, "dishonest" was a better choice than "not honest," and "forgot" was better than "did not remember." Today, broadcast journalists will report that the jury found the defendant "guilty" or "innocent" even though by custom the foreman answers the judge's query with "guilty" or "not guilty." Print journalists still write, "not guilty."

It would be hard to fault Strunk, however, for failing to anticipate specific practices that stem from the intrinsic nature of broadcast technology and communication. A broadcast writer's words must jump two hurdles on their way to the audience. They must be unambiguous to the eye of the broadcast talent who reads them and clear to the ear of the listener who hears them. Thus, broadcast writers put a premium on familiar vocabulary and conversational writing styles. For instance, contractions like "haven't," "I've," and "she's" are usually preferred, except if the shortened form may be misinterpreted. Sometimes the "not" needs to be retained as a separate word to add emphasis, but a unique negative form such as "won't" can be more distinctive than its longer counterpart "will not."

It's a good rule for broadcast writers to use their speaking voice instead of their rehearsal voice (the one we use to talk to ourselves) to test their writing. That should make you sensitive to the hissing "s" or the exploding "p" and "b". Also embedded in your writing can be homonyms such as "their," "there," and "they're" that suddenly become unclear to listeners because the words are not spelled out for them. The problems can be even more complex when writers unconsciously create homophones: "a tax on drug dealers" sounds the same to the listener's ear as "attacks on drug dealers." We might keep in mind the story of musician Louie Armstrong who once amused his radio listeners by characterizing an unusual jazz tempo as "half slow, half fast." The point is, we don't want our words to inadvertently embarrass us or the person who reads them. Write for the ear as well as the eye.

Finally, we may want to reconsider what is an acceptable level of repetition in our writing. Print journalists shift from proper names to pronouns almost immediately in writing a news story. In broadcast copy, a short name can be repeated in two successive sentences without raising the listener's hackles, a practice that makes it easier to mentally process the second sentence. Furthermore, the right measure of repetition can add rhythm and power to spoken language. Thus, Glenn Mitchell stresses the differences between *Jacqueline & the Beanstalk* and the original fairy tale by describing the revised version as a story that contains "no goose, no golden egg, no death of a giant." It is shorter to say "no goose, golden egg, or death of a giant," but not as clear or emphatic.

ENGLISH COMPOSITION AND BROADCAST WRITING

If your English composition instructor forced you to read *The Elements of Style* once or, better, twice, and you adopted its creed wholeheartedly, then you are well on your way to becoming a successful broadcast writer. Unfortunately some English composition students always go awry. These students mistakenly attribute their passing grade to a newly discovered ability to express abstract ideas with esoteric language. Worse yet, they employ this style every opportunity they get.

For that reason I want to end this chapter with a real-life example that contrasts the writing of a well-intentioned student with a skilled broadcast writer. Both spoke at an august ceremony replete with academic robes and banners—the inauguration of a new president for the University of North Carolina system. Public television carried their words across the state. The broadcast journalist, Charles Kuralt of CBS News, attended the University of North Carolina at Chapel Hill as an undergraduate. He welcomed the new president on behalf of the university alumni. The student representative, a senior at North Carolina State University in Raleigh, was the elected head of a student government forum that represented the university's 16 campuses. He welcomed the new president on behalf of all students. He spoke his 545 words first:

> It has been said that education is the instrument by which the past is preserved, the present made productive, and the future given promise. As such, the role of the university has been to serve as a vital conduit through which the advancement of knowledge can be passed. This conduit has bound itself inextricably with the ability of North Carolina's young people to be more than passive recipients of what is. Rather it has allowed them to be shapers of what ought to be. For many years the University of North Carolina has been an essential, irreplaceable crucible of learning and evaluative thought. In this crucible the friction among ideas has been the heat that generates the transformation called education. This process has manifested itself in the thousands of students that have been endowed themselves with more than a means to make a living. They've been provided with a means to make a life.
>
> In order to foster a society capable of enduring the critical transitions ahead of us, we must supply the current and forthcoming constituents of that society with the tools necessary to construct a future worthy of the proud heritage of our past. Accordingly, we must commit ourselves to the augmentation of pure learning with values that will ensure a culture based on ethics and integrity. An education is void of true meaning if it leaves a person incapable of exercising compassion, justice, morality, courage, conviction, and other factors necessary to the improvement of the human condition.
>
> With these thoughts weighing heavily on our minds, we place our trust in a leader we believe will provide the direction and distinction necessary to move the University towards these goals. In good faith, President Spangler, we support your assumption of responsibility, fully cognizant of your ability to shepherd the educational mission of our system with the same enthusiasm and vigor exemplified in your continued dedication to the advancement of education.

When one considers the dilemmas facing our state and our nation, it is an easy task to see why your leadership as chief post-secondary educator will be indispensable. The strongest forces in history have not been societies, but highly motivated persons that have comprised the society and their ideas of what it is worth living for.

Today, President Spangler, you will undoubtedly have many questions to answer and difficult choices to make. Some of these questions may be: How can this University retain and cultivate its sound commitment to ensuring the access to knowledge that makes freedom truly possible? How can we improve the content and character of our academic programs to afford the maximum educational utility to students? What can we do to keep educational opportunity open to all with the attitude and aptitude to learn?

These questions and many others are already there, and your leadership will be instrumental in providing us with answers. Surely the roads to the future are not paved in asphalt. They are paved in the education of our people in order that they may live more productive and enriching lives as citizens of this state.

In this regard, the students of North Carolina's public universities happily offer their assistance to our new president and look forward to the fruits of your wisdom and vision.

Here is a student who desperately needs *The Elements of Style*. We learn that the university is a conduit, a crucible, and, oddly, a more important road to the future than blacktop highways. For those unfamiliar with North Carolina politics, that last was for the governor, who sat nearby on the podium. Traditionally, road building and education programs are at odds in the state budget, but this ungainly metaphor made no impact on its intended audience.

Kuralt limited his remarks to 315 words:

When I was a student at Chapel Hill, I was contemptuous of the alumni. The fat, bald ones who cluttered the campus on reunion weekends, acting as if the University belonged to them. And now fat and bald, I understand at last that it did belong to them. That it does. And I speak for them this morning, the men and women, living and dead, who passed part of their lives at these schools and carried a part of these schools away with them into the state and into the world. They all return in spirit this morning, President Spangler, to bid you welcome and to put into your hands the care of their university. The one they loved so. And love so.

It will be no secret to you that alumni can be a trial from time to time and their proprietary affection for Alma Mater a burden of your office. If you wish to know the size of the burden, I may as well tell you now. The number of living alumni of the 16 schools for which you now assume responsibility is 529,592. Most of them will come to you in person to offer advice. Therefore, I shall not presume to do so. For I knew earlier than most about your character and intelligence. When you were Dicky and we were 13, I voted for you for president of the student body of Alexander Graham Junior High School. And having had no reason in the intervening years to waver in my confidence or affection, I now vote for you again on behalf of all 529,592 of us, to hold to this greater presidency in the tradition of Frank Porter Graham and William C. Friday, which is a noble tradition. And in the name of a liberating and liberalizing education, which alone can advance our state and region, and save our precious world.

16 *Chapter 1 Elements of Broadcast Style*

The audience interrupted with laughter and applause. Kuralt's speech, the shortest of the day, had the greatest impact. He focused on people's actions, not abstractions. The most surprising story was the vignette from junior high school. Few persons in the audience knew that the two men had crossed paths previously. But, for a broadcast writer, the most impressive aspect of the speech was Kuralt's assault on the rule that large numbers should be rounded off in broadcast copy. By enumerating each digit, Kuralt not only conjured up, but enlarged until it became comical, the image of 529,592 alumni bearing down on a green university president.

Yet all this was accomplished using easily pronounced words—two-thirds were four letters or fewer—and sentences that gave the speaker time to breathe. Only six times did Kuralt use words longer than 10 letters. By contrast, the student speaker used 23. They are listed next in order of appearance.

1. contemptuous
2. proprietary
3. responsibility
4. intelligence
5. intervening
6. liberalizing

1. advancement
2. inextricably
3. irreplaceable
4. transformation
5. transitions
6. forthcoming
7. constituents
8. Accordingly
9. augmentation
10. improvement
11. distinction
12. responsibility
13. educational
14. exemplified
15. advancement
16. post-secondary
17. indispensable
18. undoubtedly
19. educational
20. educational
21. opportunity
22. instrumental
23. universities

Big words are not always the enemy. But the student's long list of high-sounding terms brings to mind George Orwell's critique of what he called inflated style: political prose where the author strings together ready-made phrases that generate only a dim blur in the minds of the audience. It is telling that the student alludes to the university's "educational mission," "educational utility," and "educational opportunity," while Kuralt pinpoints "intelligence." In broadcast writing, you choose a word because it signals a precise meaning or image. You must, as Mark Twain once scoffed, "Choose the right word, not its second-cousin."

ADDITIONAL READINGS

The Elements of Style by William Strunk, Jr. and E. B. White (Macmillan, New York, 1979). In this chapter, I have only touched on what I think are Strunk's most useful principles of composition. There are, in addition, Strunk's rules of usage in case you still get "its" and "it's" confused and White's essay on writing, "An Approach to Style," that includes 21 incisive reminders.

Communication Theories: Origins, Methods, Uses by Werner J. Severin and James W. Tankard, Jr. (Longman, New York, 1988). These authors provide a basic introduction to information theory and describe its influence on communication research. Other chapters are devoted to alternative models of the commmunication process. It is well worth investigating those that help you better understand the needs of the audience. They explain "cloze" procedure in their chapter on readability.

Introduction to Communication Studies by John Fiske (Methuen, London, 1982). Fiske is a leading British scholar in the area of cultural studies. His introduction to the mass media devotes considerable space to both semiotics and information theory. Particularly interesting is how Fiske applies two basic concepts of information theory—redundancy and unpredictability (technically called "entropy")—to the study of verbal and visual messages.

The Mathematical Theory of Communication by Claude Shannon and Warren Weaver (University of Illinois Press, Urbana, 1949). This short book includes a reprint of Shannon's famous article, published originally in the *Bell System Technical Journal*, along with an explanatory essay by Warren Weaver. Unless you're on your way to a degree in electrical engineering, you're unlikely to make much headway after Shannon's five-page introduction. But Weaver's essay exploring implications of the theory for human communication is still provocative after 40 years.

2
Broadcast Script Formats

A broadcast writer must please two audiences. There is, of course, the audience at home that tunes in a program with the expectation of being entertained or informed. But there is another audience at the studio—fellow professionals including producers, directors, actors, announcers, and engineers—charged with the job of bringing the script to life. Broadcast writers soon learn to prepare their scripts in set formats that help both technicians and talent understand how they have envisioned the program. Precision and consistency are a must, because every error in a script opens the door to a multitude of mistakes when the program is produced. Let me give an example of someone else's slip up that could have ended my television news-producing career prematurely. What saved it was a prompt disclaimer from the news anchor, who suffered an extremely embarrassing moment because of someone else's error.

During the summer of 1979, journalists were literally waiting for a story to drop out of the sky. The orbit of NASA's Skylab space station was perilously low. Although long abandoned, the 20-ton monster was threatening to re-enter the atmosphere, creating a huge fireball, and just possibly flatten some structure or some unfortunate person as it smashed into the face of the earth. No matter that the earth is three-fourths covered by water or that the odds for any individual being hurt were less than one in a million. In San Francisco, where I was producing television news, no one ever wanted to let the facts get in the way of a good story.

In this case, though, it was the San Francisco *Examiner*, the original newspaper in the William Randolph Hearst chain, that decided to use the Skylab story for self-promotion. The *Examiner* offered a $10,000 reward to the first person who arrived in its lobby with a chunk of Skylab. On Wednesday, July 11, 1979, Skylab re-entered the atmosphere. NASA flight controllers calculated a trajectory that had the space station plunging into the Indian Ocean southwest of Australia at 10:08 a.m. (PDT). No one even saw a splash, but two days later, Stan Thorton, an Australian teenager, arrived at the *Examiner* lobby to stake his claim. He had a black lump of something that had hit the roof of his house in Esperance, a small coastal town in southwest Australia.

Of course, before Thorton could get his check, someone had to authenticate that his piece of debris was a piece of Skylab. The black lump was sent to the National Aeronautics and Space Administration for analysis. After days of scrutiny, the NASA scientists announced their result. They could neither confirm nor deny that the debris was from Skylab. The *Examiner*, having gained more than $10,000 worth of free publicity from the competition, decided to award the check to Thorton anyway, at one last media event to cap the contest.

As it turned out, Thorton was better in print than on TV. He was a small-town boy with a heavy Australian accent. To understand his version of English, an American viewer would have needed subtitles. So when the newswriter at my station edited the videotape of Thorton's receiving his $10,000 check, the newswriter chose a sound bite, not from Thorton, but from the *Examiner* columnist, Jeff Jarvis, who presented it. The audience could understand Jarvis. Unfortunately, when the news story appeared on the air, and we endeavored to identify the talking head with "JEFF JARVIS, COLUMNIST," the caption in the graphics computer read "JEFF JARVIS, COMMUNIST." The text flashed on the screen for only a moment, but the damage was done. I can still hear the anchor on the phone to me in the control room: "What the hell was that?!" Even a subliminal impression requires a disclaimer. When the sound bite ended, the anchor carefully chose his words: "Of course, the caption on that video was incorrect. Jeff Jarvis is a *columnist* for the San Francisco *Examiner*."

During the next commercial break, everyone focused on the script, looking for the source of the error. The writer had noted the superimposed caption in an abbreviated form—SUPER: JEFF JARVIS—with no second line. The script was not wrong, but neither was it right. If it had designated both lines of the caption, then there was at least a chance that the director would have discovered the discrepancy between script and graphics computer before it got on the air. But, as a rule, in television news, the director's responsibility is only technical and not editorial. If JEFF JARVIS in the script matches JEFF JARVIS in the computer, then the director need not question the second line of the caption. COLUMNIST had to be designated in the script as well if the director were to be held accountable for what was technically only a typographical error.

In the end, the real culprit in this embarrassing episode was the station's graphic artist, who misread the caption when typing it into the computer some hours earlier. He was resting comfortably at home while we scrambled in the control room to correct his error. Thus, every mistake in creating a broadcast can result in a multitude of errors on the air. As a broadcast writer, you do not want those errors traced to a mistake in your script. In this case, the writer was only slightly to blame. He took a short cut, never anticipating that the graphic artist would misread his typed order for a two-line caption. Ultimately, I was just as guilty for never questioning his short cut. We had both guessed wrong that the second line would be redundant for identifying the correct super. Ironically, not Jeff Jarvis's name but his title had conjured up the more unpredictable message. As the anchor said, "What the hell was that?!"

CONTROL ROOMS AND STUDIOS

To understand the rationale behind various script formats, it is useful to understand what goes on in a control room and who assumes control of what. The truth is that the control room is essentially the province of the director. The script is now in the director's care. The producer, who has conceived the program and has coordinated the writing of the script, depends on the director and the technical crew much the same way a composer depends on a conductor and members of the orchestra. If they follow the notes as written, then they are not at fault if the results are discordant. That doesn't mean, however, that directors don't give useful advice based on their experience. Changes are often made in the control room (if time permits). But, ultimately, the program producer and the writers have to create a script, anticipating what goes on in the control room, so that the notes—when played together—sound like those they heard in their own minds.

In broadcasting, the script is an arrangement for a multitude of audio and video elements. From a purely technical standpoint, good programs are created by mixing sources of audio and video into an aesthetically pleasing and intelligible pattern. It is in the control room that these audio and video inputs—some generated in the studio, others already prerecorded—are collected and mixed. Radio production is the simplest, because it entails audio sources only: people speaking, music playing, and sound effects. Technically, the one major consideration is whether these audio sources are live or recorded. In the audio control room, a single engineer mixes the various audio inputs, which generally include studio microphones, reel-to-reel audio tape, audio cassettes, self-cueing audio cartridges (carts), records, and compact disks. These devices are represented in the illustration on page 22.

Radio script formats are designed to differentiate most commonly between people speaking into microphones in real time and previously recorded voices, music, and sounds. Thus, the scripts describe what comes when and from where. There are just two major radio script types: news and

22 Chapter 2 Broadcast Script Formats

Audio sources

Microphones
Reel to reel tape
Digital audio tape
Audio cassettes
Audio carts
Records
Telephones

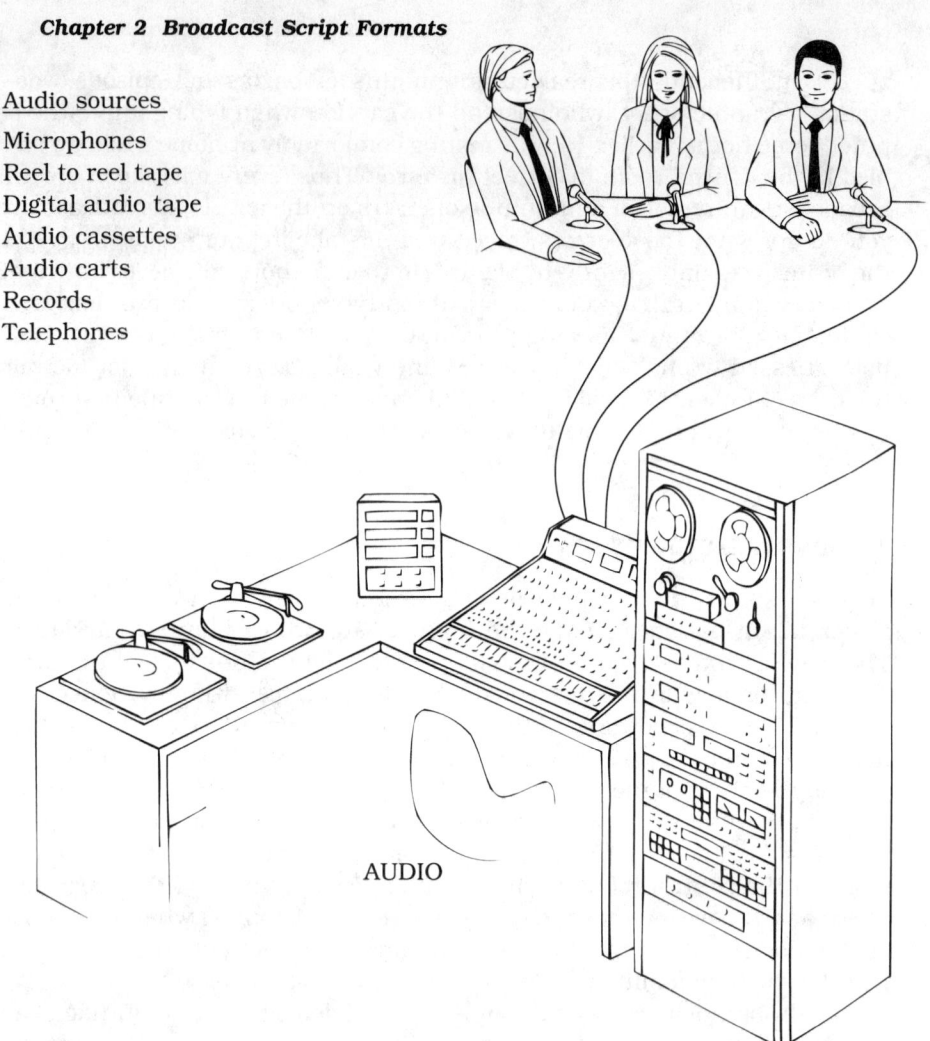

drama. They will be described first before we discuss the technical complexities of television studio production and its standard script formats.

RADIO SCRIPT FORMATS

Radio Drama

The radio drama script format is used for every type of programming except radio news. In the example that follows on page 24, a 60-second radio commercial is presented in radio drama format. The comedy team of Bob Elliott and Ray Goulding wrote and recorded this spot more than 20 years ago (when seatbelts were not mandatory). It exploits, of course, the audience's familiarity with the Dick and Jane reading primers and their simple, repetitive style, which can be skillfully reworked to create a humorous, yet repetitive advertising message.

Video sources

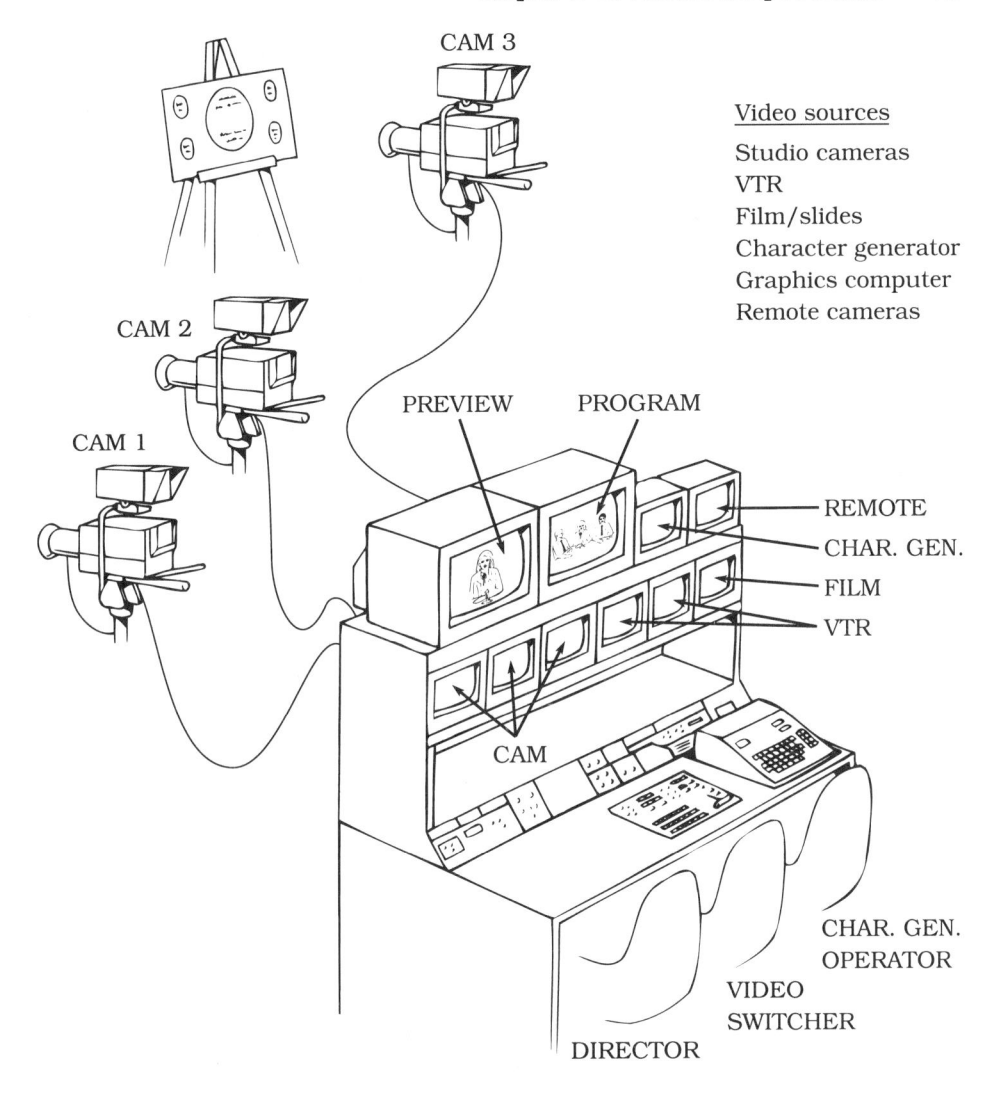

Studio cameras
VTR
Film/slides
Character generator
Graphics computer
Remote cameras

Looking more closely at the radio drama script format, however, we can see how all capital letters and normal down style typing are used to distinguish technical information from the spoken elements of the script. Capital letters identify the sources of sound, the four voices, ANNCR (announcer), TIM, JIM, and HARVEY, played by Bob and Ray in the studio, as well as the MUSIC and SOUND EFFX (effects), which are normally prerecorded on audio tape or carts. The underlining of MUSIC and SOUND EFFX serves to highlight audio elements which must be acquired from a tape library or created separately. Thus, the script indicates the type of planning and preproduction that must be done to efficiently complete a program or spot.

"HARVEY"

MUSIC: ORGAN MELODRAMA THEME FULL AND UNDER ANNOUNCER

ANNCR: Time again for Tim and Jim, Guardian Maintenance men, brought to you by your Chevrolet car and truck, Pontiac, Oldsmobile, Buick, Cadillac, and G-M-C truck dealer. Joining the boys ... an old friend has just driven in.

SOUND EFFX: METALLIC CLANKING OF MECHANICS' TOOLS UNDER

TIM: Say, Jim, isn't that our old friend Harvey, who writes children's stories?

JIM: Uh-Hmmm.

TIM: Hi, Harvey.

SOUND EFFX: CAR DOOR CLOSING

HARVEY: (HIGH-PITCHED MAN'S VOICE) Hi, Tim. Hi, Jim. Hi, Tim and Jim.

TIM: Can we help you?

HARVEY: Yes, this is my car. My car is red. See my red car.

TIM: (PLAYING IT STRAIGHT) Yes, what about it?

HARVEY: I am going away. I am going away in my red car. Go car, go!

TIM: Well, Harvey, you probably want our summer travel special then.

HARVEY: Yes, I would like your summer travel special.

TIM: Maybe a quality engine tune-up? It's another of our featured Guardian Maintenance summer services.

(MORE)

```
                                                              2.

    HARVEY:    Yes! Yes!

    TIM:       And we're also installing seatbelts, rotating tires,

               and balancing wheels.

    HARVEY:    See my dog Spot.  My dog Spot is in my red car.

               I love to run and play with Spot.  The pretty red

               car will go good.  When will the red car be ready?

    TIM:       When the big hand is on twelve and the little hand

               is on five.

                                    END
```

    Margins and line lengths are also important in script formats. Not only are they consistent to help technicians and talent decode the script, but they also provide a rough estimate of how long a production runs. In radio drama format, the line is divided into two sections. The first 10 characters in the line (columns 1–10) designate a particular voice or sound type. The next 50 characters in the line (columns 11–60) specify the text for the speaker or describe the desired sound or music. A line of text 50 characters wide takes about 3 seconds to read. So, by counting full lines of text and partial lines that extend halfway or more, the director can estimate the running time of the script. In this case it's 19 lines times 3 seconds = 57 seconds. Add in a few seconds for the organ music UP FULL at the beginning, and the spot times out to an even minute.

    Audio sources, can be either UP FULL, the dominant sound, or UNDER, a background sound. When two or more audio sources are used at once, then the script must designate which sounds are UNDER. Sound effects and music often begin UP FULL to set a scene, and are then reduced in volume to provide a background ambience. In this spot, that's true of the organ music, but the clanking sounds of the working mechanics provide only background noise. The sound of the closing car door is heard UP FULL between two elements of the dialogue.

A few final details: As in any dramatic script, there are directions to the actors. These directions are included in the portion of the script devoted to text but in all caps and parentheses so the talent will know not to read them aloud. In this script there are two directions to the actors to establish their demeanor and voices. However, writers should not try to direct the way every speech is to be given. Remember that if the script is well written, then the writer's intent should make itself known to a sensitive director. Let the director direct.

If this were a longer play interrupted by commercial messages, then it would be broken into acts. ACT ONE would appear in the first line of the script after the title, beginning at column one. ACT TWO would appear after the first commercial break, and so on.

Finally, flashbacks or even flashforwards are usually signaled to the audience by a device called a SEGUE. Technically, an audio segue consists of fading out the sound of the present scene and bringing up the sound of the flashback or flashforward scene. The term segue is generally employed in broadcasting for any device that smoothes a transition from one setting, topic, or program element to another. When the TV meteorologist finishes the weather segment with a forecast for the championship game on Saturday, and the sportscaster picks it up from there, that's also a segue.

Radio News

While the radio drama script format is extremely versatile, the radio news script format is highly specialized. Form follows function. The basic format assumes that only the newscaster is speaking live in the studio and that all other voices are recorded on audio tape. In addition, news stories are typed in double- or triple-spaced 70-character lines that are easy to read, easy to edit, and easy to time. If the anchor reads approximately 150 words per minute, then each full line of copy represents about four seconds of air time. The sample script that follows is just over six and a half lines, which times out to approximately 25 seconds. Most stories run less than a page, but each new story is typed on a separate sheet so the order of stories in a newscast can be rearranged until air time if unexpected developments occur. Each story is identified with a slug in the top left corner and is followed by the time of the broadcast, the date, and the initials or last name of the writer.

As in the radio drama format, all text to be read is typed in down style, but there's no need to designate a talent, because the newscaster does all the reading. Further, stories are usually written as single paragraphs, because multiple paragraphs result in more partial lines, which make timing by line count less precise. The triple number sign under the last line of the story indicates the end. If a story continues to a second page, then "(MORE)" is typed at

```
HUNGER
NOON NEWS
2/26/85
DAV

A group of doctors and public health experts say up to 20-million

Americans suffer from hunger at least once a month.  After a year-long

study, members of the Physicians Task Force on Hunger report that

hunger in America has reached epidemic proportions ... caused in part

by governmental cutbacks in income and nutrition programs.  The Task

Force is urging Congress to increase welfare and food stamp benefits,

and restore hunger programs for the needy.

                              ###
```

the bottom of the first page, and a new slug and page number are typed at the top of the second page.

For short newscasts and updates, the only voice heard is that of the newscaster. Longer newscasts may also include reporter stories and actualities (sound bites) from newsmakers, experts, or witnesses. These audio segments are usually recorded on short cassette tapes, known as carts (short for cartridges), which can be cued and played on a special tape player at the push of a button. The use of a CART is noted on the script exactly at the point it is to be inserted into the news story. Because it takes about a line to identify the cart's slug, its running time, and its audio out-cue (the last few words of the recorded segment), the information is usually centered on a separate line.

```
          CART:  HUNGER  (:14)  OUT-Q: "... at government offices."
```

Any tag or additional material that the newscaster is to read after the cart has played then begins flush left on a new line. The HUNGER story with the actuality added would run about 40 seconds total.

28 *Chapter 2 Broadcast Script Formats*

TELEVISION SCRIPT FORMATS

Television compounds the problems of radio by simultaneously mixing two separate channels: audio and video. Thus, one small part of the television control room is devoted to audio mixing while the major portion is devoted to the mixing of video images. The inputs that the director must monitor are many (see the control room illustration on page 23). There are three different cameras in the studio itself that the director shifts constantly to obtain specific shots of the performers. In addition, there may be remote cameras at other locations, especially for live news coverage. Meantime, video elements of the program may be prerecorded and stored on videotape, film, slides, or computer memory. For television news programs, two or more videotape recorders are systematically loaded and the tape cued to present one story after another without pause. There may also be video inputs from one or more film chains; that is, TV cameras hooked up directly to film and slide projectors. And, most certainly, the control room includes one computer that generates caption material and other text and another called a frame storer for graphics and still pictures. The videotape recorders, the live remote cameras, and the film chains add new audio inputs that must also be monitored.

In the end, then, the director must keep all these inputs straight, directing the video switcher and the audio engineer in the proper selection of inputs to create the desired output. The script, while it does not designate exactly which device to choose for the proper input, does designate the type of device used. The director will decide precisely whether camera no.1, no.2, or no.3 shoots the anchor head and shoulders and whether videotape recorder no.1 or no.2 plays the mayor's news conference story. But the script must provide technical cues to identify when the anchor is on camera and what medium was used to record visuals of the mayor's news conference.

With so much to keep track of, it's not surprising that the first television production scripts were designed to reflect the simultaneous tracking of video and audio inputs. Rather quickly, however, scripts for fictional television programming adopted a format that reflected their theatrical and cinematic character. However, there are still two readily used split-page script formats: Live-TV and TV News. We will look at them first because they graphically reflect the interplay between studio and control room in television production.

Live-TV

The Live-TV script example that follows on page 30 is for a 30-second political commercial that aired during the 1988 election campaign. The script page is split into video and audio columns, with a vertical line down the page just to the left of center. There are 1-inch margins all around and considerable white space to give the director additional room in which to "mark up" the script; that is, to add time cues and notes, designating camera shots, video sources, and verbal instructions for the crew during production. Note also that the spoken parts of the script are typed within an audio column that is 35 characters wide. Each 35-character line takes approximately 2 seconds to read. Thus, even before production begins, we can estimate the time of this spot—30 seconds—by counting lines of copy. Generally, all the partial lines will average out if we count only the ones that extend at least half way. In this case, the lines add up to 15.

Fundamentally, this ad is a testimonial from Congressman Doug Barnard, who sits on the House Banking Committee with Congressman David Price. As we can see from the audio column, Barnard does all the talking. He begins at a desk on camera (OC) and continues voice-over (VO) as the audience sees a montage of still photographs of Rep. Price at work in Washington. With three lines of copy (6 seconds) to go, Barnard reappears on camera momentarily but gives his punchline-ending voice-over while the viewer contemplates a full screen (FS) computer-generated graphic that reads: DAVID PRICE—Everything we ever wanted in a Congressman. (The actual is reproduced in freeze frame format in Chapter 7, beginning on page 129.)

Needless to say, a lot happens in 30 seconds. In the studio, we have one camera taking a close-up (CU) shot of Rep. Barnard sitting at a desk. In addition, we need two cameras focused on two easels with the photographs arranged for a smooth transition from one to the next. Photos 1, 3, and 5, must be lined up on one easel with a camera focused on it while photos 2, 4, and 6 are lined up on a second easel with its own camera. (Those photos could also be stored digitally in computer memory for recall during production.) The director tells a technician to roll the videotape and then cues Bernard, who starts reading his script off a teleprompter. While Barnard is on camera, his name is superimposed at the bottom of the screen.

Four lines into the spot, the video source changes. The director tells the video switcher to dissolve to photo no.1 on the first easel, then to photo no.2 on the second easel, then photo no.3 on the first easel, and so on. (Dissolves are the fading out of one image as another fades in. While dissolves are often used to suggest the passage of time or a major change in the setting, in this 30-second spot they reinforce the thematic flow of the visuals. If direct cuts were used, then the pace of the spot might appear too hectic, given a change in the video almost every 3 seconds.) The spot concludes with a shot of Barnard at the desk again and then the computer-generated graphic as Barnard reads the closing line.

As precise as the Live-TV format seems to be, it should be pointed out that it does not present a perfect schematic for the interlocking elements of this 30-second commercial or any other complex script. In the political ad, PHOTO #1 and PHOTO #3 are indeed matched with the first words of corresponding text. However, the match between PHOTO #2 and the audio copy is much more ambiguous. In the actual commercial, the dissolve occurs on the word "get" in the middle of the line. Sometimes, in fact, the writer may circle the precise word that corresponds to a change in video and then draw a line back to the video cue. Clearly, though, some leeway is permissible. The writer can reasonably assume that an experienced director will dissolve from photo to photo at an aesthetically pleasing pace.

VIDEO	AUDIO
	CONGRESSMAN BARNARD (OC)
CU CONG. BARNARD AT DESK	I've served with Congressman David
SUPER: DOUG BARNARD BANKING COMMITTEE	Price on the House Banking
	Committee, and his home equity bill
	is a remarkable achievement.
	(VO)
PHOTO #1 NEWSPAPER CLIPPING	It's rare for any first time
PHOTO #2 CU PRICE SPEAKING	congressman to get a major bill passed.
PHOTO #3 TWO-SHOT PRICE LISTENING	David Price may be the only one this term.
PHOTO #4 CU PRICE READING	I think his success is a real tribute to his intelligence and
PHOTO #5 TWO-SHOT PRICE TALKING	his ability to deal with people.
PHOTO #6 COMMITTEE MEETING	He brought Democrats as well as Republicans together on this.
	(OC)
CU CONG. BARNARD	And a lot of American homeowners are
SUPER: DOUG BARNARD	going to be protected by this bill.
	(VO)
FS GRAPHIC PRICE FOR CONGRESS	They can thank David Price for that.
	END

Another inconsistency in the Live-TV format is the mixing of both audio and video information in a single column. For instance, the audio column of the political ad includes the OC and VO notations that let Rep. Barnard know exactly when he's on camera. During the VO portions, he need not worry whether he's squinting at the teleprompter. He can even look down to read from a written script in front of him. On the other hand, if audio and video channels are recorded simultaneously as on videotape, then information about audio sources is often found in the video column. Accordingly, some professionals like to think about these split-page formats as divided into a left column for technicians and a right column for on-air talent. The director, of course, must coordinate both.

TV News

The production of television newscasts differs from the production of most other programming in one essential way. Much of the newscast is live, unrehearsed, and unedited. When the anchor kicks a line, the audio engineer fails to turn off a microphone, or the video switcher hits a wrong button, the viewer knows it instantaneously. As a result, writers and producers try to minimize the technical complexity of live elements in TV newscasts. In fact, TV news scripts are surprisingly simple to decode once you've mastered the alphabet soup of technical jargon.

There are, for instance, only a few basic in-studio shots. Anchor on camera (ANCHOR OC) designates a head and shoulders close-up when the anchor is reading a news story directly to the viewers. When a second video element is added to the basic ANCHOR OC shot, it is called a chromakey (CK) shot. Chromakey once referred to a specific technical process for mixing two video pictures electronically. Now it is the generic term for any shot where the camera frames the anchor to one side so that a photo, a graphic, or even rolling videotape can be inserted into a framed portion of the screen. A map inserted over the shoulder of the anchor, for instance, helps identify the story while adding visual interest to the shot. When short news items are run in rapid succession, changes in chromakey graphics mark the transition from one story to the next.

Aside from chromakey shots, the vast majority of technical notations in TV-News scripts relate to the use of videotape, abbreviated VTR or ENG. ENG, which stands for "electronic news gathering," refers both to a technology—the lighter, more compact video recording equipment that replaced film in the mid-1970s—and the special cassette tape format it employs. The audience rarely sees or hears raw videotape on the air. Rather, they watch an edited version that a reporter or anchor narrates.

Because reporters like to go home at night for dinner and not return to work for the 11 o'clock newscast, they almost always record their narrations on the edited videotape for playback during the newscast. In the script, these videotape stories are technically identified as VTR/SOT. VTR/SOT stands for "videotape with sound on tape." However, because one of the strengths of broadcast news is its timeliness—its ability to update a news story as soon as new details are known—it's often the case that the anchor reads the narration live during the news program itself. The technical notation for live narration is VTR/VO, that is, "videotape with voice over."

Straightforward VTR/SOT and short VTR/VO stories are not difficult to execute live. However, the director's task grows more complicated when VTR/VO segments are edited with VTR/SOT segments. Ordinarily, these VTR/SOT segments are not reporter narrations but portions of a taped interview or natural sounds that accompany an event (the roar of a rocket launch or music from a marching band). In these instances, the script must distinguish the SOT portions from the VO portions by noting the exact times for each. In addition, the scriptwriter must also provide an audio outcue (abbreviated OUT-Q) to make sure the director doesn't clip off a word or two owing to a split-second timing error. When the videotape is rolling, the director must give the audio engineer explicit cues: when to punch up the anchor's microphone (VO) or when to punch up audio on the videotape playback machine (SOT). Just in case the videotape machine fails, scripts often include a summary of SOT segments, often called a precis, so the anchor can ad lib the missing information.

Videotape times are spelled out in detail in the video column of the script. In the example that follows on page 33, the first segment is a 22-second voice-over, followed by an 11-second sound bite. The two segments add up to a total running time (TRT) of 33 seconds. In some newsrooms, the practice is to give the length of each segment. The TV-News format presented here designates instead the running time; that is, the time at which each segment begins. Thus, the first voice-over begins at :00, the sound on tape starts at :22, and the sound bite ends at :33. The total running time (TRT) is marked opposite the last line of the OUT-Q if the videotape ends with SOT or the last line of the VO copy that the anchor reads. A script could also call for multiple segments of voice-over and sound on tape. If you hear a TV newswriter refer to a v-b-v, it means a voice-over, sound bite, voice-over videotape story.

Like Live-TV, TV-News format uses a 35-character, 2-second line for all copy the anchor reads. On camera, time is elastic; that is, the director can hold a studio camera shot indefinitely. But for voice-over copy, the audio reading time must match the videotape running time. If the first segment of silent videotape runs 22 seconds, then the copy for it should run about 11 lines. Ideally, the anchor should finish reading the voice-over in the nick of time with only a beat before the SOT begins. Mismatches in VTR/VO portions of the script create embarrassing errors. Two seconds of silence or one second of black video can seem like forever in a fast-paced news program. Overlapping sound can make even the best-written story incomprehensible.

Two final points about timing: First, don't confuse the total running time (TRT) of the videotape with the total time of the story. The total story time (sometimes abbreviated TST) includes not only the TRT but also the anchor's on-camera lead-in and any on-camera tag after the videotape. Second, start-

```
DRUGS/REAGAN
_____ 11p
4/6/89
hsf
```

ANCHOR OC	A police SWAT team has stormed a
CK/DRUG BUST	suspected drug house in south-
	central Los Angeles tonight ... but
	it's not been a typical drug raid.
VTR/VO @ :00	Parked outside was an air-conditioned
SUPER: MAIN & 51ST LOS ANGELES	motor home with two V-I-P's ... L-A
	police chief Darryl Gates and
	former first lady Nancy Reagan.
	Neighbors say this is the third
	time since January that police have
	raided the frame house with a metal
	security door. But the first time
	it received such high-level attention.
	After witnessing the arrests, Mrs.
	Reagan voiced her dismay.
SOT FULL @ :22	(PRECIS: SAYS SHE'S MORE USE TO VISITING TEACHING AND REHABILITATION PROGRAMS. THE PEOPLE IN HERE ARE SADLY BEYOND THAT POINT.)
TRT :33	OUT-Q: "...that's very discouraging."
ANCHOR OC TAG	Police say they've arrested a total
	of 14 men and women on drug-related
	charges.

# # #

ing a new paragraph in the audio column is only helpful when it corresponds to a major technical change in the video column. Otherwise, too many partial lines are created in the script, making it more difficult to estimate how long the voice-over copy actually runs. The writer must make accurate estimates to synchronize audio with video. The producer must make accurate estimates to make sure the entire newscast fits the scheduled time period.

Three-Camera Format

Although split-page formats for television programming seem entirely logical, they're not always necessary or helpful. One of the surprising aspects of television production is that among the dozens of technical personnel involved, only one person—the director—actually works from a script. Whether they be camera operators, audio engineers, video switchers, or videotape editors, every technician simply follows the director's verbal commands. They keep in contact on headphones, ready to respond to each instruction sent their way. From this standpoint, then, the technical details that writers insert in a script provide something less than a full technical description. The director must still translate those details into a sequence of step-by-step commands. The director needs preparation time, in fact, to mark up the script; that is, to jot down notes indicating the verbal instructions for the crew.

Accordingly, the technical jargon the writer uses is not meant for the technical crew at all. It is simply a shorthand way to let everyone who is privy to the script—the producer, the director, and the talent—know how the writer envisions the actual production. That is no small matter in presenting news or commercials. A change in presentation can easily subvert the accuracy, objectivity, or persuasive appeal of the intended message. But, in a dramatic production, the director fully participates in its artistic realization. There's time to rehearse the cast and crew together and to discuss the results. A writer who is overly prescriptive about technical details in a dramatic script is bound to be overruled in rehearsal.

Furthermore, when production is confined to a TV studio, there is less uncertainty about the sources of audio and video. Normally there are three to five cameras plus microphones. The primary technical challenge is blocking out the actors' movements and then shifting cameras into position for the most effective sequence of shots. What the director needs most is plenty of white space on the page to mark the anticipated camera moves and the selection of shots. Therefore, since the earliest days of studio-produced television, TV drama has been written using a single-column format, based on a format devised originally for motion picture production.

Today the three-camera format is most commonly used for sitcom scripts. What follows beginning on page 36 is a dialogue sequence as it might have been written for the lead characters of the original "Bob Newhart" show. Remember, the sources of video and audio are generally limited to in-studio cameras and microphones. They do not require explicit notation. Instead, the major delimiting factors in the script are the acts and scene changes. The acts are created as a result of interruptions for commercial breaks. A half-hour sitcom is normally divided into two acts, although it may have a short tease or prologue at the beginning and a tag at the end. An act always begins with a FADE IN:, typed flush with the left margin, and ends with a FADE OUT:, typed flush with the right margin.

Scenes are sequenced alphabetically. The first scene is A, the second is B, and so on. A scene is normally defined as a continuous sequence of dialogue or action. When a scene ends, the type of transition to the next scene is typed flush right. The transition may be a straight cut, indicated with CUT TO:, a dissolve where one picture fades out as the other fades in, indicated with DISSOLVE TO:, or a FADE OUT. to black, which would require the next scene to begin with a FADE IN:. In three-camera format, a new scene usually begins on a new page. The end of an act is indicated END OF ACT ONE, for instance, centered on a line two lines below FADE OUT. cue. For the end of the last act, use THE END.

Following a tradition begun in the film industry, a new scene is first identified by listing the "conditions of work" for the specific set. As a rule, this one-line set description identifies the shooting location, specifies whether it is an interior (INT.) or exterior (EXT.) space, and notes the time of day for the scene. In early film production, knowing those "conditions of work" was essential for regulating camera lighting.

Immediately below the set description in the three-camera format comes a list of the characters appearing in the scene. The final technical instructions are the stage directions, which are often used to describe the mood and the fabric of the scene in greater detail. The stage directions stretch across the page in a 65-character line. Specific sound and camera cues should be written in all capitals and underlined.

Dialogue is roughly centered on the page using a 40-character line. Although character names are capitalized, the speeches themselves are in down style and double spaced. Personal directions, however, are capitalized and set off in parentheses. If a character's speech extends to the next page, it should be split between sentences, followed by "(MORE)" centered at the bottom of the page, and begun anew with the character's name and "(CONT'D)" at the top of the next page. Stage directions can also interrupt dialogue. If the action occurs during a character's speech, then once the stage directions are completed, the character's name should be retyped, with "(CONT'D)" next to it to identify the continuing lines.

Alternate Formats

Now that you've been exposed to five standard broadcast formats, let me warn you that no two organizations seem to adopt exactly the same rules. So don't be surprised to see variations in all these formats. There is, for instance, an alternative to three-camera format, called "Tape-Live" that is commonly used for sitcom production. Though the elements are basically the same, most begin flush with the left margin to give the director more room to write notes

BOB NEWHART SHOW

"Anniversary Waltz"

ACT ONE

A

FADE IN:

INT. HARTLEY'S APARTMENT - EVENING
(Bob, Emily)

BOB AND EMILY ARE FINISHING DINNER. THE TABLECLOTH, WINE GLASSES, AND CANDLES INDICATE IT'S BEEN A FANCY MEAL. BOB IS SITTING ALONE AT THE TABLE. EMILY IS COMING FROM THE KITCHEN WITH A SILVER COFFEE POT.

     BOB

  Boy, what a scrumptious dinner, Emily.

  Any special reason?

     EMILY

  (WALKING IN) You should kno-o-o-w, Bob.

     BOB

  Let's see. You paid off your department

  store charge.

     EMILY

  Oh no, Bob. This is something that

  concerns you and me.

2.

                    BOB
Your mother's coming for a month-long visit.

                    EMILY
Bob, why would I cook a special meal just to announce that my mother is coming?

                    BOB
In the movies...a condemned man always gets a special meal.

                    EMILY
(SITTING DOWN) I'm really surprised at you. Don't you know? Tonight is our anniversary.

                    BOB
Emily. I'm a stickler for dates. I just happen to know that National Applesauce Day and our wedding day don't coincide.

                    EMILY
That's not the anniversary I mean. It was 14 years ago on National Applesauce Eve that you proposed to me.

                    BOB
You expect me to remember that?

                    EMILY
Well yes. (SLIGHTLY HURT) You're the one who proposed. Who else should remember?

3.

                    BOB
Probably your parents. They'd been waiting
28 years for that night.
                    EMILY
That's enough! In my way of thinking...
the anniversary of our decision to get
married is as important as the anniversary
of our wedding ceremony.
                    BOB
In your way of thinking, dear, you'd be
celebrating your conception day rather
than your birthday.
                    EMILY
Oh no, Bob. That'd be silly. That would
make me nine months older than I really am.
                    BOB
Well...celebrating the night I proposed
would make it seem as if we're married
almost a year extra.
                    EMILY
But Bob...that's okay for an anniversary.
All those years together. That's what
couples should celebrate.
                    BOB
I'm not so sure.
                                   DISSOLVE TO:

on the right side of the page. Interestingly, "tape-live" format can be shifted right, so left-handed directors can comfortably write their notes on the left side of the page.

Such alternate formats should not distract you, however, from the main purpose of this chapter, which is to illustrate the connection between script formats and the rudimentary technical elements of broadcast production. You should understand from the start that these script formats are essential tools of the trade. They help writers organize their creative visions into game plans that producers, directors, and performers can follow. Scriptwriting errors most commonly occur because writers are careless or fail to learn fundamental concepts of broadcast production. In neither case are those errors excusable.

ADDITIONAL READINGS

The Complete Guide to Standard Script Formats: Part II, Taped Formats for Television by Judith H. Haag (CMC Publishing, North Hollywood, CA, 1988). If you're going into the sitcom writing business, this book details every possible contingency in three-camera and tape-live format.

Writing for Television and Radio, fifth edition, by Robert L. Hilliard (Wadsworth Publishing, Belmont, CA, 1991). This text, first published in 1962, is an institution. It provides sample scripts of all kinds from commercial broadcasting that can serve as models and inspiration for your own work.

3

Radio Commercials and Public Service Announcements

From a philosophical perspective, it's not surprising that advertising overwhelms the airwaves of America. In a country that exalts freedom and choice, persuasive speech is a necessity. Democracy and persuasion have always been intertwined. If ancient Athens is the starting point for our study of democratic forms of government, then it is also the starting point for our study of rhetoric: the art or science of using words effectively in speech or composition—in short, persuasion. What the Greeks and Romans could not foresee was the industrial revolution. Thanks to it, citizens have not only political decisions to make but a legion of economic ones. Without judging the merits of this social environment, it is nevertheless fair to say that commercial ads are the campaign speeches of consumer products. Each day we vote with our dollars. If we are free to choose, then we must somehow be persuaded. Similarly, the not-for-profit institutions of our society have also come to accept the notion that the broadcast media are the most effective means to persuade people to change their attitudes, donate money, or volunteer time.

The result has been an ad culture of staggering magnitude. In the mid-1980s, economist Robert Heilbroner estimated that if we were to count the stars on a clear night, they would number 3,000. By contrast, if we were to count the number of brand name products on the American landscape, they would number almost 30,000. What's more, advertising researchers have estimated that the average American family is exposed to 1,600 ads a day in the newspapers and magazines they read, the radio they listen to, the television they watch, and the billboards they pass. Given these exorbitant numbers, it's truly amazing that any one advertisement can have an effect—that mere mortals can use words and pictures to make any chosen star shine brighter than its neighbors and draw attention to itself. The challenge of that task is revealed in some additional observations about advertising effectiveness. Researchers estimate further that the members of an average family notice only about 80 of those 1,600 ads they are exposed to, and they respond to about 12.

EXPOSURE AND RESPONSE

Of all of those numbers cited, broadcast writers are most concerned about the disparity between exposure and response. How did 12 ads generate a response when 68 did not? Why is exposure not enough? Fortunately, humans are complex. Their behavior is guided by numerous contingencies: goals, experience, estimates of future success, energy levels, and attitudes, just to mention a few. People can pay attention but not understand. They can understand but not believe. They can believe but not act. The path from exposure to response is rarely cleared by a single compelling argument. In reality, it would be frightening if the audience were so easily manipulated.

Persuasive speech, then, is no simple matter. To change someone's mind or behavior requires a strategy that deals with a series of contingent situations. Developing a model of the most critical contingencies in attitude change has been a focus of psychological inquiry for more than 50 years. During World War II, when the U.S. government wanted to develop defenses against enemy propaganda, yet inculcate attitudes in American soldiers that would improve motivation, psychologists began working systematically to trace the impact of information on attitudes. In the belief that a better understanding of the circumstances that led up to the U.S. entry into the war would help improve the morale of young draftees, the U.S. Army produced a series of documentaries entitled, "Why We Fight." One project for the psychologists was to measure how well those movies worked. The results from questionnaires were not very encouraging. Enlisted personnel who watched the films did know more about the war than those who did not, but they were no more eager to fight after watching the film than they had been before. It was clear that simple exposure to information was not enough to change people's minds.

Accordingly, psychologists expanded their focus to look not only at the relationship between knowledge and attitudes but between attitudes and behavior. They found that laboratory experiments did not support the easy assumption that pre-existing mental attitudes shape social behavior. Often, the specifics of a social situation generate behavior in conflict with previously expressed opinions. For example, how often have parents or friends talked you into doing something you feared or disliked, only to discover that you genuinely enjoyed the experience, or at least felt that it wasn't that bad? Now, what was your attitude going into the event? What was it after? When did your attitude shift most dramatically? Before or after? As you might guess, psychologists have documented many cases where changes in attitude followed changes in behavior; that is, action—not information—elicited attitude change.

This point has not been lost on advertising executives either. The basic strategies they espouse—whether adapted from psychological research or developed through marketplace experience—almost always seem to focus on consumer behavior. Broadcast spots rarely run longer than 30 seconds. Within that time frame, finding a way to get consumers to act differently may be more effective than building up arguments to change their minds.

Hal Kome, a former vice president at the Leo Burnett agency in Chicago, suggests a straightforward strategy: Promise people they'll get something out of doing what you suggest. Two techniques work particularly well. One is to find a problem and show how the product will solve it. Rolaids asks, "How do you spell relief?" McDonald's tells Mom, "You (Mom) deserve a break today." Its chief competitor conjures up the munchies, "Are you hungry for Burger King now?" Kome's second technique is to propose a fantasy life and show how the product will make dreams come true. Kids' cereal, for instance, promises fun in the form of Snap, Crackle, and Pop or Tony the Tiger. Beer ads do the same for adults: "This Bud's for you" or "Miller time."

For both techniques, the advertiser provides a reason for a specific behavior instead of focusing on the merits of the product. In 30 seconds there's scarcely time for a long list of features or even a series of favorable comparisons. That level of detail is more manageable in print.

So far, of course, we've been discussing the short-term effects of persuasion at a more or less conscious level. However, we don't have to be advocates of Freudian psychoanalysis to believe that persuasive messages may have long-term effects that audience members need never be aware of. Remember that the communication process requires decoding at the receiving end. Signals must be matched with a message if their meaning is to be understood. Even if the mind initially rejects the implications of the message, then a trace is left. No matter how faint the impression, there's good reason to believe that somehow memory has been at least minutely transformed. Thus, no matter how low the involvement in viewing or listening, by virtue of processing signals from outside, the human mind may be committing new information to memory. What psychologists call "incidental learning" has occurred.

Perhaps the greatest opportunity for unconsciously affecting behavior lies in the consumer's lack of competing information or relevant experience. In the early years of persuasion research, much attention was focused on source credibility. In those years, just after World War II, people were more skeptical of an article that was published in *Pravda* than one published in the New York *Times*, even if the so-called *Pravda* article was the work of a *Times* reporter.

But, over the long term, researchers discovered what they labeled the "sleeper effect." Readers' opinions appeared to change as they forgot the source of the information on which their opinions were based. Standing in the supermarket, faced with multiple brands, consumers often have little information. They can compare price, read ingredients on the label, judge the aesthetic quality of the packaging, or search their memory for some faint trace that will help them discriminate. Ideally, a truly effective ad would have sent those consumers in search of a specific product with no interest in competitors. Failing that, however, the spot that will most completely engage their attention and information-processing capacity has the best chance of popping into their minds at the appropriate moment. Either case seems to support advertiser David Ogilvy's famous dictum: "You can't bore people into buying your product."

This memory trace may be a fact, an opinion, an image, or even an emotional feeling associated with the product. Think, for instance, how often music and jingles are used in broadcast advertising. It has become axiomatic in commercial advertising that if you have nothing to say, you say it with music. That is, if you can't make an effective verbal argument for the product, link it to a pleasant feeling. For instance, no matter how much I may deplore cost overruns at the Pentagon, I still have a generally favorable feeling about those young, shining-faced male and female recruits who are trying to "be all you can be in the Arr-rrr-my." That recruiting jingle may not be aimed at me or anyone else my age, nor have I been especially attentive when it airs, but it has left a trace through repeated exposure, and that trace may affect future thinking and behavior. What advice should I give my children if they want to join the Army as a way to pay for college? (That logical argument is embedded in other spots.) Should I vote for a senator who wants to cut the budget for national defense? Should all young people be required to enlist in some form of national service?

While on the one hand this list of questions makes these Army ads seem potentially very powerful, on the other hand it also reveals the essential weakness of subconscious strategies. Incidental learning may only cause incidental effects. On all these questions, for instance, experience serving in the U.S. military—not to mention a personal accumulation of relevant items read, seen, or heard—is bound to have greater impact than an assortment of 30-second commercials. Because these ads were not aimed at these questions, they are unlikely to displace or overwhelm an even larger store of information already lodged in people's minds.

Ultimately, we must assume that institutions incur the cost of advertising only if they are convinced it helps them meet their primary objectives. Professionals who create the commercials must develop strategies for securing those objectives first. They must define the audience and create appeals that motivate behavioral change. Considerable thought (and research) must be devoted to finding out what the audience already knows. As always, that helps the writer compose a clearer message. But, even more basic to persuasive writing, it forces the writer to confront countervailing or contradictory information that may nullify the premise of the ad.

WRITING FOR RADIO

The discussion so far has been an extremely broad one about persuasion strategies used in broadcast media. The discussion may make sense, but it will always remain abstract until you begin writing scripts of your own. As a rule, broadcast writers begin writing pure, that is, without thinking about accompanying pictures. Practice with audio comes ahead of video, like crawling before walking. Even in a television newsroom, new writers must prove themselves by writing simple readers—short news stories that the anchor reads on camera—before they can begin mixing words and video.

Generally, the better the writer, the more romantic they are about the creative possibilities of radio. Comedian Stan Freberg once did a radio commercial extolling the virtues of radio commercials. He asserted that radio was a more powerful advertising medium than television. To prove the point, he edited together a series of sound effects purporting to be the creation of the largest hot fudge sundae ever assembled. It began with the draining of Lake Michigan and ended with a helicopter flying over and dropping a 10-ton maraschino cherry onto a 700-foot mountain of whipped cream. Then he challenged television to present the same event.

The point is well taken. The radio writer can use words and sounds to create any image available in the audience's mind. To the extent that reality can be stretched and twisted, radio is particularly well suited to caricature and humor. On the other hand, radio can present documentary material that may be too shocking to look at. (When I first began writing this book, one of the reviewers said he was offended by the Murrow excerpt that appears in Chapter 1. That reaction surprised me, because Murrow's commentary about the conditions at the concentration camp is highly restrained. But I think we would all agree that within the context of this textbook, no one wants to see photographs of what Murrow described.)

A final strength of radio is the involvement it demands. The audience cannot glance at the screen to help fill in missing information or predict what's coming next. That's a double-edged sword for the writer. Each word carries a great share of program information. To make sense out of the signals, listeners must focus their attention on the speaker, screening out distractions. Thus, radio is a mentally engaging medium, a "hot medium," as Marshall McLuhan once described it. Certainly, much radio listening is done for relaxation. Recorded music on the radio often provides a background for more focused activities. But speech on the radio demands our attention. We strain to hear the dialogue of a radio mystery, fearing that we might miss some essential clue or fail to comprehend a turning point in the plot. Radio can engage both the audience's desire for imaginative play and its need to resolve uncertainty.

PUBLIC SERVICE ANNOUNCEMENTS

Persuasive writing for radio usually falls into three categories: commercials, promotion, and public service announcements. Of course, we all know what commercials are, but promotion and public service announcements may require added definition. Promotion spots are simply commercials for upcoming programming on the same station. They try to convince listeners to stay tuned or tune in at an appropriate time. Since broadcasters charge for time based on the size of the listening audience, it pays to run ads to attract listeners. During a major ratings sweep, radio stations will pay for ads in newspapers and on television in a further attempt to increase audience size.

Public service announcements (or PSAs) are ads that run for free to support programs and causes backed by nonprofit organizations or governmental agencies. While it is always the radio station's decision whether it will air a particular PSA or not, the production of a PSA may be initiated by a variety of organizations and agencies at the local or national level. Thus, it is an especially appropriate first assignment for a course in broadcast writing. Even if you never pursue a career in broadcasting, you may someday be drafted to help in the production of a public service announcement.

Broadcasters air PSAs as part of their public service mission. Aside from their legal obligation to serve the public convenience, interest, and necessity, PSAs give broadcasters a means to identify their stations with community concerns, thereby building good will in their local market. Thus, broadcasters are actually searching for what they consider to be interesting and informative PSAs. Ironically, organizations that don't have money to pay for advertising spots on radio often don't appreciate the value of the free time that stations are willing to make available. Not realizing what free air time is worth, local organizations will submit PSAs that fall far short of broadcast quality, or they will send a radio station the same news release they prepared for the newspaper, never thinking through the differences between mass media and the precise message they want to broadcast on radio. For a starter, a 30-second PSA is limited to 75 words. They need to be well chosen.

As persuasive messages, PSAs can be as diverse as regular commercials. They can range in complexity from straight readers that disc jockeys or station announcers read to prerecorded minidramas that feature professional actors, sound effects, and music. They are produced as 60-, 30-, or 10-second spots. The 30-second spot is the most popular length, although, during prime time, station managers may refuse to give up any slot longer than 10 seconds to a nonpaying customer. As you might guess, 60-second PSAs will be pushed out to fringe times when audiences are small and commercial demands are weak.

Developing Strategies

Like any other form of advertising, PSAs can't be dull. Once an organization or agency decides its prime objective and defines its target audience, it must

Chapter 3 Radio Commercials and Public Service Announcements 47

```
RADIO PSA                            Start Using:  IMMEDIATELY
NC MEMORIAL HOSPITAL                 Stop Using:   VALENTINE'S DAY
Contact:     SUDI DANNENBERG
Telephone:   555-2211                Reading Time: 30 seconds

                        "BULIMIA"

ANNCR:    On Valentine's Day you give candy hearts to the

          one you love.  But what if the one you love has

          an eating disorder?  One out of every ten college
                            (buh-LEE-mee-uh)
          women suffers from Bulimia ... an illness that

          causes binge eating and vomiting.  If someone you

          love has an eating disorder, tell them Memorial

          Hospital can help.  Memorial Hospital provides

          recovery programs designed to stop bulimia's vicious

          binge-purge cycle.  There's more to love than candy

          hearts.  Loving care can help your Valentine.
```

develop a fresh and interesting approach to the subject that will win the audience's attention. No one can say for sure how to brainstorm these new approaches, but ultimately everything people do is potential material for a PSA. So is everything people have ever read or seen. In trying to convince a person to adopt a new behavior or attitude, look for relevant connections. Start with yourself. You're a person. Think how the topic connects to your life. Then explore how it connects to other people's lives.

A few years ago it seemed as though every other young starlet was admitting that she was a closet anorexic. When I found out that the local hospital had a special program for women with eating disorders, I gave my students a hospital pamphlet and asked them to write radio PSAs to be aired on a local radio station. One student looked at the calendar and submitted the script reproduced above.

To write a good PSA, you often have to jump through three hoops; that is, satisfy three critical audiences. First, there's the station manager or program director. Do they think this message is appropriate for their audience? Is it written well enough to be read on the air? Then there's the station's general audience. We know that the vast majority of them do not suffer eating disorders, but is the information contained in the PSA interesting enough that they gain something simply by hearing it? And, finally, there's the targeted audience: young women who suffer from eating disorders and their friends. Does the PSA identify a problem in their lives and present a workable solution? A well-written PSA must meet all these demands.

For a moment, we must take a short detour from our aesthetic concerns to consider essentially practical matters. The first is the format of the script. In this case, it's radio drama. The narrow left column identifies the speaker. The wide right column contains the copy. The tabs and margins are set for a 50-character line that takes about 3 seconds to read. Not surprisingly, this 30-second PSA runs 10 lines. But, equally important to station management is the information at the top of the script. What is this? Whom is it from? Whom can we contact if we have questions about the content? What is the phone number? All these items are meant to facilitate decisions that station managers must make. In addition, they need to know the best time to air the spot. Many PSAs are tied to holidays, seasons, special events, community activities, or national celebrations. In broadcasting, timeliness is everything. Start and stop dates save announcers from the embarrassing recognition that they're reading copy that's out of date. Finally, the writer must provide an accurate time estimate for the PSA. There's nothing sacrosanct about the layout of this information at the top of the PSA. But it must be there. It sends a critical signal that the organization asking for free air time understands the radio business.

Another way that organizations and governmental agencies display their ignorance of the business is their shotgun approach to disseminating PSAs. Top-40 rock stations receive PSAs on applying for social security benefits even though their listeners may be 45 years from retirement. Meantime, the pleas of pro basketball stars to buckle up may end up at classical music stations whose listeners remain unimpressed.

Television killed off general interest radio stations like it killed off *Life* and the *Saturday Evening Post*. Radio broadcasters adopt a format for their stations that shapes all their programming. Listeners come to expect a certain type of music or content no matter when they tune in. When a radio station changes format from album-oriented rock to country music, it expects to lose one audience and gain another. PSAs that don't fit the format never hit the air. That may sound like a hard-hearted business decision, but, in truth, radio broadcasters are setting legitimate criteria for effective communication.

Every PSA is written for a target audience. Every radio format is designed for a specific segment of the listening public. PSA writers should be creating messages that fit the format of radio stations that attract their target audiences. It's as simple as that. Creating PSAs that match the format and the audience of the station shows that every effort is being made to use free air time effectively. Professional broadcasters will appreciate that effort.

Radio PSAs arrive at stations in many forms: prerecorded on reel-to-reel tape, audio cassettes, and inexpensive records or as announcer scripts to be read by station personnel. Radio station preferences vary, but, at a practical level, live scripts such as the "Bulimia" PSA have one serendipitous advantage. As long as a station announcer or disc jockey reads it, it is immediately identified with the station's personalities and sound. If the topic relates to the interests and needs of the station's listeners, then its chances of airing are good if it has been cleverly conceived and well written.

The "Bulimia" PSA, for instance, attracts our interest because it connects to a familiar holiday but raises uncertainty by questioning a traditional custom. While we're waiting for the answer, the writer shifts us to the problem she wants us to consider: She defines bulimia, identifies it as a curable illness, and tells us where to get help. Then she returns to the Valentine theme, urging us more generally to show concern for the person we love. Even if we know no one who suffers from bulimia, the intrusion into our time has not been irksome. Certainly, it has been less annoying than a hard-sell commercial. We're a bit wiser than before, and, perhaps, the PSA will actually help someone else. Further, the writer skillfully employs repetition to develop a coherent and clear message. Twice she describes what sort of eating disorder bulimia is. Twice she names Memorial Hospital as a source of help. And Valentine's Day and candy hearts receive a second mention at the end of the PSA, assuring its thematic unity.

Straight Readers

The "Bulimia" PSA was designed to be aired in early February and was aimed at a local audience: people who live reasonably close to Memorial Hospital. Before we consider more complex PSA scripts, I want to discuss a professionally written straight reader that was distributed to radio stations nationwide. This PSA was part of a packet the Selective Service System sent to broadcasters across the country. The target audience was any male U.S. citizen about to celebrate his 18th birthday. Two versions are reproduced on page 50.

Despite its national distribution, the 30-second "Register" PSA doesn't make it cleanly through all the hoops. First, it's wordy. The script runs 12 and one-half lines. It's a tight squeeze to fit that many words into a half-minute spot. Extra words are often symptomatic of a lack of focus. Indeed, the PSA sounds like it was written by a government agency. Every member of the bureaucracy had some point to make. And one of the points generates political controversy, not compliance. Is it absolutely clear, as the PSA contends, that "you're not registering for a draft"? Sure, there's no draft now, but what is the Selective Service going to do with the list in case of a national emergency? On that point, the PSA is noticeably silent.

As is often the case in broadcast writing, less can be more. In the accompanying 10-second version, the Selective Service creates a credible message by retaining only the strongest elements of its 30-second spot.

Short and swift: This PSA identifies its target audience, tells them what to do, and provides three concise arguments for compliance. If registering is truly no big deal, then 18 year olds can get the details at the post office. Interestingly, the concluding triplet of the 10-second version complements its

"REGISTER"

ANNCR: Hey guys, if you're about to turn 18, you've got to get down to the post office and register with Selective Service. Now let's get one thing clear -- you're not registering for a draft. No one's been drafted in over 10 years. You're just adding your name to a list, in case of a national emergency. Registering is easy. Just go down to the post office within a month of your 18th birthday, pick up a card, fill it out, and hand it to a postal clerk. It takes just about five minutes. So if you're about to become 18, don't forget to register with Selective Service. It's quick. It's easy. And it's the law.

"QUICK"

ANNCR: Hey guys, if you're going to be 18 this month, register with Selective Service at the post office. It's quick. It's easy. And it's the law.

own formal structure. The PSA is quick to read, easy to understand, and forceful at the end. Live script PSAs should try to meet those standards.

Testimonials

If we thumb through a 40 year-old magazine, we should not be surprised to come across an advertisement in which an opera singer endorses a particular brand of cigarettes as being especially mild to the throat. And 40 years before that, the same brand might have been endorsed by a distant relative of a European monarch. Testimonials may not be quite so popular in advertising as they once were. Audiences have grown skeptical. But, when celebrity and product are well matched—tennis champion and racket, basketball star and shoe, racing driver and motor oil—simple testimonials are one way of attracting attention to a message and heightening the credibility of its premise.

What works with commercials works with public service announcements. In fact, nationally or locally known personalities who refuse to endorse a commercial product for their own financial gain may well volunteer their time for a campaign or a cause they believe in. Georgetown University basketball coach John Thompson is a person that many young men look up to, and perhaps more importantly, someone who takes a sincere interest in the young men he coaches. So, when the Selective Service organized its registration campaign, Coach Thompson was recruited to voice a PSA that specifically emphasized his relationship with young men turning 18. Because the PSA had to be prerecorded for national distribution, the writer also added background sound effects that placed Coach Thompson at basketball practice, not in a soundproofed recording studio. The sound effects were a small touch, but they reinforced the notion of Thompson's daily contact with young men like those he was trying to persuade.

Of course, athletes aren't the only personalities who can record convincing PSAs. The Will Rogers Institute produces many PSAs, using Hollywood stars to promote better health and safety. Note how the writer of the PSA on page 52 crafted a message about accidental injuries that particularly suited television comedienne Lucille Ball.

The PSA begins and ends with references to professional comedians using misfortune to get laughs while making clear that everyday accidents are quite different: They produce pain. Not only does the writer argue verbally for a changed behavior—one out of four people will require a doctor's care—but the writer generates images of slapstick antics and real-life accidents that the audience immediately recognizes as being charged with completely different emotions. The PSA takes aim at both mind and emotions to promote behavioral change.

```
                    "SLAPSTICK"

    LUCY:    Hi. This is Lucille Ball. Slapstick comedians can
             get laughs out of taking a fall or smashing a thumb
             with a hammer. But in real life, accidents cause
             pain and sometimes permanent disability. This year
             one out of four people will have an accident that
             requires a doctor's care. But most accidents can be
             prevented by taking sensible precautions. So always
             lean towards safety. And leave the accidents to
             those of us who want to make you laugh.
    ANNCR:   This message is from the Will Rogers Institute, White
             Plains, New York.
```

Documentaries and Dramatizations

Once an organization commits itself to prerecording its PSAs, then all the techniques of radio production—multiple voices, music, and sound effects—are at the disposal of the broadcast writer. The PSA can employ documentary techniques—using the recorded statements of actual persons—or it can be a completely fabricated dramatization. What follows on page 53 is a documentary-like PSA that the United States Catholic Conference created for its campaign against poverty. This type of announcement or commercial is often called a "slice of life."

    All the elements are skillfully blended to create a coherent theme. Merry-go-round music sets the scene and continues in the background through the 60-second spot. Audio sound bites from four different down-and-out individuals are woven together to trace the origins and eventual consequences of poverty. The announcer adds just enough commentary to make the ironic theme explicit: The circle of poverty is a vicious one for its faceless victims. If the PSA has a fault, then it is its failure to specify an action to be taken. Should we send money, volunteer, or stay in school? The emotional pitch works but only for so long. As the Roman orator Apollonius once said, "Nothing dries faster than a human tear."

Chapter 3 Radio Commercials and Public Service Announcements

"POVERTY MERRY-GO-ROUND"

MUSIC: <u>MERRY-GO-ROUND PIPE ORGAN UP FULL, THEN UNDER</u>

ANNCR: Merry-go-rounds are fun...except this one. It's called poverty.

CUT #1: All of my life I had to take little jobs, you know. I've never been good enough at anything to call myself anything.

CUT #2: When we was children, we worked on the farm and in the fields.

CUT #3: We were poor. We didn't have enough bread. I didn't get the education...

CUT #4: It kind of hurts me to think about the rule being out 14, 15, and sometimes 16 hours a day in order to bring 10, 11 dollars home.

CUT #5: I had to work. I had to exist. I wish I could have gone to school.

CUT #6: I'm depressed and I'm looking for work.

CUT #7: And they see how you've been going out of work for so many months. And the guy says, "Wow, this guy's a bum."

ANNCR: A merry-go-round is no fun when you can't get off.

CUT #8: Just give me a break.

ANNCR: Help break the circle of poverty. Campaign for Human Development. United States Catholic Conference.

MUSIC: <u>UP FULL TO FINISH</u>

<u>END</u>

"STAR TREK II"

MUSIC: THEME FROM STAR TREK. THEN UNDER FOR...

ANNCR: These are the voyages of Starship ADULTHOOD. Its mission to boldly go where most 18-year-old men have gone before...to the post office.

SCOTTY: Captain, we're almost there. It's the building with the flag in front, right?

CAPTAIN: (WITH GREAT AUTHORITY) Right, Scotty. (PAUSES) Imagine. Losing 30 years in the last time warp. We're all 18 again!

SPOCK: And Captain, it's only logical that we register with Selective Service.

SCOTTY: (WORRIED) But Captain, it's gonna take forever.

SPOCK: (CUTS IN) Incorrect. Registering only takes five minutes. We just fill out a little card.

CAPTAIN: (HEROICALLY) Ahh, I can see it now...fighting the evil Spasmodians...

SPOCK: Sorry, Captain, but there's no draft. There hasn't been a draft for a decade.

CAPTAIN: Beam us down, Mr. Scott!

SOUND EFFX: SIZZLE-SIZZLE-ZAP

CAPTAIN: Excuse us, Ma'am. We're here to register with Selective Service.

CLERK: (WITH HILLBILLY ACCENT) Well, that's nice boys. (SUSPICIOUSLY) Saaaay, is the one with the pointy ears from around these parts?

(MORE)

```
                                                              2.

   MUSIC:   UP THEME, THEN UNDER
   ANNCR:   If you've turned 18, trek on down to the post
            office and register. It's quick. It's easy. And
            it's the law.
   CLERK:   Billy-Joel McGee!  I'd know your ears anywhere!
   MUSIC: UP FULL TO FINISH
                              END
```

Of all the possible formats, perhaps the most difficult to create is a successful minidramatization. In Chapter 8 we shall actually confront what it takes to write a dramatic script. Certainly, a minute is not enough time to develop the credible characters and compelling conflicts that we associate with good dramatic writing. More often than not, minidramatizations are really miniparodies of well-known plays, films, or TV serials. Just like the fairy tales we saw caricatured in Glenn Mitchell's commentary on *Jacqueline & the Beanstalk*, the writer plays on characters and situations already in the minds of the audience. The Selective Service PSA packet included three prerecorded dramatizations, "Computer Knows Best," "Tarzan and Boy," and "Star Trek II." The "Star Trek II" script is reproduced beginning on page 54 is not vintage Bob and Ray. But it makes its factual points rather effortlessly, and to some degree more honestly than the straight reader on the same topic. Just to make sure the audience doesn't overlook the basic message, the announcer sums up the serious part before we return to the woman clerk for a humorous tag. Good parodies, of course, are hard to produce. PSAs like this one can easily turn corny. You need to try them out on friends and colleagues before you let them loose on the airwaves.

This spot illustrates as well some basic rules for writing radio drama. All the voices must be unique, and rarely should more than three characters participate in the dialogue at any one time. Otherwise the audience will lose track of who's speaking. Scotty, Captain Kirk, and Spock are all easily identifiable in the first half of the spot. In the second half, the woman clerk with the hillbilly accent is easily distinguished from the announcer. Also, notice how familiar music and sound effects are used to establish the two scenes. These techniques are essential whether the drama runs 30 seconds or 30 minutes.

PSA Guidelines

PSAs can run the gamut from deadly serious messages about AIDS to light-hearted ads to promote a high school play. No matter what the topic, though, the broadcast writer strives to create as effective a message as possible. In recent years, medical professionals have been giving increasing attention to the effective use of mass media in improving the public's health. Aided by federal grants, teams of medical and media experts have mounted campaigns to change eating habits, reduce smoking, promote cancer check-ups, and cut drug abuse. Madison Avenue professionals have always contributed time and creative effort to worthy causes. But now the worthy causes are developing their own cadre of experienced professionals, ready to advise community and health organizations on how to develop PSAs.

Here are 12 guidelines from the National Institutes of Health that set standards for effective PSAs. They can serve as a checklist for almost any radio PSA script you write. For the most part, they simply review the points presented in this chapter.

- Keep messages short and simple—just one or two key points.
- Repeat the subject as many times as possible.
- Recommend performing specific behaviors.
- Provide new, accurate, and complete information.
- Use a slogan or theme.
- Be sure your message is relevant to your target audience.
- Be sure that the message presenter is seen as a credible source of information, whether authority figure, target audience member, or celebrity.
- Select a testimonial, demonstration, or slice-of-life format.
- Use only a few characters.
- Present the facts in a straightforward manner.
- Use positive rather than negative appeals.
- Use humor, if appropriate, but pretest to be sure it does not offend the intended audience.

Inasmuch as these guidelines were written for health campaigns, they are suitably cautious about humorous appeals. Entertainment values can easily overwhelm educational aims. But, when appropriate, humor is extremely effective at winning attention and creating good will. You would do well, however, to pretest humor in any PSA not only to be sure it does not offend the intended audience but also to make sure the humor works as intended, without injury to any innocent segment of the listening public.

PERSUASION AND ETHICS

For more than 35 years, there has been a book on the market called *How to Lie with Statistics*. It's my guess that it owes its popularity in some part to its title, which neatly captures the public's skepticism about any argument that uses numbers to change people's opinions. Yet, in many ways, statisticians use numbers no differently than writers use words. Numbers, like words, are used to symbolize abstract concepts. They are combined together in agreed upon ways that conjure up similar meanings at both source and destination. The problem with statistics, however, is that the mathematical language used to express ideas with statistics is unfamiliar to most of us. We fear that a fast-talking statistical expert can twist the numbers any which way in order to win an argument. Thus, the public buys books entitled *How to Lie with Statistics*. Yet to the best of my knowledge, no one has ever thought to publish a sequel, *How to Lie with Words*.

The fact is, however, that writers can lie with words, and the more expert the writer, the more difficult it may be to detect the falsehood. But what keeps expert statisticians from lying with statistics and expert writers from lying with words is a personal and professional sense of ethical behavior. In fact, the more we appreciate the fine points of writing and the fine points of statistics, the more sensitive we become to the distortions that arise when words and numbers are used fast and loose. Even when the goal is to persuade the audience, standards of truth and accuracy must be maintained. Statisticians have ethical codes and professional sanctions against lying. The same goes for broadcast writers. If a broadcast writer does not believe his or her own words, then the result is not persuasion, but propaganda.

As in every activity, gray areas requiring interpretation exist. The Selective Service PSAs we have discussed provide an interesting case study. Today's 18 year olds have no personal memory of the Vietnam War and resistance to the draft. They may at best have a dim awareness of the link between the creation of the Selective Service System on September 16, 1940, and the initiation of the military draft at the outbreak of World War II. The military draft then continued uninterrupted—whether the United States was at war or at peace—until July 1, 1973.

For those who opposed the draft, the congressional vote to reinstate Selective Service registration in July 1980 was tantamount to reimposing the draft. Naturally, the Selective Service System wanted to dispel that notion. Their argument was a narrow one, but it was technically correct. There's no war. There's no draft. Registering with the Selective Service System should not be equated with registering for a draft. Furthermore, as long as the country is at peace, there is little chance of reinstating the draft.

In the "Star Trek II" PSA, Mr. Spock ignored the larger argument of the draft critics by choosing to rebut only the 18 year old's immediate concern that he faces military service. Spock deflates that concern by debunking Captain Kirk's heroic visions of military action.

CAPTAIN: (HEROICALLY) Ahh, I can see it now...fighting the evil Spasmodians...

SPOCK: Sorry, Captain, but there's no draft. There hasn't been a draft for a decade.

However, in the straight reader version, the argument goes awry.

> ANNCR: Now let's get one thing clear—you're not registering for a draft. No one's been drafted in over 10 years. You're just adding your name to a list, in case of a national emergency.

But is it clear that "you're not registering for a draft?" To paraphrase Queen Gertrude in *Hamlet*, "The announcer doth protest too much, methinks."

The writer has complicated the argument by invoking the term "national emergency." As soon as the listener recognizes that one possible "national emergency" is "war," then indeed 18-year-old Americans could be registering for "a draft." In the event of "a national emergency"—read "war"—what the writer innocently portrayed as "a list" would become "the list" for inducting young men into the military. Unlike the writer of this PSA, Mr. Spock avoided this muddle by choosing his words carefully. Of course, we would expect nothing less from a supra-rational intelligence like Spock.

SCRIPTWRITING ASSIGNMENT

Nonprofit organizations and government agencies publish numerous pamphlets urging the public to adopt safer and healthier lifestyles and behaviors. One specific cause or campaign probably makes enormous sense to you. Using their persuasive literature as a starting point, research the topic, and write two radio PSAs urging the public to take a specific action. One of your two PSAs should be a straight 30-second reader that an announcer or disc jockey at a local radio station can deliver on the air. The second PSA you write should provide the script for a 30- or 60-second prerecorded announcement that uses sound effects, dialogue, or a dramatic or humorous situation to attract the audience's attention and make its point. As in the sample "Bulimia" script, remember to include the name of the sponsoring organization, a contact person (probably you), the appropriate dates for airing the PSA, and its running time.

ADDITIONAL READINGS

Advertising: The Uneasy Persuasion by Michael Schudson (Basic Books, New York, 1984). This is an in-depth study of advertising as a social and economic institution in America. Schudson reveals why it is so difficult to determine if advertising really works, but he finds the ad culture interesting in itself as a manifestation of what he calls "capitalist realism."

Broadcast Copywriting by Peter B. Orlik (Allyn and Bacon, Boston, 1986). Orlik's book deals with the basic building blocks of radio and television copy: station IDS, promos, PSAs, and commercials and provides numerous scripted examples. His chapter on political campaigns and issues should be helpful for the assignment in Chapter 7 when you will be writing a political spot for television.

Making PSAs Work: A Handbook for Health Communication Professionals by the National Institutes of Health (DHEW Publication (NIH) 85-2485, U.S. GPO, Washington, DC, 1985). This is a basic instruction manual for those without exposure to broadcast training. But because medical professionals are used to adapting scientific research to clinical practice, this handbook freely mixes communication research findings with practical suggestions on how to write, produce, and distribute PSAs.

4

Broadcast Interviews

In 1983, novelist Walker Percy wrote a satirical essay in script format called "The Last Donahue Show." Percy proposed an imaginary last episode of the popular talk show, dedicated as usual to the discussion of sexual behavior. This time, however, Donahue and his forthright panelists are interrupted by three dissenters. One bears a likeness to the sixteenth century French theologian, John Calvin. Dressed in a black robe, he condemns the speakers for their "licentious talk about deeds which are an abomination before God." The second dissenter is a Confederate army officer. A Southern gentleman of the old school, he upbraids these folks for the way they act and talk. "Where I come from, we'd call them [the panelists] white trash." Finally, the third dissenter speaks up. Oddly dressed in a 1950s double-breasted suit, he turns out to be a cosmic intelligence projected as a holographic image. He has arrived to forewarn the earthlings that a nuclear war between the two superpowers is imminent and to take back to his planet for study a pregnant 14-year-old panelist from the show.

    Percy, whose first novel, *The Moviegoer*, won the National Book Award, is much too realistic about the impact of mass media on the American psyche to forecast the last "Phil Donahue Show." Perhaps, he is telling us instead that nothing short of a nuclear conflagration will eliminate Donahue and his talk-show competitors from the airwaves. While mocking the conflict between solemnity and sensationalism that characterizes these programs, Percy nonetheless concedes "that the high ratings of these sex-talk shows are nothing more nor less than an index of the public's intense interest in such matters." The talk show fills many gaps in the viewer's life: a knowledge gap, an emotion gap, an isolation gap. Some experts see the shows as a surrogate for campfire gossip, an antidote to lives of quiet desperation.

When we review the full range of television programming, it becomes quite clear that talk supplies the fundamental content for a substantial portion of the daily broadcast schedule. Like Hydra, the nine-headed monster from Greek mythology, the interview program reformulates itself throughout the broadcast day. "Today," "Good Morning, America," "Donahue," "Oprah," "Geraldo," "Evening Magazine," "McNeil-Lehrer News/Hour," "Nightline," and "The Tonight Show" are among the best known examples. Only a few soap operas, for instance, can rival NBC's "Today" and "Tonight Show" for television longevity. In fact, NBC's "Meet the Press" as of 1990 is the oldest continuous-running program on network television.

Interview programs address the audience's need for information about real persons and real events. Social critics may judge those needs as serious (when a political candidate is questioned during an election campaign) or diversionary (when a television star is interviewed about a new network program). But what is similar about all talk shows is what broadcast executives have always appreciated. Even more important than talk being informative or entertaining, talk is cheap. Interview programs require no rehearsal, no editing, and no embellishments, just interviewers who know what to ask and when to ask it. Some, such as Johnny Carson, Ted Koppel, Barbara Walters, Phil Donahue, and Oprah Winfrey, command huge salaries, because their programs sustain the interest of large audiences. Day in, day out, they ask questions the audience wants to ask and, perhaps, more important, those the audience never thought to ask. The ultimate goal is to elicit an answer the audience never heard before or could never imagine. It's a skill that interviewers develop with on-air practice and behind-the-scenes preparation. Obviously, there's some degree of luck involved in every successful interview. But, as a successful scientific researcher once remarked, "Luck favors the prepared mind." It's no less true of interviewers than scientists.

REAL-TIME AND EDITED INTERVIEWS

So far, we have been discussing broadcast interviews of a special type: what we might call real-time or verbatim interviews. While these question and answer sessions may be produced within a designated time limit—90 minutes for a presidential debate, the time between two commercial breaks on the "Tonight Show," or no more than four minutes with the mayor at city hall during a "live" segment in the six o'clock news—we view or listen to such interviews in their entirety. Nothing is added or removed. We hear the interviewer ask the questions and the interviewee respond. The audience experiences a continuous event whether live or taped.

It may seem trivial to point this out, but any interview that has been recorded on audiotape or videotape can be edited to extract just highlights or even a single excerpt that for thematic or aesthetic reasons better fits the format of the program into which it is inserted: hence, the 30-second sound bite in television news, the reappearing expert in a science documentary, a mosaic of slice of life quotes in a PSA, or the hidden camera testimonials in a TV commercial. Taken out of context, however, each recorded response (called a "sound bite" in television and an "actuality" in radio) must be embedded in a new structure that accommodates its original meaning.

For every hundred interviews recorded each day, only a few are aired in their entirety. The remainder provide much needed raw material for reports, features, reviews, and other program segments where verbatim responses are interspersed with narrative and descriptive passages. Thus, the interviewer or a writer must sift through the unrefined ore for a few gems or nuggets that add color and illumination to the selected topic. In fact, one of the first talents a broadcast writer must develop is the ability to choose the right quote and provide a proper verbal setting.

While the audience may never perceive it, there are actually two stages in the production of interview programming. The interviewer must gather the information. A writer must then edit it. Certainly, the same person may perform both tasks, but, in this chapter, we will concentrate on the writer's job: editing recorded information and placing it in a meaningful context.

Gathering and Editing Information

Interviewing has always been a mainstay of journalistic practice. And for good reason. Although the journalist's job is to report on public events, to report only what they observe would require journalists to be omniscient and omnipresent. Let's say a fire breaks out in a high-rise apartment building. The journalist rushes to the scene. On arrival he or she observes half a dozen fire engines and ladder trucks parked around the building, high pressure hoses strewn about the street, apartment dwellers and passersby standing on the curb, firefighters rushing in and out the building's front door, and a few wisps of smoke from an upper story window. As observers, journalists can learn nothing more than other eyewitnesses on the street. They're observing a fire scene, but they can't even locate the flames.

Unlike other bystanders, however, journalists are permitted to be aggressive and intrusive. Immediately, the journalist begins to ask people questions, especially those in uniform, those who might live in the building, and those who might be hurt or know about someone who is. Eventually, the reporter gathers a collection of what he or she believes to be logical and coherent facts about the event. The specifics are substantiated by trusted experts like the fire chief or lesser-known participants and eyewitnesses whose personal accounts corroborate each other's. On the basis of experience in interviewing similar sorts of people, the journalist concludes that their testimony is reliable and not likely to differ from any other objective investigation. Thus, long before any official document is completed, journalists will publish seemingly objective accounts—but in their own words.

Why do journalists use their own words: to improve the speed and efficiency with which they can communicate information. Using their own words, rather than composing their account from verbatim quotes in the style of a cinéma vérité documentary, permits them maximum freedom to create a clear and coherent exposition. Perhaps the best example of purely factual expositions based on other sources of information are the entries in a standard encyclopedia. Think for a moment how each entry is written in the same voice and how rarely the prose is organized to accommodate a direct quote from an expert or an historical figure. As a practical matter, the ad lib responses of most interviewees are bound to be redundant, long-winded, imprecise, and grammatically flawed. Journalists are trained to write better than most people speak. Thus, in print, journalists are likely to use direct quotes only when the interviewee's words are so precise that they defy improvement, so remarkable that the audience wants to read exactly what was said, or so questionable that journalists want to dissociate themselves from statements they believe to be false.

In broadcasting, however, there are new dimensions to consider. Some are simply aesthetic that result from the intercutting of sound segments or video. In radio, a change of voices can renew interest in a discourse. In television, a change of faces can attract attention back to the screen. Even more important are inferences that listeners make from the interviewee's particular voice or diction. No one thinks it curious that in broadcasting an interview with a foreign-language speaker begins with the speaker's natural voice, which then gives way to a voice-over translation. However, in print, the reader would find it unusual indeed for Gorbachev's quoted comments to begin with his verbatim Russian statement ahead of an English translation. In addition, background sounds that occur in a radio actuality can expand the ambience and enhance the credibility of what is, in fact, only a partial recreation of reality. In television, viewers can read faces even better than they can read lips. Talking heads may grow boring, but when the quote is truly important, viewers want the camera to focus on the speaker's face so they can examine it for unspoken expressions.

TECHNICAL CONSIDERATIONS IN EDITING

Additional information never comes cheap. Providing the audience with not only the words, but also the actual voices and video of an interview, complicates enormously the process of editing. In print, writers have immense freedom to eliminate segments of the verbatim transcript whenever they wish. In broadcasting, writers may make their initial choices based on a written transcript, but often they create an aesthetically unacceptable discontinuity in the audio or the video channel. Words are not always spaced on audiotape as they are in print. Speech is continuous. Words mesh, making them difficult to separate. Moreover, the speaker's intonation can signal to the audience that the thought is not finished even if a syntactically complete sentence has already been spoken. Changes in background sound between two audio segments can also have a distracting effect on the audience. Listeners may wonder why noises in the background—music, traffic, sirens, raindrops—suddenly stop.

Because television is an amalgam of sound and sight, any cut in the videotape is bound to create a discontinuity in one channel or both. Even if the interviewee's words seem acceptable, the picture may not be. When a section of tape is removed, the audience perceives a sudden jerk in the action. That's called a "jump cut." As unimportant as the interviewee's movements may be, they are dutifully recorded by the camera. Before the excised video segment, the interviewee's right hand may be raised high. Now the hand drops to the desk. (Cigarette smokers can create havoc on videotape.) Some other video must be patched over the gap, starting a second or two before the jump cut and extending just past it. The inserted video must make sense. For instance, in interviews, we often see a cutaway picture of the interviewer earnestly listening. Because the camera must focus on the interviewee, cutaways must be shot before or after the interview itself unless a second camera is available. When only one camera is available, close up pictures of the interviewer listening and asking questions are often reshot after the interview.

But at this point in the text, the logistical planning and actual practice of video editing can only be hinted at. In reality, it is too early to discuss in detail the demands of television production. That will come later. For the rest of this chapter, then, we will focus on the presentation of interviews on radio. We will work from printed transcripts, recognizing, of course, their inadequacies. But, at the same time, one important distinction between video and audio editing should become apparent. Every cut in videotape requires a rather distinctive video solution, dependent on the availability of alternative but thematically related shots. In audio editing, most cuts work as envisioned or very nearly so. Most problems arising from mismatches of intonation or background sound are resolved by lengthening (or shortening) the selected actualities. And, as we shall see, if all else fails, the writer can include the information (if not the actuality) by using a conventional narrator to voice those remarks. Thus, purely technical dilemmas need not overwhelm the writer's vision when creating scripts from audio materials.

AN INTERVIEW WITH CANDIDATE QUAYLE

By now the 1988 presidential election campaign has been incorporated into encyclopedias and history books. For the most part, these authoritative accounts are presented with a minimal amount of quoted material. As in every campaign, much of what is said is forgotten soon after election day. What may be ironic in this case is how hard the press corps had to fight to get a genuinely original response from any of the candidates. In particular, Republican campaign officials kept journalists away from Vice President Dan Quayle, who, as the junior senator from Indiana, had little experience in deflecting sharp questions.

One of the few reporters who broke through the campaign armor was Nina Totenberg, at that time the legal correspondent for National Public Radio's "All Things Considered." She caught up with candidate Quayle on a campaign bus in Illinois. She must have sat on the aisle seat with Quayle against the window. Armed with a tape recorder, she collected enough material for an extended interview feature that aired on October 18, 1988.

As you read this excerpt, you will see that Totenberg's narration, which provides the setting for Quayle's sound bites, is woven from personal observations and interviews with other people associated with the vice-presidential campaign. Try then to imagine all the sources of information that were available to Totenberg as she created this profile of the vice-presidential candidate.

ANCHOR INTRO: Throughout this campaign, wherever Michael Dukakis goes, and no matter how bad or good a day he's having, he unloads one surefire zinger—a jab aimed at George Bush's running mate, Senator Dan Quayle. Stung by all the ridicule, Quayle declared his independence of his so-called handlers a week ago. N-P-R's Nina Totenberg joined Quayle on the road this week—in the Midwest—to see how things are going for the 41-year-old Hoosier.

TOTENBERG: Dan Quayle laughingly admits it. He may have been the first male bimbo in America, the first public man to be viewed as just a pretty face with no brains.

QUAYLE: It was inevitable that it was going to happen to somebody. And I think it, unfortunately I had to be the target...that this bimbo thing was going to be applied to men some day. And I hate it! And I know what some of the unjustified charges of some women in the past have been, and I think it's (*PAUSE*) It's rather despicable, and I think I'll outgrow it and get over it, but no, I don't like it one damn bit!

TOTENBERG: You're a born-again feminist.

QUAYLE: (*LAUGHS*) Just about. I know what they're saying.

TOTENBERG: Although Quayle officially claimed his independence from his handlers seven days ago, little about his campaign has changed. The speeches are the same. The handlers are still there. And there seems to be no disagreement between staff and candidate. So what's the difference? Except that now he does talk to the press.

QUAYLE: I'd say that that's probably the major difference...is uh accessibility, communicating uh with the media, and the comfort zone. I've been on the national campaign trail now since August 15th. It took a little time to get used to it, and it took a

Chapter 4 Broadcast Interviews **67**

TOTENBERG: little time for the campaign, the national campaign to get used to me.

TOTENBERG: Quayle insists that his independence was his idea...that he was angered by the belittling statements about him in the press, even from Bush staffers. But many observers of the campaign believe Quayle's declaration of independence was the ultimate handlers' ploy...a last attempt to give the beleaguered vice-presidential candidate some stature. Plucked from obscurity to join the national ticket, Quayle, since his independence day, is back in relative obscurity or as close to it as Bush campaign officials say privately that they can arrange. While Bush tours the big cities and the major media markets, Quayle is sent to small towns to face uncritical local media coverage and carefully screened audiences. His campaign stops are beautifully orchestrated. The pictures of them on local TV news are gorgeous. In the background are bales of hay, farm equipment, pumpkin patches, and always, lots and lots of American flags. His message is patriotism, American values, and freedom.

QUAYLE: George Bush and I are committed to preserving freedom, and FREEDOM IS WHAT MAKES THIS COUNTRY THE GREATEST COUNTRY IN THE WORLD! (*A CRESCENDO OF SCREAMS, CHEERS, AND APPLAUSE FROM AUDIENCE*) THANK YOU AND GOD BLESS YOU!

TOTENBERG: The stump speech has few specifics, so in an interview on his bus tour through rural Illinois, I asked Quayle to elaborate.

QUAYLE: Well, the first freedom that you want to protect is the freedom of our country. I mean the freedom of our country means... our country, the constitution, our government. We have a free government, and we want to maintain that freedom. But freedom means a lot of different things...freedom of speech, freedom of religion, individual liberties.

TOTENBERG: You mentioned freedom of religion. Do you think Jehovah's Witnesses should be free to refuse to say the "Pledge of Allegiance" in school, if it violates their religious principles to do so?

QUAYLE: I think that the "Pledge of Allegiance" legislation that has been passed at the state levels on having a teacher lead the class on the "Pledge of Allegiance" is perfectly proper, and they have the freedom to lead in that "Pledge of Allegiance," and I don't think it's going to infringe on anybody else's freedom.

TOTENBERG: But you realize that a teacher who's a Jehovah's Witness, who felt that was a violation of his or her faith, would be violating a criminal statute if he or she refused to lead the "Pledge"?

QUAYLE: We have freedom of religion and we have a free legislature...an independent government that passes laws, and the courts of this land uphold and take freedom of religion very importantly. And to my knowledge—and we'll see if the courts get into this—that the "Pledge of Allegiance" statutes that have passed meet the constitutional test of freedom of religion.

TOTENBERG: No, Senator. They've been struck down every time.

QUAYLE: Well, I don't know. There's a lot of various laws on the books. The one from Massachusetts hasn't been struck down. The one that the governor has here in Illinois. I don't think it's been struck down.

TOTENBERG: They've never been enforced.

QUAYLE: (*PAUSE*) Well, they're on the books.

TOTENBERG: Quayle's answer reveals that although he's gotten more sure-footed, there's still dangers for him in an unstructured situation. Bush and Quayle have hit Michael Dukakis hard for vetoing a state law that made it illegal for a public school teacher to refuse to lead a class in the "Pledge of Allegiance." Although the legislature overrode the veto, that law and others like it have not been enforced because of a 1943 Supreme Court ruling that declared unconstitutional a similar state law. Although Quayle is a lawyer and worked for the state attorney general in Indiana, he apparently did not know that...

As surely as Totenberg pieced this feature together, we can disassemble it into its original parts. The report runs a total of nine minutes and ten seconds. In the first four minutes and 48 seconds transcribed above, Totenberg gradually involves the listener in increasingly complex topics. She devotes 36 seconds to the looks versus intellect question, one minute 49 seconds to the orchestration of Quayle's campaign, and two minutes 23 seconds to the religious freedom versus "Pledge of Allegiance" question.

Totenberg wastes no time in convincing us that this interview is unlike others we might have heard. She allows herself only nine seconds to set up Quayle's first response in which he not only acknowledges the legitimacy of the "bimbo" question but also laughingly concedes that his experience has made him a feminist fellow traveler. Totenberg has attracted our attention. Note, however, that we never hear the question that prompted this response nor do we know much about the circumstances under which it was obtained. Instead, Totenberg formulates in as few words as possible a fitting introduction to set up the "bimbo" actuality. Written at another time in another place, the set up creates a context for the quote to come and alerts the audience to the unexpected. The key word is "admits." Totenberg has elicited from Quayle a remarkable statement.

While the audience is musing over Quayle's admission, Totenberg starts to build a more substantial structure in which to embed other excerpts from her interviews. Now she's ready to report on the "handling" of a vice-presidential candidate (as promised in the anchor's lead-in). Once again, we never hear Totenberg's exact question, but in her set up to Quayle's response she gives the audience an indication of how she might have posed it. "So what's the difference?" she asks rhetorically, and then answers, "Except that now he does talk to the press." That last awkward phrase, it should be noted, is forced by the nature of the Quayle actuality itself. To use Quayle's recorded words, Totenberg has to let the audience know what he's referring to when he says, "I'd say that that's probably the difference...." Quayle talks about his changes abstractly. He's accessible, he's communicating with the media, he's now comfortable. Totenberg cuts through the abstract talk by reducing it to a concrete image: "Now he does talk to the press."

Through the first one minute 15 seconds of the report, we hear Quayle for almost 50 seconds. That's how it should be in an interview. But then Totenberg takes over for a 55-second monologue. The reason is efficiency. In truth, there's not much else new to say about the Quayle campaign. She sums it up as quickly as she can. It's important, however, to notice the techniques she uses to validate her description. She paraphrases Quayle ("Quayle insists...") rather than using direct quotes, relies upon the "many observers of the campaign" to give alternative explanations, and characterizes the campaign generally by noting items that everyone is free to observe.

This narrative style is what journalists call objective. A better term might be intersubjective, meaning that other members of the national press corps as well as the mainstream audience of "All Things Considered" would probably draw similar inferences and highlight the same elements of the campaign if they were to witness these events for themselves. However, like the seventeenth century theologian, the Confederate officer, and the alien intelligence who showed up in Percy's version of the "Donahue Show," people with vastly different points of view could rationally interpret these campaign events in ways we would find hard to imagine. Certainly, Dan Quayle's partisans might take exception to some "objective" elements in Totenberg's report.

Totenberg concludes her description, however, with an actuality from the wind up of a Quayle stump speech. The enthusiastic crowd responding to the simple message validates much of what she has described in her own words while providing a natural transition to the probing questions that are to follow. In just 22 words beginning, "The stump speech has few specifics," Totenberg sets the stage for an uninterrupted segment of her interview with Quayle. The tape rolls for one minute 40 seconds in which we hear six responses from Quayle as Totenberg questions him on the conflict between laws mandating that teachers lead their classes in reciting the "Pledge of Allegiance" and a 1943 Supreme Court decision that upheld freedom of religion.

For the first time, the audience is actually listening in on a continuous dialogue. Because nothing is being cut out, no additional context need be inserted. When Totenberg says "you," we know she's addressing Dan Quayle and not us. We're along for the ride sitting in the seat just behind the two of them. In the background, we actually hear the continuous grinding of the bus's diesel engine. Only after Quayle gives one final justification—"Well, they're on the books"—does Totenberg interrupt the scene.

Reassuming her role as reporter, Totenberg reviews what appear to be rather superficial answers from a candidate who's likely to become vice president of the United States. The irony, of course, is that to support her contention, Totenberg uses actualities that in other circumstances would be a waste of time. It is clear that Totenberg, who normally covers legal affairs for National Public Radio, is competent to sort out the issues. But Quayle's sound bites are essential precisely because they reveal how inexpert he is on a campaign issue that the Republican media advisors had chosen to emphasize.

SELECTING VERSUS CONDENSING

When I was first adjusting to the frenetic pace of television production as a newswriter in San Francisco, one of the most senior reporters at the station tried to reassure me that the hectic routine would become manageable once I learned the techniques of the trade. "It's just a matter of learning how to condense the stories," he told me. The advice had the ring of truth, but it was only a half-truth. Unfortunately, the word "condense" connotes a uniform compression of information. To simply condense news was to strip the stories of all the detail that made them unique or all the background information that added perspective.

In the mid-1970s, in fact, veteran TV news reporters voiced strong objections when outside consultants began advising TV news directors to pick up the pace of local newscasts by cramming more and more stories into a single program. Reporters who were used to devoting three or four minutes to a packaged report were now told to wrap them up in less than a minute and a half. Many squeezed not the fat but the life out of their stories. They skipped over details that provided color, and they left out background that provided insight. Their work suffered.

In editing a verbatim interview, however, one of the major challenges of nonfiction broadcast writing must be addressed: making selections. If the job were to condense the interview, then the writer need only paraphrase it as concisely as time constraints demand. In reality, however, the writer's first job is to select the most telling actualities or sound bites and then consider what context they require to retain their meaning. If anything is compressed in the script, then it is the context that supports the quote. This is what broadcast writers need to be truly adept at condensing. They must learn how to create an economical setting that enhances the sound bite. Keeping this goal in mind, we will examine next the verbatim transcript of an interview that was published in a news magazine and imagine how a broadcast writer might have created a radio interview feature if the dialogue had been recorded on tape.

Radio Interview Feature

One of the largest organs of the American mass media system is all but invisible to the general audience. Almost every major corporation, business, or institution in this country has a public relations department whose aim is to promote free favorable mass media coverage of their organization's activities. Because the production of broadcast quality video for commercial TV requires expensive equipment, most organizations can only guide the producers and reporters who are assigned to photograph their activities and interview their representatives. But when it comes to radio and print, they can create their own programming and distribute it by mail or telephone. Each day newspapers are besieged by news releases, written like news stories for publication. Similarly, radio stations may telephone a toll-free number for prerecorded actualities and edited interview features.

Whether or not a particular newspaper or radio station relies on these prepackaged materials depends on the size of their staffs (do they have the resources to cover the event themselves)—and on their trust of the organization's intent (is its coverage biased due to self-serving organizational goals). For small radio stations with limited resources, programming produced by independent news organizations, university news bureaus, and even governmental agencies may be acceptable.

It is not uncommon for the interviewing and the writing of the interview feature to be done by two people. Thus, a student writer can realistically gain practice writing and editing a radio interview feature by using an interview from a print source rather than by conducting or searching for one that must be transcribed from audiotape. What we have reproduced next is the first eight questions and answers from a 1500-word verbatim interview on job hunting that originally appeared in *U.S. News & World Report*. While the remaining two-thirds of the interview certainly included useful and interesting information, an experienced broadcast writer would recognize that the excerpt reprinted here provides more than enough material for an informative two-minute radio feature. Remember, the point is to select, not to condense. What remains of the interview may provide material for one or two additional features. Quite simply, broadcast writers adjust to the programming conventions and formats of their medium. Take a look at this interview and then think how you might create a structure for Mr. Challenger's most interesting sound bites. The Q-numbers serve as reference points for the analysis that follows.

Q1. Mr. Challenger, millions of Americans are looking for jobs. What's the best way for them to go about it?

A. The best way to find a job is to go out and visit company after company. The more people they can see, the quicker they're going to get a job. What young people tend to do is stay home and wait for somebody to call them. It doesn't work.

Q2. Where are the best leads on job openings?

A. People don't normally get jobs that are open unless they have very specific academic backgrounds. The average person with a liberal-arts degree, such as a B.A. in economics, gets a job by pounding the pavement and making his own opening because somebody likes him.

72 *Chapter 4 Broadcast Interviews*

What I emphasize is: Don't write letters. You don't get jobs that way. It's too easy for the person at the receiving end to throw the letter away.

Q3. Does it help your job search to know someone on the inside of the company you're applying to?

A. It always helps to know somebody. About 40 percent of all jobs are obtained through somebody you know.

Q4. Are there disadvantages to knowing someone on the inside?

A. Only if they think you're not nice. But it's almost invariably a plus.

Q5. What about sending out blind resumes? Are they worthwhile?

A. One of the greatest misconceptions among job hunters is the value of resumes. Resumes lose more jobs than they gain. A resume is basically a crutch so that when you walk in the door and someone says, "What do you do?" you hand it over and say, "Here's my resume." That's the wrong approach because more often than not, you'll get pigeonholed. For example, if your resume says you are sales oriented and the employer has an advertising-marketing job, right away it will tend to knock you out of the running.

Q6. You advise your clients not to even have resumes?

A. I advise them to have three or four, with each one emphasizing different strengths and abilities. That way, the resume matches what the employer is looking for. Then I tell them, "Take the resumes with you, but don't hand one over unless somebody asks for it."

Q7. How would someone just graduating from school have enough experience to justify more than one resume?

A. Easy. If you're facing an employer who's looking for a gregarious, outgoing person, you'd produce a resume that emphasizes how active you were in school, including all the extracurricular projects you were involved with.

If it's an employer who wants someone who spends all of his time working, your resume would emphasize all the summer jobs you've had—how, for example, you never took a day off in summertime.

Q8. Besides having a resume in your pocket, what other preparations should you make for a job search?

A. The most important thing is to know yourself. This means you should sit down prior to starting your job hunt, and depending upon your job experience, write anywhere from a page to 100 pages about yourself, so that you know everything you've done. You need to do this to prep yourself so that you can sell yourself in the most effective way possible.

This magazine excerpt runs 550 words. That means on audio tape the verbatim material would run for approximately three and a half minutes. If a normal radio feature runs two minutes or less, how might a broadcast writer achieve such economy? First, just like a PSA, a short radio feature must have a thematic focus. The experienced broadcast writer would rather explore one provocative theme than superficially touch on three or four. In this portion of the transcript, Challenger's unexpected critique outlining the misuse of resumes provides a near perfect focus. Of course, there's related material about employment leads, contacts, and inside help, but the experienced broadcast writer feels no compunction about dismissing these warm up questions.

Another way the broadcast writer achieves economy, of course, is by shortening the selected sound bites themselves. However, the broadcast writer's freedom to edit individual sound bites would be severely limited except that, by convention, the broadcast writer is also free to substitute a new narrative voice for that of the original interviewer. This transformation has become so natural to listeners that we scarcely bother to contrast the two formats or think much about them when they both appear in the same report (as in Nina Totenberg's report on Dan Quayle).

As we discussed earlier, in a verbatim interview, the reporter and the subject are talking to one another. The audience simply eavesdrops. But, in an edited feature, the reporter need no longer even pretend to converse with the subject. (That's why someone else, in fact, can conduct the interview if necessary.) Instead, the reporter talks directly to the audience, setting up and commenting on the sound bites as they are aired. The dialogue form is maintained only to the extent that two voices are heard. The original questions—whether asked by the reporter or not—are replaced with continuity; that is, new narrative material that thematically organizes and joins the selected sound bites.

The sample radio feature script which follows is based on the Challenger interview. Because we are familiar with the original questions and answers, we can compare the sound bites in their new context with their original plácement in the verbatim interview. By convention, a double slash is used to denote deleted words within an edited sound bite.

Like every composition, this radio feature has a beginning, middle, and an end. The times devoted to each section are different, but each part has a distinct purpose. In the beginning section, the broadcast writer must simultaneously propose a topic that will attract the attention of the audience and create a credible and imaginable setting for the discussion. In this case, the writer attracts interest by quickly hinting that the feature will contradict ("But maybe not") conventional wisdom about job hunting while introducing Challenger as a consultant and expert. A vital point to recognize is that the audience must get a chance to hear Challenger as soon as possible. And so, some of the material about the setting ("Challenger, who was on the University of North Carolina campus to...") is held in abeyance until we have convinced the audience that the interviewee has something worth listening to.

The middle of the feature—its basic substance—is drawn from Challenger's responses to questions five through eight in the original interview. Here we most clearly see how the writer can save time by sharpening quotes and paraphrasing essential background information. The reporter re-enters the dialogue, not so much to rephrase the interviewer's original question but to announce a shift in the topic. The continuity between Challenger's first and second sound bites efficiently summarizes all the most important

"JOB RESUMES"

ANNCR: While most college seniors have their sights set on graduation this time of year, the most ambitious are already searching for a job. The first step is usually to write a resume. But maybe not. According to career counselor James Challenger, a resume can hurt more than it helps.

CHALLENGER: One of the greatest misconceptions among job hunters is the value of resumes // A resume is basically a crutch // you walk in // and say, "Here's my resume." // more often than not, you'll get pigeonholed // if your resume says you are sales oriented and the employer has an advertising-marketing job, right away it tends to knock you out of the running.

ANNCR: Challenger, who was on the University of North Carolina campus to take part in a seminar on career planning, tells his own clients to prepare three or four resumes ... each one emphasizing different strengths and abilities. Even new grads with little experience can target their resumes.

CHALLENGER: If you're facing an employer who's looking for a gregarious, outgoing person, you'd produce a resume that emphasizes // all the extracurricular projects you were involved with. // If it's an employer who wants someone who spends all his time working, your resume would emphasize all the summer jobs you've had.

(MORE)

```
                                                               2.
        ANNCR:       Challenger says the most important thing for the
                     job hunter is to know thyself.
        CHALLENGER:  This means you should sit down and write anywhere
                     from a page to 100 pages about yourself, so that
                     you know everything you've done. You need to //
                     prep yourself so that you can sell yourself in the
                     most effective way possible.
        ANNCR:       And what's the best way to find a job?
        CHALLENGER:  Go out and visit company after company. The more
                     people they can see, the quicker they're going to
                     get a job.
        ANNCR:       For the School of Business at the University of
                     North Carolina at Chapel Hill, I'm Carroll Hall.
                                     END
```

material that originally appeared between Challenger's fifth and seventh response. Even more remarkable is the reporter's continuity just before the third sound bite. The writer actually has the reporter voice part of Challenger's own answer as a way to set up Challenger's specific advice.

To reiterate, there are two types of movement in an interview script. Of course, there's a forward progression as the reporter and interviewee explore the topic. But there's also a repeating cyclical pattern. General information provided by the reporter sets up each new response from the interviewee. Indeed, most communication is based on a movement from the general to the specific. In every sentence, there are some essential elements understood beforehand by speaker and listener. And it is on this base that new details are added. Psycholinguists call this the "given-new" contract. Every communicated thought is predicated on "given" information that the speaker and listener share. Once the "given" information is established, the "new" information can be conveyed.

As we have seen in the verbatim interview, most questions and even the beginning of most interview responses try to establish this general ground of conventional beliefs and given information. Only then can truly new information be conveyed. During the interview itself, questions are often designed to be open-ended and exploratory. The interviewer doesn't want to close off discussion. The interviewee also feels compelled to start answering even before ideas are fully formulated. As in any first draft, some words are imprecise while others turn out to be repetitive or useless. In preparing a script, however, writers know what new information they want to convey. The goal is to do it within a framework that relies on a minimum of preparatory or contextual information.

Finally, every script must have an end. In live broadcasting, we have all heard interviewers apologize that they have run out of time. In a scripted feature, that is scarcely acceptable. The audience expects either a summary from the reporter or a particularly well-chosen remark from the interviewee. Thus, the writer may save for the end a quote that is particularly effective because of the emotion or insight it generates. In this interview feature, the writer has used Challenger's first interview answer to end the feature. The reversal may seem odd, but it provides a useful counterpoint to everything that precedes it. If the resume is not the key to getting a job, then what is? The warm-up question from the original interview becomes the pay off in this two-minute feature. It is important to emphasize that the broadcast writer is never given license to reorder sound bites in a way that distorts the speaker's meaning or unfairly represents them. But, to paraphrase Strunk and White on the design of a composition, an interview feature "must follow closely the thoughts of the interviewee, but not necessarily in the order those thoughts occurred."

INTERVIEWS AS PSEUDO-EVENTS

The use of verbatim interviews as a source of content in the mass media represents a revolution of sorts. Historian Daniel Boorstin has pointed out that until the middle of the nineteenth century, newspapers focused on real events and public occurrences, and only as the audience's demand for exciting information began to grow did verbatim interviews become acceptable subject matter in newspapers. Mass media historians tend to identify Horace Greeley's interview with Mormon founder John Smith as the first modern newspaper interview.

Boorstin believes the subsequent legitimization of those interviews has subverted society's notion of what constitutes real and relevant public events. The so-called press conference, he argues, is often only a pseudo-event that is skillfully manipulated by public relations experts to create an image for a business client, institution, or governmental agency. This public confusion about what constitutes real news, Boorstin feels, is an anathema to democratic forms of government that operate intelligently only when the electorate is sufficiently informed to choose wise leaders.

In this chapter we have seen that interviews—no matter what their form—are an essential data-gathering method employed by the mass media. What may be more important is how the data are communicated, and this is determined by writers, editors, producers, and other professionals who shape the content of mass media programming. Those data can be selectively incorporated into new scripts or communicated verbatim. As the plethora of talk shows on radio and television suggests, however, many verbatim interviews are broadcast live or "live on tape" not only because they are cheap to produce but the audience seems to enjoy the implied spontaneity of an unedited format.

This fascination with spontaneity is not peculiar to the popular audience alone. A recent essay in the *American Scholar* laments the fashion among literary magazines to publish verbatim interviews with lesser-known poets and novelists because many of those interviews seem pompous and self-serving. Previously, renowned authors who had arguments to make about literary theory would write carefully reasoned essays. Now the pages of literary journals are filled with off-the-cuff remarks of poets popping off in response to an interviewer's casual question. Quite clearly, these journals are succumbing to the readers' entertainment as well as information needs. What editing a verbatim interview permits—in addition to more efficient communication—is the opportunity to adjust the ratio of information to entertainment in the broadcast version.

SCRIPTWRITING ASSIGNMENT

Imagine you are applying for a part-time job at the campus news bureau. In addition to writing and mailing out press releases about campus activities, the office wants to begin producing two-minute radio interview features to be distributed free (by telephone) to radio stations across the state. To choose among applicants for this writer/producer position, the director of public affairs—who will voice the feature—is requiring everyone to submit a sample script.

The feature is based on recorded interviews with either faculty members or recent visitors to the campus. Normally it would include the following three elements:

1. A 25-second introduction, including a standard open, an indication of the topic, an introduction of the interviewee, and some indication of the interviewee's qualifications for speaking about the topic.
2. One minute and 20 seconds of excerpts from the interview along with appropriate continuity to provide transitions and set-ups for the interviewee's responses.
3. A 15-second close that provides a summary statement and a standard close.

Because this is an audition script rather than an actual production, it is not necessary for you to conduct an original interview. Instead, you can use a verbatim interview that has been published in a national magazine sometime in the last two months. Try to choose a published interview with someone who might be invited to speak at your campus. In your script you may refer to the interviewee as a guest speaker or as a guest lecturer.

The proper format for this assignment is radio drama format. A two-minute feature should run about 40 lines. You can adapt your standard open and standard close from the edited interview script presented in this chapter. Keep a copy of the magazine interview in case any questions arise about your choice of quotes or interpretation of the answers.

ADDITIONAL READINGS

Creative Interviewing: The Writer's Guide to Gathering Information by Asking Questions by Ken Metzler (Prentice-Hall, Englewood Cliffs, NJ, 1989). Metzler reminds his readers that the 30-second sound bites and confrontational news conferences we see on television should not define the state of the art. The book covers every aspect of the craft, with one chapter devoted to broadcast interviewing.

The Image by Daniel J. Boorstin (Harper & Row, New York, 1961). Boorstin's book only begins with the problems of news media coverage of pseudo-events. As an historian, Boorstin is concerned with our mistaken notions about reality. He surveys the American scene and sees heroes replaced by celebrities, travel replaced by tourism, and ideals replaced by images.

Telling the Story: The National Public Radio Guide to Radio Journalism edited by Larry Josephson (Kendall/Hunt, Dubuque, IA, 1983). Three of NPR's reporters—Robert Krulwich, Scott Simon, and Deborah Amos—contribute chapters on creating radio features, Susan Stamberg is interviewed on interviewing, and another section of the text provides an in-depth discussion of audio recording, editing, and production techniques. Best of all, National Public Radio Educational Services (Washington, DC) has developed a set of three audio cassettes to accompany these chapters.

"Thought Experiment: The Last Donahue Show" in *Lost in the Cosmos: The Last Self-Help Book* by Walker Percy (Farrar, Straus & Giroux, New York, 1983). If you haven't been introduced to the writing of Walker Percy, this is a good place to start. Read the entire book if you have time. It's a witty, ironic, and very intelligent commentary on the human condition in the late twentieth century.

5

Radio News

In the first act of John Adam's opera *Nixon in China*, the former president emerges from *Air Force One* on an airstrip near Beijing. The moment is historically charged. Nixon, the veteran cold warrior, looks perplexed. "We live in an unsettled time," he begins singing in a rich baritone voice. "We live in an unsettled time," the libretto by Alice Goodman continues. "Who, who, who, who, who are our enemies? Who, who, who, who, who are our friends?"

The aria this fictionalized Nixon sings is called "The News Has a Kind of Mystery." It is a remarkably fitting title. For American journalists, Richard Nixon has always been a kind of mystery. Broadcast coverage of the Vietnam War, the trip to China, and finally Watergate was so compelling that it convinced a generation of young people that investigative journalism was a more noble profession than medicine or law. More than a decade later students may not idealize broadcast journalists, but one thing is still for sure: Broadcast news has a kind of mystery.

NEWS VALUE AND INFORMATION PROCESSING

For the beginning journalist, that mystery is often reduced to a list of rules about content and news value. The rules about the content of a good news story are universally expressed as the five Ws: Who, What, Where, When, and Why (or How). More problematic is the concept of news value. Most lists of what constitutes news value mention terms such as impact, magnitude, prominence, oddity, timeliness, and proximity. Thus, to be newsworthy an event must be characterized in superlatives: the most important or the most extreme, involving the best known or the most unusual, having occurred most recently, and closest to home (real or psychic). There are, of course, always exceptions to the rules that define news. In those instances, journalists rely on experience, answering the question "What's news?" with the response an exasperated Supreme Court justice once gave about pornography: "We can't define it, but we know it when we see it."

One reason that we can't define news (but know it when we see it) is that our ability to recognize the significance of a news story is intimately related to our ability to make sense out of the story's unexpected details. Experienced journalists understand this process intuitively, using stylistic tricks to make sure the audience pays attention to what they think is interesting and important information. Curiously, the best way to explain this cognitive notion of news value is to describe a computer in New Haven, Connecticut, that has spent a decade learning to read news stories hot off the Associated Press wire.

Experiments in programming this news-reading computer conducted by two Yale University psychologists, Roger Schank and Robert Abelson, have provided considerable insight into the complex processes involved in reading and understanding news stories. It turns out that programming a computer to extract the correct meanings from strings of words with punctuation—what we commonly call sentences—is a formidable task. You may have thought that you could teach a computer a little grammar and a lot of definitions and let it combine the meanings of words to come up with the meaning of a text. The problem with that approach is that a computer is often too literal minded. Once, for example, the computer was stumped by a story that said "San Francisco was shaken" after the assassination of Mayor George Moscone. The computer thought an earthquake had taken place.

The computer does seem to do better, however, when it has an overview of the story. For example, Schank and Abelson programmed their computer with stereotypical scenarios for certain types of news stories and directed it to show that it understands what it is reading by summarizing the relevant details. Primed with a generic scenario for train crashes, the computer summarized a seven paragraph train wreck story in three sentences: A TRAIN HIT A TRAIN IN MEXICO. 17 PEOPLE DIED. 45 PEOPLE WERE INJURED. The odd first phrase—"a train hit a train"—reflects the computer's literal way of reporting a head-on collision.

Psychologists who study the way people process language realize that humans are dependent as well on some type of mental device that gives structure to incoming sensory information. Often called "schemas," the most highly developed of these mental frameworks is what Schank and Abelson call "a script": a stereotypical sequence of events that is frequently called up from memory to specify the roles of participants and their expected actions. No one has ever seen a script, but at least hypothetically humans are believed to use them to make sense out of a story or even decide what to do next. At the crack of a bat, a baseball fan knows to watch the ball, not the batter. That's because the batter can be expected to run to first base, but the path of the ball and its implications for the game are unpredictable.

A popular example that psychologists have studied is the script for going to a restaurant. The sequence of major events includes (1) being seated, (2) reading the menu, (3) ordering the meal, (4) eating the food, (5) paying the bill, and (6) leaving. Script theory specifies that most people will subconsciously call up this type of mental framework when the word "restaurant" appears in a text. The reader thus establishes a context for the details to come. The sequence of events is so well known, in fact, that a reader would think something is amiss if the characters in a story were to sit, read the menu, and leave.

An interesting point is that a reader recognizes the deviation from standard behavior whether the characters are fictional—like Jake Barnes and Lady Brett in *The Sun Also Rises*—or factual, like George and Barbara Bush. From an information-processing approach, fictional and factual texts share many of the same formal elements, and this raises some interesting implications about the possibility of news reports being purely objective.

Another indication of the power of scripts to influence our perceptions is what happens when we intentionally reorganize the sequence of events. If, for instance, the characters (2) read the menu, (3) order, (5) pay, (1) sit down, (4) eat, and (6) leave, the reader must call up the script for a fast-food restaurant to make sense out of the passage. Scripts permit what computer scientists call "top-down processing": the ability to fit diverse pieces of information into a fixed pattern or model that makes sense at the outset. The reverse is called "bottom-up processing." In bottom-up processing, not only must we identify the pieces of the puzzle, but we must arrange them in a meaningful pattern. That requires conscious mental effort, like sorting out the relationships between variables in a mathematical story problem.

The key point for broadcast newswriting is that scripts underlie our easy understanding of news stories. A chief goal of every high school civics textbook is to familiarize young people with a script that underlies much of the news reported nightly from Washington. That script is often encapsulated in a diagram entitled, "How a Bill Becomes a Law." The text normally elaborates on the role of congressional committees, the intricacies of legislative procedure, and the influence of lobbyists and White House tacticians, but the diagram itself outlines the stereotypical sequence of events: A majority of both houses of Congress must pass the bill, the president must sign it, or the Congress must override a veto. The bill then becomes a law. Without that script, listeners would find it difficult to interpret a phrase such as "Senate split on arms cut" or to distinguish "a House amendment" from "a new addition to a family dwelling."

But scripts, it seems, are not only important in helping us understand news stories. The degree of abnormality in an otherwise commonplace script seems to be at the heart of defining what news is. Every student journalist is trained to find out "Who, What, Where, When, and Why." The first four denote the routine information gathered for all news stories. But the answers cannot be routine. At least one must be abnormal to attract the public's attention.

Think of the scripts that framed the major international news stories as we moved from the 1980s into the 1990s. Beginning with friction between the Soviet Union and the Western Democracies after World War II, the Cold War script had anticipated continued Marxist rule from Poland to Bulgaria, unending tension in a divided Berlin, party-controlled elections in the Soviet Union, and East Germany remaining a separate Communist state. Beginning in late 1989, however, we witnessed a succession of events in Eastern Europe that challenged our 40-year-old Cold War script.

> The new president of Czechoslovakia is *who*? A formerly imprisoned playwright.
> The Berlin Wall is doing *what*? Crumbling.
> Free elections are taking place *where*? The Soviet Union.
> East and West Germany will unify *when*? October 3, 1990.

A cascade of unpredictable events forced a major reassessment of our Cold War script. Reporters in search of Why, constantly uncovered facts that forced us to amend our scripts or adopt new ones. In turn, these revised scripts prompt us now to re-evaluate old facts in a new light that provides additional surprises. In the end, then, it is these deviations from normalcy that distinguish news from simple facts and information, a distinction that humans, but not computers, can sense and even enjoy.

Newswriting, therefore, demands a considerable amount of professional judgment. If readers and viewers react unconsciously to abnormalities in commonplace scripts, then any unexpected deviation in a well-known script can provide the novelty we seek. Thus, the mass media—always concerned about attracting the attention of larger audiences—may exploit our physiological need for stimulation as a matter of habit, even when they mean to inform us. The challenge of broadcast newswriting is to select daily events and occurrences that are noteworthy and present them within a mental framework that makes their significance obvious to the audience. As Ezra Pound once wrote, "Literature is news that stays news." Put in those terms, writing broadcast news can challenge the full range of intellectual resources that a liberal arts education is designed to provide.

THE 30-SECOND READER

The bread and butter of broadcast newswriting is the 30-second reader. About 75 words or less, fashioned into four to six simple sentences, this is the basic unadorned news story that forms the basis of every radio newscast. The newscaster tells the story in no more than 30 seconds, often as few as 15, based on information transmitted to the studio by telephone, teletype, facsimile, or any other technology for storing and communicating messages, including a reporter's brain. But for the purpose of its on-air presentation, the listener hears it exactly as the newscaster voices it—with no other accompaniment.

"Readers" can be written from long wire service stories or even from newspaper articles, which means that beginning broadcast writers can practive writing "readers," using a good daily newspaper. AP and UPI editors perform essentially the same task—though on a more timely basis—for customers who subscribe to their broadcast wire services. The broadcast wires provide news summaries and headlines that disc jockeys and announcers can "rip and read" directly on the air. Radio news, of course, can be packaged in technically more complex formats that include the recorded voices of participants, witnesses, and reporters, but in writing the 30-second reader, broadcast journalists demonstrate the fundamental skills of their profession: the ability to recognize news when they confront it and create the spoken texts that communicate it.

GETTING THE LEAD RIGHT

All news stories begin with a lead. All good journalists know how to write them. NBC network anchor John Chancellor describes leads as "the keynotes, the overtures, the tee shots of newswriting. Properly crafted, the lead answers questions before they are asked and promises more answers to follow." For the beginning journalist, crafting the lead is a formidable task. Usually, print journalists are instructed to summarize the story providing the five Ws—Who, What, Where, When, and Why—in a single introductory sentence. As you can imagine, the result is often an unwieldy, graceless statement that starves the lungs for oxygen if ever spoken in a single breath. Accordingly, the essence of writing a lead for broadcast news is to establish a context that conjures up an underlying script in the audience's mind and to announce the most glaring and significant abnormality that has occurred. Among the newswriter's most important tasks is to select and emphasize the particular Who, What, Where, or When that makes the event a news story. That's how the broadcast lead "answers questions before they are asked" while recognizing that it "promises more answers to follow": the secondary Ws and the all-important "Why?"

Often, the underlying script can be conjured up with a minimum of fuss. By the last year of the Reagan administration, four words—"The White House says..."—generated the context for a broad range of normal scripts: President Reagan is spending the weekend at Camp David, President Reagan opposes any new tax increase, or President Reagan supports George Bush's candidacy for president. None of those items generated much excitement. But six months before the end of President Reagan's second term, the sentence, "The White House says chief of staff Howard Baker is resigning," was news. As vague as the underlying script might have been, the public had a notion of what the White House chief of staff does, and "resigning" is not part of the daily routine. In eleven words the broadcast newswriter conjured up a context and described a glaring and significant abnormality. Once it was heard, the audience had new questions, including When, Why, and, if known, Who would succeed Howard Baker as White House chief of staff. Underlying this basic script was also the memory of Baker's predecessor Donal Regan resigning after run-ins with Nancy Reagan.

Of course, establishing the context for a news story in the lead is not always that simple. Perhaps the most important television newscasts I ever produced were in reaction to the killing of San Francisco Mayor George Moscone. Assassinations of public officials are without doubt abnormal and significant. But the impact of this story was magnified a hundredfold because Dan White shot to death both George Moscone and Harvey Milk. If you know something about San Francisco city politics in 1978, then you can understand my point. But if you lack that knowledge, you lack the context for fully understanding how unusual a news story this event was. Across the continent in Bangor, Maine, the broadcast lead should have been written: "A San Francisco city councilman is accused of murdering the mayor of San Francisco and a fellow city council member." The audience's understanding is based not on knowing names but on knowing the scripted roles for city officials. Even the most uninformed listener understands that murder is not a tolerable political activity in a major U.S. city.

Incidentally, this example should reinforce a common rule for writing broadcast news. Never lead a story with an unfamiliar name. In many cases, an individual's title or role is more important than his or her name in establishing the underlying framework that makes the story comprehensible and newsworthy.

Generally, the more significant the news story, the easier it is to write a satisfactory lead. The most significant news stories are usually based on institutions, persons, and situations with which the audience is familiar. Hence, the context can be established almost without effort: "The White House says...." But sometimes the unexpected Who, What, Where, or When are not of great magnitude or moment. In that case, journalists may select the lead on the basis of interest rather than significance. If the Australian ambassador to the United States holds a news conference, what was the most interesting thing said? Often, broadcast journalists will be advised to pretend they are describing an event, a speech, or a public occasion to a friend. What is the first thing they would tell their friend? Make that the lead.

For especially complex or psychologically remote stories, the lead may require at least two sentences. The first establishes the context, the second gives the new information. Thus, for stories dealing with economics, science, or foreign events in which the United States is not directly involved, the lead may be: "The economy continues to heat up," "Researchers are reporting a breakthrough in the treatment of Alzheimer's disease," or "A shakeup in the British cabinet tonight." Ultimately, though, the broadcast journalist is seeking to achieve the most economical use of language possible. With a minimum of words, a suitable backdrop has to be developed that highlights the new information conveyed. The lead need not be memorable, but it must always work.

IDENTIFYING THE SOURCE

News stories are distinguished not only by the use of leads but also the use of attributions. Journalists do not create information. They gather it. And a significant portion of every news story is dedicated to revealing the sources of information on which the story is based. If Howard Baker unexpectedly resigns as President Reagan's chief of staff, then the information must be attributed to a reliable source: Baker himself, the president, a White House press secretary, a former (or future) Tennessee law partner, or even an unnamed administration official. In an abstract sense, attributions allow the audience to verify statements in a news story. They imply that the reporting is accurate and attest to the reporter's objective attitude.

What is true in print is doubly important in broadcasting. Newspaper stories are printed in black and white, but radio news is communicated using a human voice. All too easily a listener can take exception to a statement voiced by the newscaster. Unless that statement is attributed to a specific source, the listener's irritation or skepticism about the news may seep into his or her evaluation of the anchor's credibility. Incontrovertible facts do not need attribution nor, ironically, do universally held prejudices, but, if there is a glimmer of doubt, partisanship, subjectivity, or prophecy in a statement, then it needs an attribution. Otherwise, someone in the audience will become upset at the anchor for injecting personal opinions into the news.

The one problem with attributions is that they make sentences more complex. They add an extra layer of packaging. It is not enough to say that the Republican candidate for governor is leading the Democratic incumbent. "According to the latest Gallup poll" must be added. Print and broadcast, however, have come to quite different conclusions about where attributions should be placed in a sentence. Print journalists prefer attributions at the end: "The warehouse fire broke out in a first floor office and spread from there, said arson investigators." Broadcast journalists demand that they be placed at the beginning: "Arson investigators say the fire broke out in a first floor office and spread from there." Both have good reasons.

Print journalists, who are especially sensitive to grammatical forms, want the topic of the sentence—"the warehouse fire"—and the grammatical subject of the sentence to be one and the same. That focuses reader attention on the primary topic of the story.

Broadcast journalists, however, have three major reasons for ignoring this rule. The first is the one just alluded to. Attributions remind the audience that the surprising, incredible, or controversial assertions made by the newscaster are not his or hers but are those of other authorities or interested parties. Second, attributions at the end of sentences are not the conversational norm. When talking with friends, we are more likely to place the source of information, if given, at the beginning of a statement: "My doctor says smoking will cut three years off my life." And, finally, because the validity of an assertion may be highly dependent on the source of information, it can be misleading to withhold that element until the end of the sentence. For example, if the assertion is that the president cannot avoid raising taxes to reduce the budget deficit, the listener's evaluation will be substantially different depending on whether the statement is attributed to the president, a top assistant, or a leader of the opposition party. Furthermore, to make a controversial or incredible assertion and then withhold the source of information until the end of the sentence forces the listener to reprocess the assertion within its new context. While newspaper readers can stop processing the text at any time, broadcast listeners must ignore what's next if they want to reconcile second thoughts engendered by a questionable source.

TIMELINESS

One other important difference between print and broadcast journalists is how they deal with time, especially in the lead. Newspapers work on a 24-hour cycle. Broadcast news may be updated every hour. For a print journalist there is nothing embarrassing about leading a story with an event that occurred in the previous 24 hours. But, for the broadcast journalist, there's always the need to make the story as timely as possible, to update the story from the most recent report that might have occurred only an hour ago. The story must be written in a style that highlights the most current situation. As a result, lead sentences are almost always expressed in the present, present perfect, or future tense. By implication, the news is immediate.

If a fire breaks out in a warehouse Monday night, then Tuesday morning the broadcast lead inevitably deals with clean up operations, damage estimates, or arson investigations, any one of which may convey a more current perspective on the story. If a political leader makes a major announcement, then the broadcast lead almost always reports it in the present tense: "The president says...." And, if that lead grows weary, then the updated story leads with reaction to the announcement, reported in the present tense.

Obviously, this emphasis on immediacy can grow artificial and diminish credibility. Time sequences for real events should not be distorted beyond comprehension. In fact, once the lead is delivered, the sequence of events may be related in the past tense. But within the limited time frame of broadcast news, potentially significant facts are always excluded. Searching for a link that ties the event to the present may help the writer uncover an important detail or perspective that reporters failed to grasp when the story was still breaking.

AN ABBREVIATED STYLEBOOK

While the script format for radio news is the simplest of all broadcast formats—set margins at 10 and 80 and double or triple space—the script itself must be typed in a fashion that precludes any doubt about how the newscaster should read the text. Every word, indeed every symbol in the text, must be familiar and unmistakable. Thus, the beginning newswriter must adopt a whole series of conventions aimed at diminishing the amount of mental effort that the newscaster must expend in reading the copy. The only major debate still raging is whether news scripts should be written in down style or all capitals. Many traditionally minded journalists prefer to type their scripts in all capitals, because broadcast wire teletypes print stories in that style. But researchers in information processing argue that down style writing—because it is the more prevalent print form—is easier to read. Indeed, capital letters that initialize sentences and proper nouns help the reader decode the text.

Particular conventions of broadcast newswriting even extend to punctuation. Ends of sentences are still marked with periods, and short pauses are marked with commas. But you also use an ellipsis (a series of three periods...) to designate longer pauses, and a pair of dashes (typed as double hyphens --) to set off primarily parenthetical information. Semi-colons are not used because the two independent clauses that they might have joined will be written as two separate sentences. And a colon is rarely used because you will rarely write a long list in apposition to a noun.

What follows should give you an indication of the most important stylistic conventions in broadcast news scriptwriting:

Abbreviated words, except for Dr., Mr., Mrs., Ms., and an occasional St. (as in St. Louis) are always written in full in broadcast copy. What might be Gov. Smith or Lt. Smith in newsprint is Governor Smith or Lieutenant Smith in broadcast copy. Abbreviated words are not only ambiguous, but the time they take to say is underrepresented in the script.

Acronyms, if very well known like FBI or NASA, can be used in broadcast scripts. However, you must be explicit about how they are to be pronounced. The letters in F-B-I must be separated by hyphens (not periods) to designate that each letter should be read separately. More complex examples are N-C-double-A or N-double-A-C-P. Acronyms such as NASA or OPEC, which are to be read as if they were whole words, should be typed without periods, spaces, hyphens, or any other punctuation between letters. In some cases you may want to mention an organization by its complete name in the beginning of the story, the Internal Revenue Service or Indiana University, for example, and then use appropriate acronyms, I-R-S or I-U, on second mention.

Typewritten symbols are almost always avoided, because they can easily be misperceived and the space they demand on paper rarely reflects the amount of time they require to be said on air. Thus, the $-5°$ temperature reading in Fargo, North Dakota, becomes negative five degrees or five degrees below zero, and the basketball team's star center is six-foot-eleven-inches, not 6'11". The same general principle applies to the typographical symbols for percent (%), dollars ($), at (@), and (&), or the slash (/), which has multiple uses and meanings. Even AT&T becomes A-T-and-T to the hard core broadcast newswriter.

The use of arabic numerals is constrained in broadcast newswriting as well. Numbers from 0 to 11 are almost always written out, especially "one" and "eleven," so they are not confused with the letters "1" and double "1." Numbers from 12 to 999 are written in numeral form. Beginning with a thousand, however, the writer usually tries to round off any specific number so that it can be expressed in larger units such as hundreds, thousands, millions, or billions. The result is a compound term that may use both numerals and word forms. The number 2,765 may well be written as "almost 2-thousand-800" or "nearly 28-hundred." If the precise number is crucial, then you would write 2,765 as 2-thousand-765. The number 95,624 becomes 95-thousand-624 and 241,041,545 becomes 241-million-41-thousand-545. In reality, you actually replace the comma in the numeral form with an explicit term (-million- or -thousand-) that expresses what the comma stands for.

As numbers increase, so does the writer's need to simplify them. The annual federal budget is now in 13 digits, more than "one-trillion dollars." There are more than "240-million" Americans, and the median cost of a one-family home in the San Francisco Bay Area is more than "187-thousand dollars." When reporting extremely large dollar amounts, broadcast newswriters may designate fractional amounts as well. "Ten B-one bombers" cost "two-and-a-half billion dollars." The proposed federal budget is "one-point-three trillion dollars." Writing out numbers in this unequivocal form not only helps the anchor read them more easily, but it readily reveals to the writer numbers that are simply too unwieldy for aural communication.

There are some familiar numbers, however, for which these rules do not apply. Calendar years (1776, 1984, 1991) are always written in numeral form. Calendar dates are usually written using ordinal forms (January first, February 22nd, April 15th). Hyphens may be used to designate how telephone numbers (5-5-5 1-2-1-2), street addresses (11-84 Hamilton Avenue), and other special numbers (I-R-S Tax Form 10-99) are to be pronounced. Simple fractions should be written out (one-half, one-third, one-quarter). Other ratios should be expressed as percentages.

Quotation marks are another problem for the broadcast newswriter. The anchor does not voice them, and the audience does not see them. However, sometimes, when a statement is particularly memorable or controversial, we may want the audience to know that the words the anchor is reading are precisely those the newsmaker said. If no taped actuality is available, then the quoted material may be signaled with a conventional phrase such as "in her words," "as he put it," "what she called." The oratorical approach—"And I quote.... End of quote"—is usually reserved for those rare occasions when anchors need to dissociate themselves unequivocally from what the newsmaker said. In all cases, keep direct quotes short. It is also good practice to set direct quotes off in quotation marks (even if there is no aural cue for the audience) so that producers or anchors who edit the script know those are the spoken words and not a paraphrased version.

Pronouncers should be provided for unfamiliar names and places. If the newscaster will be uncertain about how to say a word, then include a phonetic spelling in parentheses immediately following the word. Most newswriters model their phonetic spelling systems after those the wire services use. Words are divided into hyphenated syllables with special attention given to the pronunciation of vowels. Some examples from the Associated Press include Mikhail Gorbachev (Mih-kah-EEL Gor-bah-CHOV), the Straits of Hormuz (Hawr-MOOZ), and Bobby Rahal (RAY-hawl). When the AP wire is in all caps, the accented syllable is followed by a single quotation mark (for example, RAY-hawl becomes RAY'-HAWL). Thus, we can appreciate an added advantage of down style typing. It permits the writer to use all capital letters as a way of emphasizing or accentuating an element in the text.

To copy-edit broadcast scripts, even to change a single letter, you must blacken out the entire word and rewrite it directly above. If one or more words are to be deleted, then they must be similarly obliterated and an arrow drawn to indicate how the text connects. Only a few words can be added to any typed line in the script. They should be printed above the appropriate line and their insertion point indicated. Only a few corrections may be made in this way before the script becomes too messy and must be retyped. The changes should cause minimum distraction for the on-air talent.

WRITING THE BROADCAST VERSION

Now that the essential elements of writing broadcast news have been explained, you should be more than ready to try writing your own scripts based on stories prepared for the print media. Your objective is to inform the audience with some degree of insight about a significant or interesting event that has occurred in the previous 24 hours. Your script is limited to 30 seconds or less, which means you have 75 words or fewer to make your point.

What follows is an AP wire story, which student broadcast newswriters have translated into broadcast news copy under deadline pressure. Those who succeeded (1) composed a timely and interesting lead, (2) provided essential information logically and clearly, and (3) remembered to attribute the most controversial statements to original sources. Their first task, however, was to read the story carefully, making sure that they understood it. Broadcast newswriters cannot tell a story clearly unless they understand it clearly.

> BOSTON (AP)—Hunger has reached epidemic proportions nationwide, leaving up to 20 million people vulnerable to fear and illness because of economics and conscious government policy, a group of doctors and public health experts said today.

The report by the Physician Task Force on Hunger in America follows a year-long investigation by researchers who traveled back roads, opened refrigerators and searched out "the human face of hunger."

In its report, the task force found that despite the nation's economic recovery, "hunger is getting worse, not better." The evidence: growing lines at soup kitchens and food pantries, upsurges in infant mortality, and widespread testimony about malnutrition among the elderly, infants and the unemployed, the report said.

"Clearly, lack of food is not the cause of hunger in America," said the report titled "Hunger in America: The Growing Epidemic." The task force was headed by J. Larry Brown of the Harvard School of Public Health. According to the authors, hunger is due to the lingering effects of recession, combined with Reagan administration cutbacks in income and nutrition programs, which have left 35.3 million Americans below the federal poverty line.

"Hunger is a problem of epidemic proportions across the nation," the report said. "While no one knows the precise number of hungry Americans, available evidence indicates that up to 20 million citizens may be hungry at least some period of time each month."

"The recent and swift return of hunger to Americans can be traced in substantial measure to clear and conscious policies of the federal government," the study charged.

The authors called on Congress to increase welfare and food stamp benefits and ease eligibility requirements; restore free and low-price meal programs to the schools; expand the Women, Infants and Children nutrition program and offer more meals for the elderly.

In Washington on Monday, assistant White House press secretary Anson Franklin said the administration had not received the report.

With $120,000 in grants from a dozen foundations, the task force reviewed previous studies on hunger and added to that data through interviews and field studies.

Like many news stories these days, this story is a report on the publication of a report. We can infer that a news conference was held, but the logistics of this media event in Boston are not as significant to the audience as the compelling (if awkwardly stated assessment) that "up to 20 million Americans are hungry at least some period of time each month." Quite naturally, most students seized on that fact for their lead and then devoted the remainder of their story to answering why. The radio news script reproduced on page 91 is an example of a fundamentally good story that does exactly that. Note in particular how identifying the source of the information—the attribution—sets the context for the unexpectedly large statistic. Note also how the writer uses the present or present perfect tense to convey a sense of timeliness about the information he has provided.

Still, there are improvements that can be made. First, does the audience know anything about the Physician Task Force on Hunger in America? A standard rule of broadcast journalism is never start a story with an unfamiliar

```
HUNGER
NOON NEWS
2/26/85
DAV

According to the Physician Task Force on Hunger, up to 20-million

Americans suffer from hunger at some period of time each month.  After

a year-long study, the report states that hunger has reached epidemic

proportions nationwide and is caused in part by governmental cutbacks

in income and nutrition programs.  The authors of the report have

called on Congress to remedy the situation by increasing welfare and

food stamp benefits and re-establishing hunger programs for the needy.

                              ###
```

name. Very often a descriptive phrase is more meaningful to the audience than a formal title. For the lead, at least, we can substitute "A group of doctors and public health experts" for "the Physician Task Force on Hunger," providing a richer framework of expectations at the beginning of the story.

Now for a second point. Must the writer adhere to the awkward language in the published report? The answer is no, as long as the writer can competently paraphrase the quote. In this case, we can almost see the survey question that generated the phrase "some period of time each month." To find out how often people went hungry, the interviewers most likely provided a check list of progressively longer time periods as possible responses: "Last month did you go hungry at least once per day? once per week? once in four weeks? not at all?" It may be important to social scientists to sustain this technical precision in their report, but broadcast journalists will look for a more economical phrase. They will collapse "at least some period of time each month" to "at least once a month." Thus, the new lead becomes "A group of doctors and public health experts say that up to 20-million Americans suffer from hunger at least once a month."

Next we can make a few simple changes to smooth out the flow of ideas in the second sentence. In the lead of this story, the writer has attrib-

Chapter 5 Radio News

```
HUNGER
NOON NEWS
2/26/85
DAV
```

A group of doctors and public health experts say that, ~~up to 20-million~~
Americans suffer from hunger at ~~least once a~~ month. After
a year-long study, *members of the Physician Task Force on Hunger say the problem* ~~has reached epidemic~~
proportions *in America...* ~~caused in part by governmental cutbacks~~
in income and nutrition programs. *The Task Force is urging* ~~Congress to~~ *increase* ~~welfare and~~
food stamp benefits, and *restore* ~~hunger programs for the needy.~~

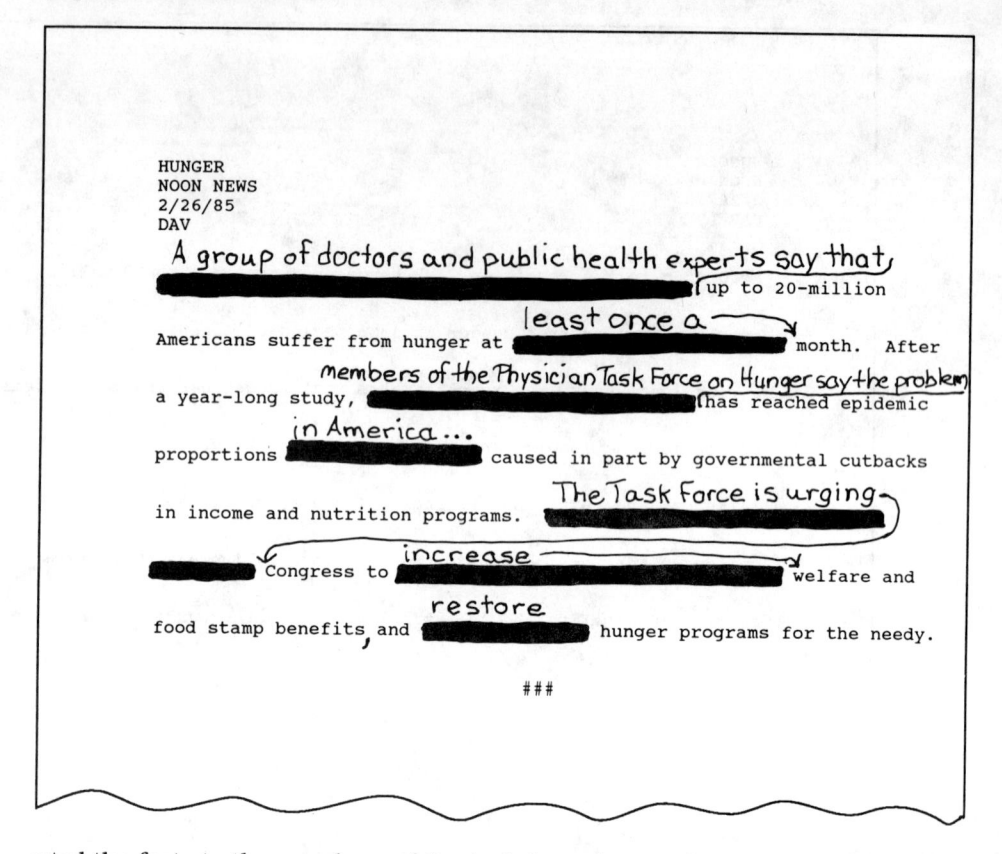

###

uted the facts to the members of the task force, but in the second sentence the writer quoted not them but their report. There is a subtle shift in the frame of reference here: from experts answering questions to a published report opened to a particular page. The question is for what reason? Why not continue to report the story as if the task force members were being interviewed? Besides, now that we have dropped the official name of the group in the lead, we may well want to restore it in the second sentence: "After a year-long study, members of the Physician Task Force on Hunger say the problem has reached epidemic proportions in America...caused in part by governmental cutbacks in income and nutrition programs." Note how the ellipsis permits the simple attachment of the explanatory clause at the end of the sentence.

Finally, we can cut portions of the last sentence. The writer has done a good job of summarizing the various measures Congress may take, but we can be even more economical: "The Task Force is urging Congress to increase welfare and food stamp benefits...and restore hunger programs for the needy." With these final cuts, the story runs 75 words. The first version was 81. The revised version is pencil edited as an example above, but a script with this many changes should be retyped. (The corrected version actually appears as the radio news script example in Chapter 2.)

Questionable Leads

It may be helpful to review as well a few false starts for this story. One student began, "According to a recent report, hunger in America has reached epidemic proportions." The substance of the lead is worthy, but the vague reference to "a recent report" diminishes any notion of timely reporting. Another student began, "Hunger is a problem of epidemic proportions across the nation according to a report by the Physician Task Force on Hunger in America." Obviously, the writer has broken the rule against placing an attribution at the end of a sentence. But even if no such rule existed, then the writer should still be sensitive to the possibility that the listener will miss the first word of the story—hunger—and not know what sort of epidemic the newscaster is reporting.

Finally, students need to be careful about gimmicky or sensational leads. They can do more harm than good. One student tried to generate added interest by starting with a question. "Feeling hungry lately? You're not the only one." You can decide for yourself whether the tone is appropriate for this story. But direct questions to the audience are used sparingly in broadcast news, because they are used with such frequency in commercial spots. No journalist wants the audience to confuse broadcast news with advertising messages. In another case, a student began the story, "America is starving. That's what a physician task force report called Hunger in America has discovered." First we must question whether a "report" can "discover" anything. But, in addition, the structure of the lead is questionable. This combination of a short, emphatic lead followed by a qualifying "That's what" pops up all too often in broadcast news. To put it briefly: Start over. That's what you should do if this ready-made phrase springs to mind.

SCRIPTWRITING ASSIGNMENT

Choose three major news stories printed in your local newspaper that are attributed to AP, UPI, or another prominent wire service. Try to choose one international, one national, and one regional story. Then rewrite them for broadcast on a local radio station. No story should run longer than 40 seconds (that's long by commercial radio standards), and the time for all three should total no more than a minute and a half.

Be sure to use proper radio news format, observing all the stylistic rules outlined in the text. Set your margins at 10 and 80, double or triple space, and write only one story a page. If questions arise about a story that cannot be resolved from the print version alone, then consult other sources (including earlier news coverage) until you clear up the confusion. It could be that the wire service has made an error. In any event, you cannot write the story clearly until the story is clear to you.

ADDITIONAL READINGS

The News Business by John Chancellor and Walter R. Mears (Harper & Row, New York, 1983). Chancellor, the former NBC "Nightly News" anchor, and Mears, the Washington Bureau Chief for AP, join forces to discuss what makes news stories newsworthy and how to write them effectively. Because most of the advice is based on experience, you can read the book as a primer on newswriting or as an introduction to the news business. The chapters on leads, color, and sources are especially perceptive.

Reading and Understanding: Teaching from the Perspective of Artificial Intelligence by Roger C. Schank (Lawrence Erlbaum Associates, Hillsdale, NJ, 1982). This is as painless an introduction to script theory as I have been able to find. Schank informally discusses how he would teach a child to read given what he has learned from programming a computer to read. Especially interesting for broadcast writers is what Schank has to say about how humans make sense of the words their brains process. After reading Chapter One on the elements of comprehension, you can skip ahead to Chapter Four on language and memory and to Chapters Six, Seven, and Eight, which deal with background knowledge.

Writing News for Broadcast, 2nd edition, by Edward Bliss Jr. and John M. Patterson (Columbia University Press, New York, 1978). The standard against which veteran instructors judge all broadcast newswriting textbooks. Bliss worked for 25 years as a writer, editor, and producer at CBS News, so the book is filled with CBS lore.

6

Television News

For many years now, the *Columbia Journalism Review* (CJR) has entertained its readers by reprinting unintentionally humorous headlines and clippings from U.S. newspapers. Among my favorites are slip ups involving newspaper photos and their captions. In one case, a Milwaukee newspaper inadvertently printed a standard U.S. weather map with its various symbols for highs, lows, rain showers, and snow flurries above the caption, "Shaded parts of map locate areas occupied by Israel since 1967." In another case, a Florida newspaper published a story about major renovations at the state capitol, but inadvertently printed a picture of the building upside down. The caption read, "State pays $11.3 million to make capitol look like this." Those two newsphotos aptly illustrate how easily technical problems can arise when pictures are used to illustrate the news.

Not only can the placement of a photograph get mixed up but so can the intended connection between words and pictures. The CJR once made that point emphatically with a clipping from a suburban New York newspaper. The locally shot newsphoto shows a well-dressed matron standing in front of her home, inexplicably grasping the lamp post next to her. Perhaps the photographer suggested the unusual pose to liven up the static composition, a good idea until the news editor added his say. The caption identified the woman as a civic leader and then some: "Jane Butcher, on the walk of her home in White Plains, is president of the United Way of Westchester—only the second woman in the nation to hold a similar post."

To put it bluntly, then, mixing words and pictures, or audio and video, requires a particular sensitivity to the workings of both channels of communication. Like the print journalist who failed to "see" that Mrs. Butcher was literally holding a post, few writers make the transition from print or radio to television without further instruction. Often they need coaching from those more experienced who know when to let the video tell the story and, equally important, know when it cannot. Perhaps the most crucial lesson to learn is that only a few extraordinary videotape sequences can tell the whole story. Most spot news video requires verbal narration to clarify its journalistic significance, which means a skillful writer must provide it.

NEWS VALUE OF VIDEOTAPE

Some years ago, CBS reporter Mike Wallace handled a report for "60 Minutes" about a Texas lawyer who argued that compact, concealable, snub-nosed hand guns should be outlawed by the Consumer Product Safety Commission because those guns were an inherently dangerous and defective product. At least that's what he concluded from the high rate of criminal and accidental shootings in which those guns, known as "snubbies," were implicated. The lawyer's approach to the problem of gun control was a unique one and worthy of coverage. But the problem for the producers of "60 Minutes" was how to visualize what was at best a legal and intellectual controversy.

The video shots begin all too predictably. We see the lawyer going into court. We see him lecture law students. We see rows of those snub-nosed revolvers lined up in glass cases in a gun store. The video begins to drag. That's when the producers went to work, skillfully using archival film and video sources to heighten the salience of this controversy. Wallace reminds the audience that the "snubbie" is not simply the criminal's weapon of choice. It is apparently preferred by people who try to kill American presidents. We then see and hear John Hinckley's 1981 attack on Ronald Reagan. The video cuts to another crowd scene and Wallace's narration continues. Snub-nosed revolvers are used by people who try to kill presidential candidates as well. We then witness Arthur Bremmer's 1972 assassination attack on Alabama governor George Wallace. That sequence is followed by screams and shouts for a doctor moments after Sirhan Sirhan guns down Senator Robert Kennedy in a Los Angeles hotel in 1968.

The series of shooting scenes finally ends with a less momentous, but no less violent, event. On screen are the grainy, slow-speed pictures of a wall-mounted surveillance camera. It shows the back of a checkout counter clerk and a male customer facing him and the camera. Wallace narrates, "Of course, it's not just politicians. It's everybody...including this store owner...whose killing was recorded by a security camera." The voice-over stops. The sound on tape plays up full. We hear three muffled shots, followed by warbly screams. A gunman flees in jerky slow motion, and a panicked woman customer approaches the store owner, who has slumped to the floor out of camera range.

This videotape montage is both instructive and paradoxical. It is instructive, because it displays an acute sensitivity to the optimal use of words, pictures, and natural sound in broadcast news reporting. With just a few words of narration, Wallace identifies each scene. Then, after a moment's pause, the natural sound of the gunfire elicits from the viewers the same sense of dread that it had once evoked among the photographers, reporters, and bystanders who had witnessed the actual event. The video—along with natural sound of voices—then tells the story. That's the dramatic upside to TV news.

The downside paradox is this. With the exception of the *Challenger* space shuttle explosion in 1986 and the Apollo moon landing in 1969, this minute-long montage of assassination attempts may have exhausted the sum total of unscheduled news events of national importance that were recorded on film or videotape during the past two decades. The truth is that an actual news event is rarely captured on video. Instead, it is reconstructed from eye-witness reports, authoritative observations, and after-the-fact video. The job of the television journalist is to decide what the story is and then judge how much information the video channel can actually contribute.

The range of video information forms a continuum from high to low that a good television journalist intuitively measures. When events such as an assassination attempt or an explosion take place with cameras rolling, the videotape is literally overloaded with information for the viewer to process. We even play the tape in slow motion to give the viewers extra time so that they can scrupulously examine the countless details that might hold an additional clue about how the event came about or might have been avoided. The journalist writing the script knows that no words are necessary. Let the viewers focus their attention unconditionally on the screen. The only audio should be the natural sound that was simultaneously recorded.

More commonly, however, news stories are based on a series of events that occur over a longer time span, not just a matter of minutes, but hours or even days so that at least some of the seminal occurrences are recorded on video. President Bush meets with the heads of state from western Europe and Japan to set economic policy. We see the leaders arriving for talks and hear the outcome at a news conference after but do not see the discussions that led up to their key agreements. A disgruntled employee sets fire to a hotel restaurant kitchen, forcing evacuation of the entire building. We see smoke billowing from second floor windows, firefighters entering the building, hotel guests evacuating, and downtown traffic tied up at rush hour, but certainly not the the fire spreading from the kitchen to the ballroom or even the firefighters beating back the flames. In these cases, there may be short segments of sight and sound that will be shown without narration, because they convey a realistic sense of being there. But the reporter's narration or the anchor's voice-over copy must tie these separate elements together. Without those words, much of the meaning of the video would be lost.

More often than TV news professionals would like to admit, cameras miss the main event and record only the aftermath or reaction: twisted metal instead of the collision; higher prices at the gas pump but not the chain of events that forced the costly jump; the defendant arriving at the courthouse but not the exchange of briefcases that led to spy charges. Indeed, there are important news stories that must be told even if the video can only identify a person or picture the scene. In those cases—and there are many of them—an inventive reporter teamed with a good photojournalist and video editor can use video to illustrate important elements in the story. Ultimately, though, a coherent exposition of events requires a logical and precise verbal explanation of what occurred. TV journalists learn to make the best possible use of recorded video by putting the most dramatic pictures at the beginning of their reports to attract attention to the screen, but the news value of many pictures in a detailed report would be indecipherable without an almost constant verbal commentary.

One remarkable new tool for TV journalists is computer-generated graphics, which are becoming affordable to produce at even the smallest station. Abstract economic data can be displayed as a graph. A map or diagram can be devised to show the territory in question or the hostage scene. If no camera recorded the senator's statement, a photo and the printed quote can be joined on a computer screen. A new medical technique or a disastrous mechanical breakdown can be illustrated using animation. It must be remembered, however, that these computer graphic techniques require a heavy investment in time, even if the hardware is cheap. Furthermore, as merely symbolic representations, they divorce the story from its real-life setting, making some reports look more like cartoons than news events. There are, of course, in television news strict ethical prohibitions against staging events or failing to adequately identify historical re-enactments or after-the-fact simulations. Undetectable digital mixing of video from two diverse sources provides new ways of picturing a news story but encourages increased skepticism about the credibility of video portrayals.

JUDGING VIDEO INFORMATION

One way to judge the informational value of available videotape is to use the same criteria we employ when evaluating the news story itself. How unpredictable are the events recorded on videotape? Is the space shuttle *Columbia* blasting off on a routine orbital mission? Or is it being launched for the first time after a substantial overhaul mandated by the *Challenger* disaster? Is the mayor holding her weekly news conference in the city council chambers? Or is the deputy mayor on the steps of city hall announcing that the mayor has suffered a heart attack? Does the video show an abandoned house in a run-down section of Los Angeles the morning after a drug bust? Or do we see the former

First Lady touring the crime scene with the chief of police only moments after narcotics officers raided the house? Of course, the value of the pictures in these cases is bound up with the value of the story. But imagine for a moment that those were not news events but sporting events. When would you want the color commentator and even the play-by-play announcer to just be quiet so you can watch what's happening without interference?

Sometimes, the video can be so rare and unexpected that its spectacle value far exceeds its news value: the First Lady at a drug bust, a fully formed funnel-shape cloud looming on the horizon, or, as viewers saw in the "60 Minutes" feature, a fatal armed robbery attempt. As individual events, each deserves a place in a locally produced TV news program. But do New Yorkers need to watch a Los Angeles drug raid, Californians a Kansas twister, and Midwesterners a violent hold up whose location is never identified? The answer is yes and no. Yes, to the extent that the pictures are informative and provide a window on the world. No, if more pressing local, national, and international stories are squeezed out of the news program as a result.

In the late 1960s, a Harvard Ph.D. student, Edward Epstein, sat in on the operations of NBC News for four months straight. Among his most telling observations was the way in which network reporters, producers, and editors put a premium on film that recorded action and, therefore, created an organizational system that was adept at generating and procuring such stories regardless of geographic locale.

The irreverent title of his published report—*News from Nowhere*—aptly reflects the most serious consequence of letting video opportunism overwhelm journalistic judgment. The problem continues to vex thoughtful broadcast professionals as the improved technologies for collecting and disseminating video pictures increases the raw stock of footage from which to choose. Interestingly, an inventive broadcast newswriter can often help resolve the dilemma. Like the surveillance camera footage in the "60 Minutes" feature, the video need not tell the whole story but, rather, just a part of a larger and more significant one. Pictures are so rich in information that they are truly multidimensional. A few well chosen words can direct the audience to focus on specific details of a video image, its exemplary nature, or its universal significance as exposition of the news story requires.

MATCHING SIGHT AND SOUND

Broadcast journalists often compare the structure of a TV news story to a set of twin towers. One tower is constructed of video segments, the other of audio. Broadcast journalists try to keep the two in rough alignment, but the match is never perfect. Many times, as we have discussed, video of the specific circumstances referred to just doesn't exist. Often, skillful writing enables a generic shot to be substituted. But, in many instances, the video must momentarily mark time as the audio advances the story. After five or ten seconds, however, the divergence can subvert the intended communication. If the video succeeds in capturing the viewer's attention, then the viewer may well ignore the audio until it crosses paths with the video again.

Even more crucial, though, are the differences between verbal and visual logic. Quite early on, broadcast newswriters recognize that video information is more cumbersome to present than verbal information. Reciting a list of the last five U.S. presidents—Bush, Reagan, Carter, Ford, and Nixon—takes just over two seconds, but it would take almost 15 seconds to show pictures of each at a pace that viewers could process without feeling rushed. When writing to video, you soon learn to focus on one person, one place, or one issue at a time, and then move on to the next. The video image, while reinforcing the writers words by invoking precisely the reality referred to, also constrains the writer from making rapid transitions from place to place or person to person.

Photojournalists and video editors give considerable attention to what they call "establishing shots." Writers must also. Normally these are wide-angle or long shots that roughly define the physical area in which a sequence of shots is to take place. Generally, we see a wide shot of the courtroom before we see a close-up of the defendant, the entire airplane before the damage to the tail, the playing field before the pitcher winds up and the batter swings. The wide shot is the big picture that reveals how the many small parts are potentially related.

Sometimes, photographers will begin with a close-up of an important element in the story, but not for long. Almost always they will zoom out to establish the entire scene and hold the shot until the viewers get their bearings. Establishing shots are crucial sources of information for the viewers. Normally they're held on the screen a solid four or five seconds and longer if they record relevant action. Ultimately, every thematically related sequence of film starts with an establishing shot. Thus, when an establishing shot occurs, the writer should take special care to begin a new sentence that identifies at least indirectly what the audience is viewing.

PIECING TOGETHER VIDEO AND AUDIO

The relationship between video and audio in a reporter package is intricate. However, through practice the experienced broadcast journalist learns to exploit the interplay between words and pictures almost unconsciously.

When time permits, the reporter may first edit the video, experimenting with the order and length of shots, to create the optimum visual impact. Under deadline pressure, though, broadcast journalists are more likely to view the video and then write their narration with certain key shots and interview segments in mind. Once the narration is written and recorded, the videotape editor often pieces together the audio segments of the videotape first and then lays in the corresponding video shots.

To understand how this works in practice it helps to disassemble the video and audio elements of a completed reporter package.

Chapter 6 Television News **101**

On the following pages, I have separated into its component parts a local San Francisco television news report describing a fire in a high-rise apartment building. By carefully comparing the video freeze frames and the reporter's narration, you can begin to recognize how video and verbal information are pieced together to create effective establishing shots, interview sequences, and narration in a television news story. Once you view the freeze frames and read the matching audio cuts and shot descriptions, take a look at my comments below and review the audio and video components again.

Note that the freeze frames and shot descriptions are identified by the time at which they would appear if you were viewing the videotape. The audio segments are simply numbered as cuts one to ten. Remember also that this split-page presentation is not a standard TV news format. Normally there's no reason to type such a detailed list of shot descriptions and audio cuts unless the videotape editor must assemble the package without the writer being present.

* * *

Now that you have looked over the freeze frames and a written description of the reporter package, here are some major details. Since the telling of the story relies more heavily on the audio track than the visuals, my comments will be organized so they correspond to each of the ten audio cuts.

CUT #1: The first sounds we hear are the natural sounds of sirens, engines, and voices to create a sense of presence at the fire scene. Nevertheless, the opening words of the narration identify exactly what the audience is looking at. The establishing shot begins as a close-up to draw attention to the volume of the smoke, which could appear quite small eight stories below at street level.

CUT #2: There are, of course, no interior pictures of the fire's breaking out. The narration diverges from the video but moves quickly to the inhabitants of the apartment who can be pictured. The man in the apartment where the fire broke out gives an eyewitness report.

CUT #3: The eyewitness is a French cultural attaché. His English is broken and hard to understand. The reporter cuts him off once the audience gets an idea of how the fire started and advances the story with her narration.

CUT #4: Now that the basic story has been established, we find out it has an amazing twist. The hero—a city bus driver who lives in the neighborhood—excitedly relates the details of the rescue. Even so, his extended interview is reduced to three main quotes. Generic shots of the smoky building are used to cover the jump cuts. These covering shots are called "B-roll."

CUT #5: The reporter's narration now continues the theme of escape and evacuation. The action she's describing occurred inside. However, the inside shot we see was taken during mopping up operations when it was safe for photographers to enter the building. The shots that follow are exteriors, but they do show the victims referred to.

102   Chapter 6   Television News

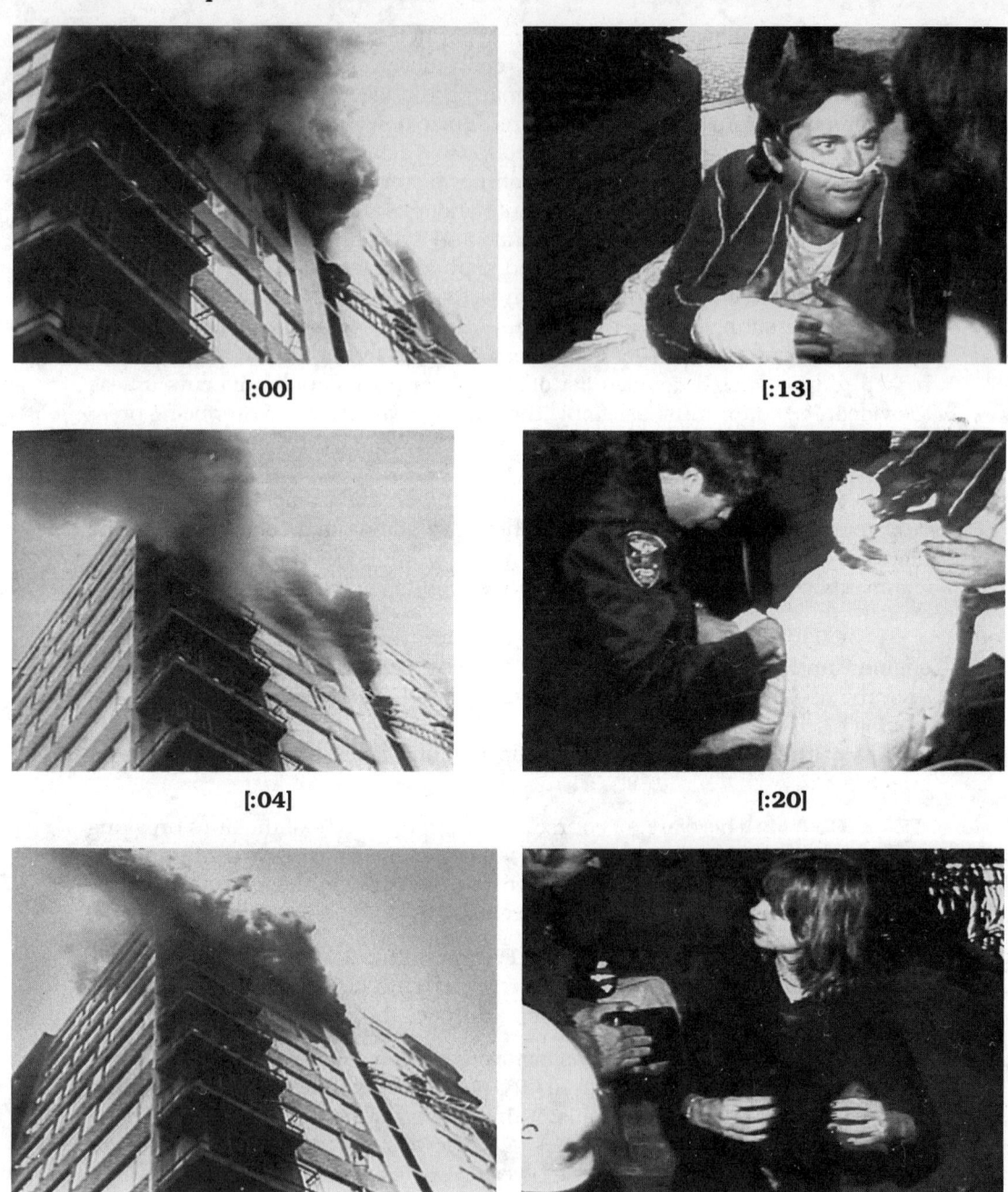

[:00]

[:04]

[:08]

[:13]

[:20]

[:26]

VIDEO	AUDIO
	CUT #1
[:00] TELEPHOTO SHOT OF BLACK SMOKE POURING FROM UPPER STORY WINDOW. ZOOM OUT TO REVEAL...	(NATURAL SOUND) Black, heavy smoke billowed out of windows and stairwells by the time the fire called to three
[:04] FIREMAN ON LONG EXTENSION LADDER CLIMBING TOWARDS WINDOW	alarms. It started in an eighth floor apartment. The couple inside that
[:08] LONG SHOT HIGH RISE IN SMOKY HAZE	apartment were just having breakfast when they noticed their sofa in flames.
	CUT #2
[:13] VICTIM IN BATHROBE	"You know the radiator. The radiator was close against the sofa. And the sofa... well... probably..."
	CUT #3
[:20] TILT DOWN TO RESCUE SQUAD ATTENDANT BANDAGING LEFT LEG	His hands and legs were burned before he was able to escape. The woman ran
[:26] YOUNG WOMAN IN DARK COVERALLS	out to the balcony where she was trapped for several terrifying minutes before she was saved in a daring rescue.

104 Chapter 6 Television News

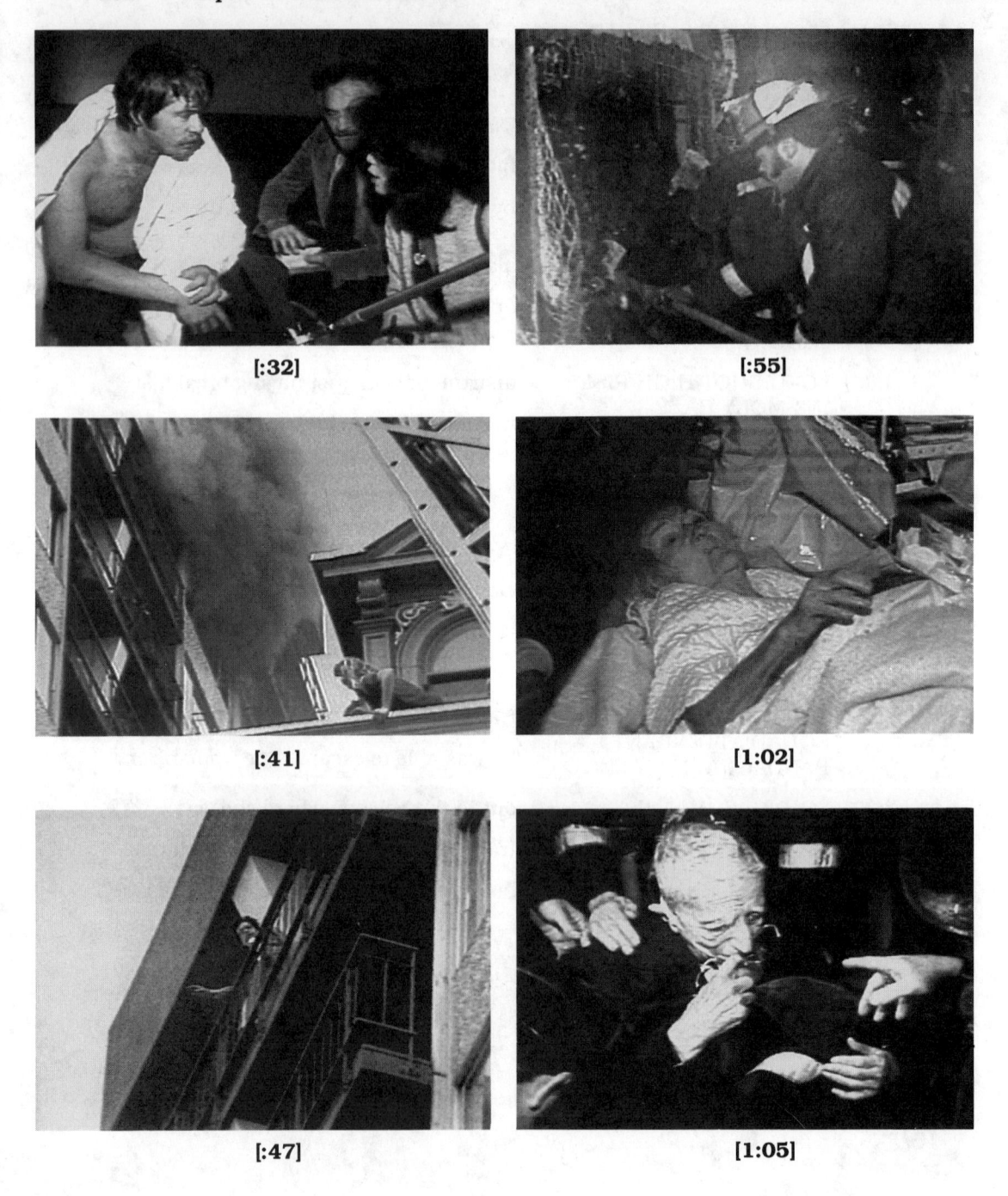

[:32]

[:55]

[:41]

[1:02]

[:47]

[1:05]

VIDEO	AUDIO
	CUT #4
[:32] YOUNG MAN, NO SHIRT, WITH TOWEL OVER SHOULDERS	"I just hopped the back fences. I live across the street here...and went over the rooftops...and got onto the ledges and pulled myself up to the ledges. I was
[:41] WIDE SHOT BUILDING WITH SMOKE SPEWING OUT	waiting to see if she...just keep her there until...but then the smoke got bad. So
[:47] LONG SHOT BALCONIES, WOMAN STANDING OUTSIDE	I just climbed up...I went up about six floors on the outside. I heard her screaming and...I looked. Yes, she was screaming bloody murder."
	CUT #5
[:55] TWO FIREMEN IN HALL, AXING AWAY AT PLASTER	The fire was confined to one apartment and the hallway of the eighth floor. The tenants who lived below escaped
[1:02] FRAIL WOMAN ON STRETCHER	through stairwells. Many of them still n shock by the time they got outside
[1:05] ELDERLY MAN TAKING OXYGEN	Rescue crews were concerned with the people who lived above the eighth floor.

106 Chapter 6 Television News

[1:09]

[1:31]

[1:14]

[1:35]

[1:22]

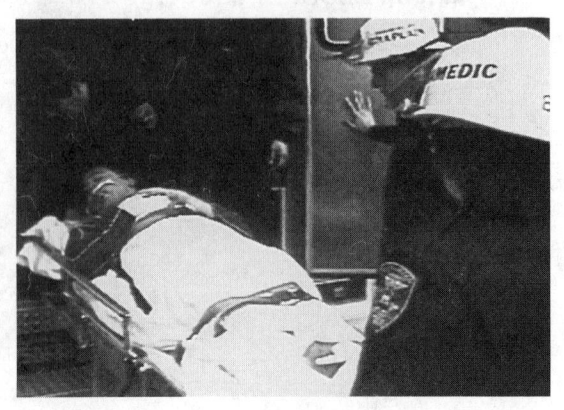

[1:40]

VIDEO	AUDIO
	CUT #6
[1:09] FIRE CHIEF WITH AIDE	"…(NATURAL SOUND)…See these people up there. We want to get them to the
[1:14] FIREMEN INCHING UP AERIAL LADDER, CAMERA ZOOMS IN	roof. There's no reason to put them on the aerial ladders."
	CUT #7
	The people did move upstairs on their own. And most of the injuries were minimal.
	CUT #8
[1:22] CLOSE UP FIRE CHIEF	"Most of the victims here this morning were from inhalation…inhalation of smoke. A Type-One building holds the fire within the confines of where it starts
[1:31] TELEPHOTO SHOT OF FIREMEN AT TOP OF LADDER	…but that doesn't mean that with all the plastics in these modern buildings that
[1:35] FIREMAN CATCHING BREATH AT WINDOW	it's not an intense, heavy, smoky fire to fight. And that's exactly what we're faced with this morning. The firefighters
[1:40] LOADING VICTIM INTO RESCUE SQUAD VAN	had to evacuate the people from above the fire to the roof…getting them clear of the heavy smoke concentrations."

108   Chapter 6   Television News

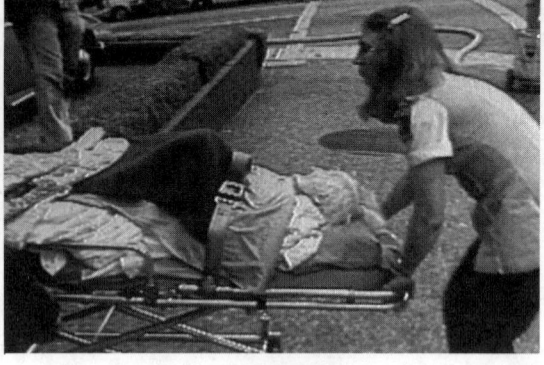

[1:47]

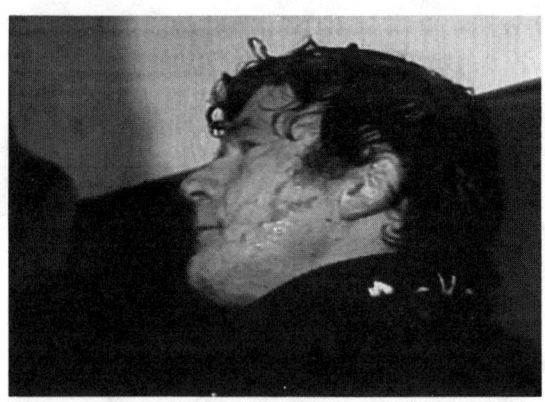

[1:58]

[1:51]

[2:02]

[1:53]

[2:11]

VIDEO	AUDIO
	CUT #9
[1:47] FIREMAN BEING HELPED TO RESCUE VAN	Several firemen were treated for smoke inhalation. Some were taken away by
[1:51] FIREMAN IN VAN	ambulance, but their injuries were minimal. Meanwhile the Red Cross was
[1:53] VOLUNTEER GIVING COFFEE TO WOMEN IN ROBES	on the scene passing out hot coffee to shivering victims…dressed only in
[1:58] FRAIL WOMAN MOVED TO RESCUE VAN	robes. The fire was under control in about an hour. The firemen fighting
[2:02] SLOW PAN OF SMOKY HIGH RISE	the blaze said it was like an inferno nside. Officials say the building was up to code, and that was one major reason the flames did not spread to other apartments.
	CUT #10
[2:11] REPORTER ON CAMERA	"More than a hundred people live inside this building and most of those residents are elderly. But due to quick thinking and efforts by the fire department, everyone was able to escape. In San Francisco, I'm Linda Yee, Newscenter 4.

CUT #6: The reporter's narration sets up this segment of video and natural sound: cinéma vérité of the fire chief directing rescue operations as the firefighters battle the eighth floor blaze. Note that this is the only segment in the entire report when the audience simultaneously sees and hears nothing more and nothing less than the ongoing event.

CUT #7: Neither the audience nor the fire chief can see people moving up the interior stairwells. But the video can illustrate what the fire chief sees: the aerial ladders with firefighters, not residents, moving up on the outside of the building.

CUT #8: The audience sees and hears the fire chief again, but this time as he responds to reporters interviewing him on the scene. Editing the fire chief's responses into a short but coherent statement creates a series of jump-cuts, which are covered by a montage of thematically related B-roll shots. The most striking shot is the firefighter catching his breath at an open window as the chief describes the blaze as an "intense, heavy, smoky fire."

CUT #9: The reporter adds a few essential facts, which are matched specifically with the shots of one firefighter receiving aid and residents receiving coffee. By now the fire scene has been so well established in the audience's mind that the shots can move more freely from one scene to another.

CUT #10: This summarizing statement with the reporter on camera is traditionally called a "stand-up close." It places the reporter at the scene, reinforcing her credibility as a first-hand observer.

CYCLE OF TELEVISION NEWS

In actuality, the reporter package just discussed was the work of a four-person team that included a reporter, photographer, sound technician, and videotape editor. All devoted a good portion of their work day to filling just over two minutes of news programming. It should come as no surprise, then, that part of the reason a picture is worth a thousand words is because it costs so much in equipment, time, and effort to obtain one. Realistically, when television news teams do succeed in capturing a story on tape, they are not about to air that video just once and then search out new visuals for the next newscast. More likely they will attempt to update the story with new verbal information—easy to acquire by phone or from news agency teletypes—and recut the existing videotape to accommodate the latest information.

If the story originally aired as a reporter package on the 6:00 P.M. news, then on the 11:00 P.M. program the reporter's narration is stripped away and replaced with voice-over copy that the anchor reads live from the studio. In most cases the story will be allotted less air time simply because it's not as timely as it was five hours earlier. The reasoning is straightforward.

Unless the story has taken an unpredicted twist, much of the information may be repetitive for those viewers who tuned in earlier in the evening. An especially telling or emotional sound bite may be retained, but often they lose their impact because of repeated exposure or new developments in the new story. The newswriter can always paraphrase whatever key information the sound bite provided in the anchor's voice-over copy. Alternatively, there may be another sound bite, not used in the original report, that is particularly salient given the focus of the updated story.

As a rule, particularly good videotape coverage of a news event will wend its way through a 24-hour cycle of news programs, appearing first, for example, as a reporter package at 6:00 P.M., then as a recut at 11:00 that night, again as part of the local news update inserted into the network morning news shows, and finally on the noon news. At that point it becomes file footage to be used again when a program producer judges that new developments in the story warrant a follow up. By contrast, routine interior shots from a news conference or public hearing may air only once as a brief anchor voice-over with sound bite in the next occurring newscast, that is, unless the reporter and photojournalist devise a means for visualizing the major issues raised or decided there.

The high-rise apartment fire story generated enough interest to be broadcast throughout the 24-hour cycle. In this case the fire broke out in the morning, so the first shots of the heavy black smoke were quickly cut into a simple voice-over story for the noon news. However, to effectively tell the rescue story, the reporter needed additional time to write a narrative track and select the best sound bites while the videotape editor had to piece those audio parts together and then lay in the B-roll. That meant that the reporter package aired first on the 6:00 P.M. news.

At 11:00, the producer was faced with a story that was already twice reported and more than 12 hours old. Yet people would still be talking about what the front-page headline on the San Francisco *Examiner* had described as a "Human Fly Rescue." It was scarcely breaking news, but, as a human interest story it could be placed at the end of the local news segment, giving the anchor and the meteorologist something to talk about before the topic turned to weather. A sample anchor VO script follows on page 112.

In this recut, only the hero's sound bite is retained, and much of the detail about the evacuation is eliminated. The voice-over (VO) portions before and after the sound on tape (SOT) run 20 and 10 seconds, respectively. With the 22 second SOT segment, the total running time (TRT) of the videotape (VTR) is 52 seconds. Add another 12 seconds for the anchor lead-in and 8 seconds for the tag, and the total story time (TST) is 1 minute 12 seconds. More than a minute has been deleted from the original reporter package, which required an anchor on camera lead-in of its own.

Already familiar with the original package, you can easily imagine which visuals would be retained, including the hero's sound bite with its B-

```
SF HI-RISE RECUT
_____11p
12/29/80
hsf
```

ANCHOR OC	Six San Francisco residents are in
CK/HI-RISE FIRE	the hospital for observation
	tonight after a high-rise apartment
	fire in Pacific Heights ... but the
	outcome could have been worse if
	not for a heroic neighbor.
VTR/VO @ :00	The smoky, three-alarm fire broke
SUPER: 1800 PACIFIC AVE	out in an eighth floor apartment
SAN FRANCISCO	this morning when a radiator
	ignited a plastic-covered sofa.
	The couple inside got separated in
	the smoke. The man escaped with
	burns to his hands and legs, but
	the woman found herself trapped on
	the balcony...until a daring city
	bus driver came to her aid.
SOT FULL @ :20	(PRECIS: DRIVER EXPLAINS HOW HE
SUPER: BILL BRISBANE	CLIMBED THE BALCONIES TO REACH THE
BUS DRIVER	WOMAN AND THEN PULLED HER DOWN AND
	LED HER THROUGH A LOWER FLOOR
	APARTMENT)
	OUT-Q "...screaming bloody murder."
VTR/VO @ :42	Fire Chief Andrew Casper says fire
	fighters were able to lead most of
	the residents to safety ... thanks
	to the two smoke-free stairwells in
<u>TRT :52</u>	the ten-story building.
	(MORE)

```
SF HI-RISE 2-2-2
ANCHOR OC TAG              The six hospitalized residents are
                           all elderly.  Doctors are having
                           them stay overnight just to be
                           sure they suffered no serious
                           injuries.
                                    ###
```

roll intact. Unlike the narration for the reporter package you saw before, this example was written as if it were an actual script for the news program. The left column, therefore, provides precise technical information including supers and time cues.

The one writing strategy that should be evident here is letting the anchor in the studio deliver information for which there are no satisfactory videotape pictures. You may not have time to completely update the story in the lead, because it's a basic rule of television to show the videotape as soon as possible. But there is a fortunate congruence between current information, which can be used to update the lead, and information hard to visualize because it was gathered by telephone or gleaned from the wires.

If you watch television news conscientiously, you'll soon realize that this is a common technique. The anchor leads with the verdict, the election result, or the final death toll, bits of information, however essential, that were still unknown when the videotape was being shot. Thus, the voice-over videotape segment of the story may be chronologically older. It may only recap details of the final arguments, the day's voting, or the fatal accident.

Good writing to visuals is a recurrent problem in every TV newsroom. It generates many memos. The executive producer who wrote the memo on page 114 sent it to all the producers, reporters, and writers in the newsroom. It's a succinct summary that carries with it the flavor of day-to-day newsroom operations.

If I have any qualms about this memo, they relate to item six. If broadcast journalists were to blindly match copy to video for every shot, then anchors and reporters would soon deliver the news in a style reminiscent of amateur photographers narrating home videos. Clearly, the relation between narration and video cannot be explained with an all purpose example. Indeed, this entire chapter has been devoted to the question, and, yet, it has only skimmed the surface.

```
KRON MEMORANDUM

FROM:  Dave McLean                        DATE:  Sept. 19, 1980
TO:    Producers, Reporters, Writers      RE:    Writing

It is painfully obvious that our writing is less than inspiring.
It should not be necessary to remind you of basics, but
apparently it is.

1.  The story must be factual.
2.  Proof read for grammatical errors and/or misspellings.
3.  Use simple declarative sentences.
4.  Write interesting leads that invite the viewers to stay for
    more.
5.  It must be complete.  Don't leave unanswered questions.
6.  The copy must match video.  Be specific.  "The mayor cut the
    ribbon, cameras dutifully captured the ceremony, dignitaries
    applauded and the champagne flowed."  While the viewer is
    hearing that copy, he/she should be seeing the mayor cutting
    a ribbon followed by cameras followed by applause followed
    by pouring champagne.
7.  Do not copy scripts from previous newscasts.  Rewrite and
    advance the story.  Update it.
8.  The scripts must contain supers, TRT's, out-cues, and precis.

I expect all of you to achieve a degree of excellence in these
areas.  I will continue checking scripts and will be paying
particular attention to item #6.

Thanks for your help.
```

A POSTSCRIPT ON DOCUMENTARY PRODUCTION

Learning to write documentaries would seem like a natural next step after learning to write for television news, but it is rarely a realistic step. Here's why. As a student, you rarely have access to the equipment you need to shoot a film documentary, so you must invent pictures for your script. The result, no matter how much research you do, is not a script but a proposal, because the first lesson of documentary making is that you almost never capture on videotape or film exactly what you planned. The one realistic alternative, if a tape recorder is available, is to write a radio documentary, an option which I will explain later.

Once this caveat is understood, it is nevertheless useful to contrast video documentaries with television news reports. One area where documentaries fundamentally differ from news stories is in their reach and scope. News reports focus on events and their short-term effects. Documentaries focus on processes and their long-term impact. If we can imagine a continuously running motion picture camera recording all the workings of our society, then daily news reports focus on individual frames of the movie while documentaries show long sequences.

Looking at just snapshots, journalists can usually identify the facts of the event—the who, what, where, and when of the story—without much controversy. That's why day-to-day journalistic reporting gives the illusion of being strictly objective. In general, hard news reporters do not stray very far from the snapshot of the event. If necessary, reporters can roll back through a few frames to provide some background information that helps explain why the event occurred. And depending how much time has elapsed, reporters can roll the movie ahead a few frames to predict with some confidence what its short-term consequences might be. But as journalists begin to relate one snapshot to another, their reporting becomes more interpretative and subjective, taking on the qualities of news commentary.

Some events, however, are of such magnitude that they generate intense interest in the processes that led up to them and, in turn, the multitude of effects that they will generate in the future. For recent events, of course, we can roll the film only a few frames into the future, but if our giant camera has been running continuously in the past, we can roll back into the movie a great distance, providing perspective on our subject.

As we investigate the significant changes that occur from frame to frame, we are, in fact, piecing together events to reveal the underlying process. Documentaries are educational when we learn about processes we were unaware of. They provide insight and even shock us when they reveal processes more complex or vastly different from those we had always imagined. In the language of cognitive psychology, effective news stories exploit commonly shared scripts, but effective documentaries go much farther: They have the power to create or revise them.

Editing Video Documentaries

A more subtle difference between the two forms exists because documentary producers do not face the same daily deadlines that news producers do. The extra time permits a different sequence of editing and writing that puts a higher value on visual aesthetics. While newswriters and reporters tend to write the voice-over portions of their scripts before the video is cut, documentary writers and reporters first work closely with their editors to achieve what they feel is an optimum selection and arrangement of shots. Only then are the words added.

What they are looking for are sequences of shots that flow together and tell a story with a minimum of narration. In the best of circumstances, each of these visual sequences helps to illustrate an important aspect of the subject the documentary deals with. These building blocks are then arranged in a logical order of presentation. An important part of the writer's job is to smooth the transitions from sequence to sequence.

Visual sequences don't magically fall together either. They are shot by photojournalists who are sensitive to the needs of videotape editors, who try to arrange shots so they tell a logical story. Even in the high-rise fire story, we can catch glimpses of how the photojournalist and the videotape editor worked together to create visual sequences. Most obvious is the shot of the firefighter overcome by smoke being helped to the rescue van [1:47], followed by a close-up shot inside [1:51]. More shots of his receiving oxygen were not used. In another case, our fire victim in his bathrobe [:13] whose hand and leg we see bandaged [:20] is also pictured on a stretcher as he is lifted into the rescue van for a trip to the hospital [1:40]. In the freeze frame, we can just barely recognize his striped robe.

An even more interesting sequence is that of the frail woman on a stretcher [1:02] whom we see for a second time when she is wheeled toward the rescue van [1:58]. The sequence is interesting because it is truncated before it reaches its dramatic conclusion. In a third shot, never used, we see that the elderly woman has a dedicated female companion who looks after her. As the rescue squad workers raise the woman's stretcher into the back of the van, the female companion tries to climb aboard so she can continue to comfort her crippled friend. But a rescue worker stops her, pointing toward the cab up front where she must ride. The backdoors are shut, and the companion gives an anguished look as she realizes that her friend's care is now the responsibility of unknown persons.

No doubt, the photographer was pained that this poignant shot was left out. In a documentary production, time might have been found to finish this small drama. For the six o'clock news report, however, additional facts about the fire and one last shot of the smoky building were judged more essential. That is not always the case, however. Newsroom practices are always in flux. Broadcast journalists like to know their stories are not only journalistically accurate but are having an impact on their audiences. Human-oriented visual sequences seem to be easier for the audience to comprehend while generating greater emotional effects. Obviously, conflicts arise because the best arrangement of the video does not always support the journalistic focus of a breaking news story. But more and more TV newsrooms are trying to achieve visual effects that were once only expected in documentary production.

Radio Documentary Writing

At the start of this postscript on documentary writing, I mentioned that writing a radio documentary script was a feasible project to further develop nonfiction writing skills. That's because access to a cassette tape recorder is all that's necessary to collect the raw material for radio documentaries. And with the addition of an inexpensive telephone pick-up microphone and a long-distance telephone budget, students can enlarge the scope of their research well beyond the confines of the campus to deal with regional and even national issues. Students need only listen to National Public Radio's "All Things Considered" a few evenings to see how often and how effectively interviews can be conducted by phone.

What students cannot obtain without broadcast-quality equipment, though, is broadcast-quality sound. Thus, they need to gather audio materials with the clear understanding that the actualities they capture on tape will need to be rerecorded if they ever want to produce the radio documentary they are scripting. Nevertheless, radio is an extremely versatile medium. Interview segments are the major component of most documentaries for obvious reasons. Eyewitnesses can describe events, and experts can explain causes and predict consequences. In television, of course, the writer needs video of the speaker or relevant B-roll. But, in radio, the mind's eye fills the screen.

Planning a Radio Documentary   When covering breaking news stories, veteran reporters can often rely on previous experience covering similar events to guide their information gathering activities. Each interview seems to lead them to another valuable source until they collect all the information they need. This strategy may be appropriate for some types of documentaries, but in most cases a surer route to success is diligent research and careful planning. The first step is to research the subject and create a detailed outline of the proposed documentary. The outline should reveal the scope of the project by enumerating the specific topics and issues to be covered and by suggesting a list of appropriate persons to be interviewed.

Whom you actually interview and record depends in great part on how deeply you want to explore each topic or issue and how effective an interviewee you can find. From your preliminary research, which should entail both print sources and informal interviews, you should be expert enough to speak knowledgably about the subject yourself. But just like any other type of radio production, part of the appeal of a documentary is the opportunity it provides the audience to meet new and different people. As a simple matter of pacing, the more time your documentary devotes to a particular topic or issue, the more likely the audience will appreciate hearing another new voice. Good interviewees are people who can orally explain or describe the topic with more insight, verve, or emotion than a reporter reading from a prepared script.

Interview Questions   To the extent that you have prepared a comprehensive outline, the questions you need to ask in an interview will be fairly obvious. Generally the subcategories in your topic outline will guide your questioning. But gather audio materials with an open mind. When something the interviewee says opens an unexpected vista, it's your job to explore it. In fact, as most books on interviewing will tell you, successful interviewers are inevitably the ones who listen most attentively to the interviewee. They are always ready to throw away a prepared list of questions in favor of more interesting ones that arise in the course of a conversation.

Remember also to ask your interviewees exactly what qualifies them as experts or eyewitnesses. Answers to those questions—especially from experts—may elicit routine responses, but they provide essential information needed to set up controversial statements. Information that establishes the interviewee's credibility is often crucial when the listeners try to weigh the importance of an interviewee's recollections and opinions.

Organizing Audio Materials The final step in the process is editing and organizing audio material into a coherent report. You might assume that assembling a documentary is just a matter of organizing material according to the original plan. But that is almost never the case. What you have actually captured on audiotape is almost always different in some critical way from what you remember recording, and certainly far different from what you originally thought you would record. As a result, expect to make changes in the structure of your script.

The first task is to make a transcript of all the interviews, or at least listen to all the interviews and transcribe those parts that might be used. In most cases, these will be interview segments that describe events, give examples, reveal opinions, and display emotions.

Once these prime actualities are selected, organize from both the bottom up and from the top down. As you did with your radio interview feature, cut out redundant elements in the interviewee's recorded responses and then imagine how the individual sound bites might fit together into thematically related units. Like the videotape editor who tries to construct logical video sequences, try to create audio sequences that develop a theme or explain a topic. At that point you'll be close to writing the continuity or narration, but not quite. You also need to develop an organizing structure for the documentary.

The challenging part is that there is no one way to organize the audio material. To keep options open, it may be helpful to write down various audio sequences on separate three-by-five cards. Even sound bites that are good, but don't fit in anywhere, can be recorded on individual cards. The cards make it easy to try different arrangements of the material. One final suggestion is to adopt an organizing system that both print and broadcast journalists find useful.

The *Wall Street Journal* Formula This organizing strategy is attributed to the *Wall Street Journal*, which, aside from publishing financial news, has a tradition of printing a long feature story daily on page one. The lengthy article always occupies the far right column and then continues on an inside page. The information in the story is reputed to be handled the same way every day. Each article has three parts: an example, an explanation, and an evaluation.

This is how this organizing strategy works. The example section, which is usually just three or four paragraphs, serves to focus the reader's attention on a single event or personal incident that epitomizes an interesting social issue or phenomenon. Next comes a long explanation section, which weaves together quotes drawn from interviews with participants, witnesses, experts, and other interested parties. Finally, the evaluation section considers anew the original example and provides a range of summary quotes from the most thoughtful of the interviewees. Interestingly, the *Journal*'s formula can be adapted to structure radio documentaries as well.

The opening segment should focus on one or two sound bites describing a specific incident that exemplifies the main issues or phenomena to be discussed. For a longer documentary, let one of your interviewees tell an especially poignant or relevant personal anecdote. Ideally, those sound bites will convey emotional feelings as well as information.

By far, the explanation section of the script will be the longest part. Excerpts from the audio interviews will provide both information and opinion, covering all of the major topics and most of the subcategories from your original outline. It may be that some subcategories were overlooked or not well covered during the initial interviews. You may be able to cover them briefly in the narration. Otherwise, if they're absolutely essential, you'll need to conduct further interviews to complete the script.

Finally comes the evaluation section. Some of those sound bites that are especially good, but do not seem to fit in anywhere are probably evaluative comments that can now be used to sum up the issues. Then, to give the script a satisfying sense of completion, the closing narration should remind the audience of the opening example and consider for a final time its important implications.

The *Wall Street Journal* formula will not solve all the problems of creating the best possible organization for a documentary script. It is doubtful that it can make up for lackluster interviews. Inspiration and ingenuity help, too. But the order of presentation is so natural that I would expect its rhetorical roots can be traced back to Aristotle. The strategy is one to remember for organizing video documentaries as well. Television is particularly good at presenting one compelling example to represent the whole. Once the emotion-laden event is shown, then the stage is set to develop the explanation and evaluation sections by fitting together interview segments and B-roll.

SCRIPTWRITING ASSIGNMENT

For this assignment, you will write two scripts for a local 11:00 P.M. TV newscast based on reporter packages that have appeared earlier that evening. The first step is to record an early evening network newscast and select two stories to re-edit and update for later broadcast. One re-edited story should be a simple voice-over videotape recut, using the best 20 to 30 seconds of videotape from one of the reporter packages. Your 11:00 version should include a 10 to 15 second anchor lead-in that updates the story and a voice-over narration timed to complement the video sequence you've selected.

Your second story should include a 15- to 25-second interview sound bite in addition to the standard anchor lead-in and voice-over videotape segments. You may want to write an anchor on-camera tag for this story so it does not end abruptly on the sound bite. If you have sufficient video material, you can also structure the story as a "v-b-v." That's newsroom jargon for a sound bite sandwiched between two voice-over video segments. In that case, you can dispense with the anchor on-camera tag.

Assuming that you don't have round-the-clock access to a wire service, use the next morning's newspaper as a source of information for updating your 11:00 stories. As a rule, the deadline for a morning newspaper is about the same as that for a late night television newscast, so the producer of an 11:00 P.M. news program has the same wire service information to work from as the editor of a morning edition newspaper.

Remember that the voice-over (VO) copy should complement the video but need not literally describe it. There are, however, two especially critical situations. The first sentence of the VTR/VO should almost always establish for the viewers what they are looking at, and voice-over narration that precedes a sound bite should provide a set up for—but not parrot or paraphrase—what the audience is about to hear. You may also want to designate chromakey graphics for the ANCHOR OC portions of the scripts. But make sure that the visual information they provide directly corresponds to the anchor's copy. Otherwise they become visual distractions.

ADDITIONAL READINGS

Air Words: Writing for Broadcast News by John Hewitt (Mayfield Publishing, Mountain View, CA, 1988). Hewitt was one of the brightest television news producers in the San Francisco market throughout the 1970s before he started teaching full time. He compresses much experience and insight into this textbook, which lays out the nitty gritty details of TV newswriting and production.

ENG: Television News and the New Technology by Richard D. Yoakam and Charles F. Cremer (Random House, New York, 1989). This text both instructs the reader in the use of electronic news gathering technology and documents its impact, especially on live and long-distance remote coverage. It provides technical diagrams to detail how videotape recording and editing work as well as broadcast scripts to illustrate the interplay between words and video.

News from Nowhere: Television and the News by Edward Jay Epstein (Vintage Books, New York, 1974). Many changes have occurred in video technology since the mid-1970s, but this case study is still the best introduction to the ethos of network television news.

Television Field Production and Reporting by Frederick Shook (Longman, New York, 1989). This is an advanced textbook that unequivocally advocates the primacy of video material in the planning and production of television news coverage. In that respect it is perhaps overly optimistic that pictures can tell the story. But, as a result, the book explains the techniques of broadcast photojournalism with extensive detail.

7
Political Commercials

A year after the 1968 presidential election, a book by a 26-year-old reporter from Philadelphia, Joe McGinnis, reached the best-seller list. It bore the provocative title, *The Selling of the President*. McGinnis had been an inside observer in the Nixon campaign. His major thesis was that Nixon had been sold to the American public through a massive advertising effort just like any other new commercial product. One of McGinniss's chief sources was Roger Ailes, a young television consultant hired by the Republican National Committee, who, 20 years later, would be George Bush's media advisor. McGinniss's account of the campaign admittedly overlooked the strong political forces that helped Richard Nixon eke out a victory, but the book did serve to raise troubling questions about the propriety of using mass marketing techniques in election campaigns.

Whether candidates can be sold like products or not, the parallels between commercial and political advertising are inherently interesting and important. Accordingly, in this chapter, we will discuss the form and content of television advertising solely in terms of one controversial category: political spots. We will look at the work of two pioneers in the field of television political advertising, outline the production elements in a representative political ad, and discuss a general technique for planning television ads, known as storyboarding. The goal is to make you a more knowledgeable consumer of television advertising and a more thoughtful student of contemporary election campaigns.

122   Chapter 7   Political Commercials

HAMMER-IT-HOME FOR EISENHOWER

Madison Avenue got its first shot at selling the presidency on television in 1952, when advertising executive Rosser Reeves created the first ever TV spots for a presidential candidate in a series called, "Eisenhower Answers America." In an interview with broadcast journalist Bill Moyers, Reeves recalled how he organized this historic ad campaign. Reeves first heard Eisenhower speak at a political rally in Philadelphia. The World War II hero was a "singularly inept" speaker. In a single speech, said Reeves, the General covered 27 different topics. In the end, no one knew what the Republican nominee for President really stood for.

Reeves was an advocate of the "hammer-it-home" school of advertising. He was determined to simplify Eisenhower's message. Reeves chose just three issues—corruption, high prices, and defense—and then hammered them home. Eisenhower filmed a series of answers on a single day. Later Reeves recruited housewives, businessmen, farmers, and veterans to ask the questions. The film segments were then spliced together to create the television spots.

Here are two examples of what the 20-second question and answer exchanges sounded like. Except for a lettered title card with a small oval portrait of Eisenhower, the audience saw only talking heads, no other visuals.

ANNCR: Eisenhower answers America...

HOUSEWIFE: General, both parties talk about bringing down food prices. How do we know which party to believe?

EISENHOWER: Well, instead of asking which party will bring prices down, why not ask what party put prices up? Then vote for a change.

* * * *

ANNCR: Eisenhower answers America...

VETERAN: I'm a veteran, General. What's wrong down in Washington? Graft, scandal, headlines. How can you fix it?

EISENHOWER: Here's how. By your vote, we'll get rid of the people who are too small for their jobs, too big for their britches, too long in power.

By today's standards, these spots appear remarkably unsophisticated, but it should be remembered that in 1952 the Republican and Democratic presidential campaign committees were still spending more on radio than on television time. Equally important, though, was Reeves' own philosophy of advertising. Reeves advocated what he called the "U.S.P.," the unique selling proposition. The man who had stuck Bic pens in electric drills to show how durable their ballpoints were and thought up the M&M slogan—"melts in your mouth, not in your hands"—didn't believe the audience could grasp complex ideas about products or politics. As he explained to Bill Moyers in an interview before his death in 1984:

> Most advertising men get tangled in their own underwear....You have to be terribly simplistic....You have to take what the product has, reduce it to a few essentials that are meaningful to them, put it in a memorable television commercial, and spend the money. It's a very simple business!

Two points seem especially crucial here. First, ads cannot summarize or condense a broad range of ideas. An ad campaign must be focused on a few issues. And within a single spot, it may only be possible to deal concretely with a single (albeit vital) aspect of that issue. Second, what Reeves calls a unique selling proposition must be expressed in terms the audience can understand and is likely to remember.

If there's a disparity between Reeves' first political spots and his most memorable product commercials, it exists in the realm of visualization. The Bic pen in the high-speed drill, the pounding hammers of the Anacin headache animation, and the messy and clean hands of the M&M anouncer each visually reinforced the ad's verbal claims. But, in "Eisenhower Answers America" we see only talking heads: a close shot of General Eisenhower intercut with the faces of "average" Americans, recruited from among the thousands of out-of-town visitors who in 1952 came everyday to tour New York City's Radio City Music Hall. At the presidential level, at least, campaign spots are now expected to reflect the same high quality production values that ads for commercial products do.

DEEP SELL FOR JOHNSON

In the world of persuasive messages, Reeves clearly represents the no-nonsense approach that attempts to define a need and show how the product fills it. But campaign advertising can take a more subconscious approach: playing on the voters' fantasies and their nightmares. American voters got their first real exposure to this type of spot in 1964 in an ad that was so powerful that it was aired only once. The 30-second commercial, created by Tony Schwartz, who was then an executive at the Doyle Dane Bernbach agency, came to be known as the "Daisy" spot. It showed a young girl counting as she slowly removed petals from a flower. When she reached nine, she was countermanded by an adult male voice from a public address system. The official voice began at 10 and counted backward to zero. That was the cue for a montage of nuclear explosion shots with natural sound. After a few moments, the rumbling thunder faded and an audio excerpt from a speech by then President Lyndon Johnson was heard voice-over:

> These are the stakes, to make a world in which all God's children can live, or go into darkness. Either we must love each other or die.

As the screen faded to black, a simple lettered message appeared: "On November 3rd, Vote for President Johnson."

That 30-second spot between segments of "Monday Night at the Movies" ignited a firestorm of reaction. Five years later in his book, *The Responsive Chord*, Schwartz recounted the episode. To Schwartz, the controversy erupted because of what people, especially Republicans supporting Senator Barry Goldwater, read into the spot—that Goldwater might actually use nuclear weapons if he were to become president. To those Goldwater partisans who cried foul, Schwartz rejoined that nowhere in the ad does he ever show or even mention the Republican nominee. Using auditory and visual stimuli, Schwartz had been able to evoke within the audience a subconscious feeling that had tremendous impact on their choice of presidential candidates.

Schwartz calls this technique a "deep sell," because it explicitly depends on the viewer's ascribing intensely personal feelings and meanings to a set of stimuli. Because those feelings and meanings are already in the viewer's mind, the stimuli simply serve to conjure them up. While critics would say the viewers are being manipulated, Schwartz doesn't see it that way at all. He argues that viewers are actively participating in the communication process. They complete the message just like they might be called on to interpret a Rorshach pattern. And because the meaning is one that they have supplied from their own context, they're more likely to take appropriate action on election day. Says Schwartz: "Television is an ideal medium for surfacing feelings voters already have, and giving these feelings a direction by providing stimuli that may evoke the desired behavior."

If you find that philosophy disquieting or even sinister, you are probably not alone. It makes it sound as if television is designed to circumvent the rational thinking processes that supposedly guide our democratic form of government. But much of what Schwartz argues is consistent with some of the basic notions of communication theory. Indeed, in Shannon's model of communication, messages are never transmitted, only signals, which evoke messages or conjure up new combinations of messages at the destination. That intense feelings may be associated with some of those messages stored in memory should not be surprising. The deeper question is whether voters will be satisfied to respond unthinkingly to their evoked feelings or will they be prompted to delve more systematically into the cause of their emotional reaction.

At best, the "Daisy" spot cleverly implied that Goldwater was more likely to use nuclear weapons than Johnson. But the implication was guided by a set of shared memories. Kennedy's civil defense fall-out shelter program, the Cuban missile crisis in October 1962, and the nuclear test-ban treaty that followed all spoke of the threat of nuclear war. In addition, there were the statements by the candidates themselves, in particular Goldwater's support for the use of tactical nuclear weapons and an off-hand remark that perhaps someone should lob a bomb into the men's room at the Kremlin. Taken together in 1964, the inference that the ad was referring to Goldwater may have been unavoidable

A generation later, however, much of this needs explanation, especially at a time when the thought of nuclear war is less threatening. Time has transformed Senator Goldwater from a radical rightwinger to a conservative statesman, while President Johnson's reputation as a social reformer has been overshadowed by his decision to escalate the U.S. involvement in the Vietnam War. Ironically, the most tragic aspect of the "Daisy" spot was that it was not germane to the real issues that would face the next president. Not nuclear war but Vietnam was the conflict that would confront America for the next decade, and, as journalist Bill Moyers, who was then a special assistant to President Johnson, has ironically noted, at no time in the 1964 campaign did the candidates confront that issue.

TYPES AND FUNCTIONS OF POLITICAL SPOTS

There is no universal model of the steps in a political campaign, but Edwin Diamond and Stephen Bates in their book, *The Spot*, provide a useful typology of political commercials. In reviewing some 500 spots used over a 40-year period, they proposed that most political media campaigns go through four phases characterized by four types of ads: ID spots, argument spots, attack spots, and, in the final days of the campaign, what have been informally dubbed "personal vision" spots.

When Richard Nixon chose Maryland Governor Spiro Agnew to be his vice-presidential candidate in 1968, the media response was Spiro Who? Agnew responded in admittedly Madison Avenue parlance that his name was not a household word, but it would be. And it was. For thousands of would-be elected officials, name recognition is their first task. Once we descend from the high-profile races for national office, the voting public can be shockingly ill-acquainted with the candidates. In a general election, party identification may be enough to win a vote but not in primaries when candidates are running against members of their own party. For some voters, familiarity with a name can be enough to tip the scales in favor of a particular candidate. In local elections, billboards with the candidate's name, photo, and slogan may be more cost effective than broadcast spots that are infrequent because air time is expensive.

Identification spots can take all sorts of formats. The most ambitious spots take the form of minidocumentaries, using snapshots to tell the candidate's life history. Predictably, John Glenn used film of his historic space flight to identify himself to voters when he first ran for U.S. senator in Ohio and dusted off the film again for the presidential primaries in 1984 and 1988. President Bush, who flew combat missions during World War II, had to bail out three times. Military photographers caught one rescue on film, dramatic scenes that ended up in Bush's identification spots beginning in 1980 when he first sought the Republican presidential nomination.

Women politicians can exploit similar opportunities. In a heated race for the Democratic gubernatorial nomination in the 1990 California primary, San Francisco Mayor Diane Feinstein introduced herself to voters statewide with footage taken moments after the November 1978 assassination of Mayor George Moscone. The videotape shows a flushed but composed Feinstein, who was then president of the San Francisco Board of Supervisors, informing news reporters that Moscone had been killed and that fellow supervisor, Dan White, was the assailant.

Candidates not so lucky to have cameras in the right place at the right time have tried other strategies. If the candidates perform well in front of the camera, they can speak for themselves. They can be shown in their office or their living room, at their farm or their ranch, on a horse or an athletic field, anywhere that helps identify their achievements and favorable aspects of their character. Others let their parents talk about them as candidates, especially if they're not well known among older voters. And—in what Diamond and Bates assert is now a cliche—candidates with long, difficult names present interviews with randomly selected voters mispronouncing the candidate's name and then getting it right. Presumably, viewers practice the name until they get it right, too. Because identification spots must visualize a narrative history and a name, it is admittedly difficult to create an original approach for every new candidate.

The argument phase of the campaign is characterized by spots that establish the issues the candidate intends to pursue. As we have seen in Reeves' development of the "Eisenhower Answers America" series, the candidates cannot afford to address every issue. They must focus on a handful that set the agenda for their campaign. Certainly, there was nothing sterling about the visual presentation of the Eisenhower spots, but as presidential campaign scholar Kathleen Jamieson has written, Reeves selected "from the smorgasbord of issues being addressed in the speeches...those that pollster George Gallup had discovered were most important to the American people." Jamieson's assessment of Reeves' contribution is especially telling, because it focuses the interplay between the selection of issues and the results of public opinion research.

Politicians are not statesmen when it comes to spotlighting issues. Their vision—or that of their media advisors—may extend no farther than election day. Thus, the handful of issues they pursue are likely to be those most effective at winning votes. Not only are polls used to see what matters to the voters but small groups of voters are interviewed in depth in focus groups to see if a particular spot generates the desired reaction. Focus groups played an important role in the 1988 presidential campaign. On the strength of focus group reactions, Roger Ailes, George Bush's 1988 media advisor, designed a hardhitting campaign that focused on three decidedly non-national issues: laws requiring school children to recite the pledge of allegiance, pollution in Boston Harbor, and prison furlough programs for violent criminals. As depicted in the Bush campaign spots, each one appeared to press what media professionals call the voter's "hot-button."

As the 1988 Bush campaign demonstrated, candidates can exploit negative issues as well as positive ones. Sooner or later, candidates create ads that attack their opponents. Trailing candidates create them as they desperately attempt to close the gap in pre-election polls, but frontrunners also employ them to protect their leads. The "Daisy" spot wasn't the only negative spot Tony Schwartz created for President Johnson's 1964 campaign. Less than a week later on "Saturday Night at the Movies," another Schwartz spot showing a girl licking an ice cream cone reminded viewers about the danger of radioactive fallout from above-ground nuclear testing. Senator Goldwater's vote against the nuclear test ban treaty was depicted as a vote in favor of letting radioactive fallout contaminate food and water supplies.

Two negative spots from President Johnson's media advisors didn't make it on the air. One that linked Goldwater's no vote on the test ban treaty to dangers for pregnant women was rejected for lack of scientific evidence. Another that associated Goldwater with the Ku Klux Klan, because Klan leaders had urged people to vote for him, was judged to be unfair. Goldwater had repudiated the KKK. The spot promoted guilt by association. While negative ads are effective at generating strong emotional reactions, they are not always the answer. No one can be sure of all their repercussions, not to mention the moral and ethical dilemmas they often pose.

According to Diamond and Bates, no matter what the advertising strategy may have been, most campaigns try to conclude on a positive note. Come the last week of the campaign, politicians try to reveal their personal vision for America after the election. The exercise is all the more agreeable if their previous spots have ensured a future of relative obscurity for their opponent. In other words, they think they've got the election won. In presidential and other major elections, the candidates routinely schedule a half-hour talk on election eve that somewhere includes the line, "I see an America...." In any case, the rule is to use "personal vision" spots during the last days of the campaign to recapture the positive tone and idealism that presumably motivated the candidates to seek elective office.

It should be increasingly clear that these various forms of political commercials did not arise by accident. Each type serves a particular campaign function. ID spots are used to make an unknown candidate better known. They increase the candidate's name recognition and visibility. The argument spots provide a forum for developing and explaining the candidate's position on issues. Concurrently, these ads may define (or redefine) a candidate's image by emphasizing positive personality traits such as honesty and competence or by linking him or her with certain demographic groups. Attack spots are used to turn the tables on the opposition by showing how one's opponent is on the wrong side of an issue, has broken promises, or supports elite interest groups. Not surprisingly, attack spots can boomerang. Even if the message strikes the target, the ads can generate negative effects against politicians who initiate them. As a result, political consultants often suggest that other partisan groups, not the candidates themselves, sponsor such ads.

While every spot is designed to win votes, the personal vision spots, coming at the end of the campaign, may be designed with multiple ends in mind. Campaign organizers are hopeful that in addition to providing a kinder, gentler form of persuasion, personal vision ads will serve to rejuvenate worn out campaign workers, increase voter turn out at the polls, and raise money for final campaign efforts. Those can be, of course, incidental effects of almost every type of spot. But the point to remember is that some types of ads serve special functions better than others. Media consultants earn their fees when they choose the type of ad that best serves the needs of the campaign.

MECHANICS OF CAMPAIGN SPOTS

One inescapable conclusion after 40 years of election campaigning on television is that no candidate can afford to be careless about media messages. A poorly executed campaign spot is a waste of huge sums of money. Worse still, a thoughtless ad can blow up in the candidate's face. Effective spots, then, must begin with research about the candidate, the issues, and the electorate and, when possible, be tested with small audiences before they are broadcast. From among a smorgasbord of possibilities, only a few promising ideas are selected and ultimately scripted for both sight and sound.

The range of formats are as vast for political spots as they are for everyday commercials. They can be documentaries, testimonials, issue dramatizations, straight question and answer, staged news conferences, sidewalk debates, bandwagon spots that depict the excitement of the campaign, and even introspective ads where the candidate talks on camera about a particular issue or goal. Looking at just one script in detail, however, will help enumerate the many production details that must be considered.

In 1986, Rep. David Price was only one of a handful of candidates who unseated an incumbent congressman. A professor of political science at Duke University in Durham, North Carolina, Price was also state chairman of the Democratic Party before he threw his hat into the ring. Two years later, he had to report back to the electorate to retain his seat. One of his spots is illustrated here. (The Live-TV script was used as an example in Chapter 2.)

The Price spot combines two common forms used in political ads. The audio track presents a testimonial. The video uses a photo montage to portray a "slice of life." Voters are skeptical both of politicians and advertising. Accordingly, political spots must overcome the voters' disposition to reject the message outright. The testimonial in this sample comes from a politician, but one whose southern accent unmistakably marks him as someone who's in synch with voters' values. The visual slice-of-life approach also works to establish credibility. Slice-of-life spots may be composed of video segments from actual news broadcasts or other documentary-like footage. In this particular spot, still photographs are used.

Chapter 7 Political Commercials 129

I've served with Congressman David Price on the House Banking Committee and his home equity bill is a remarkable achievement.

It's rare for any first time congressman....

to get a major bill passed.

130 *Chapter 7 Political Commercials*

I think his success is
a real tribute....

to his intelligence
and his

ability to deal with
people.

Chapter 7 Political Commercials 131

He brought Democrats as well as Republicans together on this.

And a lot of American homeowners are going to be protected by this bill.

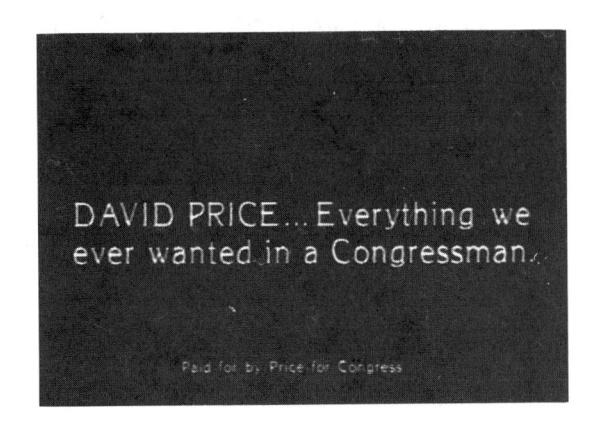

They can thank David Price for that.

132 Chapter 7 Political Commercials

CONVEYING VISUAL IDEAS WITH STORYBOARDS

The Price spot was not a very expensive one to create. The Philadelphia ad agency that produced it had only to hire a still photographer to take pictures of Rep. Price on the job and arrange to have Rep. Barnard's scripted testimonial videotaped in a Washington, D.C., studio. The elements could then be combined using fairly straightforward production techniques.

As the budget for a video production enlarges, however, the need to pretest its visual concept increases. One major problem is that using words to describe the video elements of a spot is often cumbersome and ineffective. Thus, rather than verbally detailing what the video shots in a commercial will look like, the creative team in charge of producing a television spot will often draw a sequence of simple sketches that roughly picture what the finished spot will look like. Those visual aids are known as "storyboards," and they are often crucial in convincing a potential client that the spot as envisioned by the ad agency will be an effective one.

It would be easy to confuse this explanation of a storyboard with the series of captioned photos already shown for the Price commercial. That type of display is more precisely known as a "photoboard," created from freeze frames of the completed spot. Like blueprints for a new structure, however, the storyboard can only represent in sketch form what the finished product will be. The storyboard is composed of a series of drawings that lays out the visual sequence of the spot, shot by shot. It is a planning tool that outlines what types of shots are desired and necessary to convey the message of the ad.

The storyboard sketch that follows (on page 133) of a generic politician at his desk should give an idea of how the first shot in the Price commercial might have been illustrated as part of a storyboard. Every frame in a storyboard consists of four main parts: (1) a sketch, (2) video directions, (3) spoken audio, and (4) special effects. Because the Price commercial used a sequence of nine shots, the storyboard would have had nine frames, numbered 1 through 9, as well.

Storyboard Techniques

Storyboard sketches need not be masterpieces. They can be drawn in pencil, erased, and redrawn until they bear some resemblance to reality. Perhaps the hardest thing to draw are human figures. One approach suggested by graphic artists is to draw men using rectangles to depict heads, bodies, arms, and legs and to draw women using triangles. The point is to find a consistent method. Even stick figures will suffice.

More important in regard to storyboard techniques are special considerations about the video format of television. First of all, although television screens vary in size, they all have a four-by-three aspect ratio. In other words, even though screen sizes are based on diagonal measures, the ratio between

CAMERA:
MS CONGRESSMAN DOUG BARNARD AT DESK.

AUDIO:
I'VE SERVED WITH CONGRESSMAN PRICE ON THE HOUSE BANKING COMMITTEE, AND HIS HOME EQUITY BILL IS A REMARKABLE ACHIEVEMENT.

SPFX:
SUPER OF CONG. BARNARD HOUSE BANKING COMMITTEE.

screen width and screen height is always four to three. A 20-inch screen must be 16 inches wide and 12 inches tall and a five-inch screen must be four inches wide and three inches tall. Thus, whenever a storyboard sketch is drawn for a TV spot, the frame of the sketch must be a third wider than it is high. For the purposes of composition, however, graphic artists often divide the height and width of the screen into equal thirds.

This simple procedure, which is based on what graphic artists call the "rule of thirds," divides the area of the screen into nine equal rectangles. The lines determined by the opposing corners of the center rectangle are called the dynamic axes. These two diagonal lines and the four points that determine them are given special attention when composing any scene. Rather than centering items in the middle of the screen (which would make the composition overly symmetrical and static), you should try to place the more important visual information—the eyes of a central character, a product name, or any other key element—at the corners of the center rectangle or along one of the two dynamic axes. To the trained eye, this technique markedly improves the dynamic quality and clarity of the shot.

To illustrate this concept, look at the sample frames (on page 134) depicting a man and a bear on a mountain ridge. They may not seem very political, but the bear is a traditional symbol of the Soviet Union, and the sketch is fashioned after a famous Reagan spot used in the 1980 presidential campaign that urged a strong defense as the only way to combat Soviet power.

134 *Chapter 7 Political Commercials*

PAN RIGHT FROM BEAR TO MAN

TILT UP TO REVEAL BEAR AND MAN ON RIDGE

ZOOM IN TO MAN AND BEAR

TRUCK RIGHT TO TRACK MAN RUNNING AWAY

The story goes that the creator of the ad actually used photos he clipped out of magazines to devise his impromptu storyboard. Notice how the man's head is located at one axis point and how he's looking down at the bear, which stands at another axis point. The angle of the man's vision follows a strong diagonal line that runs through these opposite corners. In fact, even if the composition is balanced on the right and left like the storyboard frame of the politician at his desk, notice how the eyes are placed on the upper horizontal line, not in the center of the frame. Indeed, if you examine all the still photographs from the Price spot, you'll see that the "rule of thirds" guides the framing in almost every case.

Designating Camera Shots and Moves

As the sketches for a storyboard are drawn, they need to be labeled as well. In reality, the verbal information placed next to the video, audio, and special effects labels is nearly the same as the audio and video information that would normally appear on the accompanying Live-TV script. There are, however, some specific storyboard notations that must be used.

Typically, the framing of a shot is described by using the terms long shot (LS), medium shot (MS), or close-up (CU). They defy any absolute definition because the relationships between them vary depending on the subject being photographed. But we can outline the differences fairly well in terms of human anatomy. A long shot shows the entire body, a medium shot is from the waist up, and a close-up shows just the head and top of the shoulders. Obviously, there are intermediate forms of these shots such as a medium long shot (MLS) from the knees up or a medium close up (MCU) from the chest up. There are also extreme forms. For example, a shot of the man and the bear on the mountain ridge would be described as an extreme long shot (ELS) while a tight shot of the man's eyes or the bear's teeth would constitute an extreme close-up (ECU).

In addition to the framing, the video instructions designate specific camera movements such as pan, tilt, or zoom. As illustrated on page 134, storyboard artists have developed a series of symbols to designate those movements on the sketches themselves. For a pan (short for panoramic shot) where the camera is swiveled horizontally, a bold black arrow is drawn above or below the frame. The direction of the arrow indicates the direction the camera swivels. For a tilt shot where, as the name implies, the camera is tilted up or down, the movement is designated by a bold black vertical arrow drawn on either side of the frame. A zoom shot, where the focal length of the lens is adjusted to make the frame larger or smaller, is designated with an arrow pointing toward the corner (for a zoom-out) and emanating from the corner (for a zoom-in). An additional convention is to use a dotted-line rectangle to define that part of the frame at which the zoom begins or ends.

In addition to the pan, tilt, and zoom, the camera may also truck left or right and dolly in or out. In both cases the entire camera is moved. When the camera trucks left or right, it usually tracks some object moving within the frame. When the camera dollies in or out, it moves closer to or farther from the subject to change its relative size within the frame. The result is very much like a zoom but with less optical distortion.

One final storyboard convention is the use of a broken arrow, slightly smaller than the type used to indicate camera moves, to designate the movements of people, animals, or objects in the frame. It is crucial, however, to remember that a broken arrow only indicates action within the frame. It does not specify how the camera should be positioned to record that action. If a candidate for office is depicted jogging past the Capitol, a broken arrow will only emphasize the fact that he or she is running in a certain direction. If the camera is to follow the action, then you must draw a bold black arrow pointing in the same direction under the frame. Otherwise, the sketch would depict a figure entering the frame on one side and disappearing on the other as it runs past a stationary camera.

136 Chapter 7 Political Commercials

As a rule, each sketch in a storyboard represents one shot, that is, one starting and stopping of the camera. Thus, the sketches are numbered sequentially. Occasionally, however, the camera movements in a long-running shot are too complex to capture in a single sketch. Two or more sketches may be required. But since the component sketches are all part of the same shot, they retain the same number for identification, but a lettered suffix is added to designate the precise order in which the reframing occurs. Thus, sketches 2A, 2B, and 2C would illustrate the proposed camera movements and the resulting visual images of the second shot in a storyboard.

Storyboard Applications

While storyboarding has become a major planning tool for advertising agencies, the truth is that Madison Avenue actually borrowed the concept from Hollywood. As cartoon animators became more ingenious in developing story lines and visual tricks during the 1930s, they developed a need for some type of scripting device to outline the high speed action and fantastic transitions they envisioned. The written word was simply inadequate.

The practice of creating storyboards first developed at Disney Studios, where teams of animators mapped out their visual ideas by pinning up sketches on a board. Each sketch was drawn on a separate piece of paper so the proposed sequence of events in animated films could be adjusted to improve the pace and flow of action. Hollywood directors have also adopted storyboard techniques to map out complex live action scenes and special effects. Alfred Hitchcock, himself a graphic artist, was among the the first to promote their use. More recently, Steven Spielberg has employed storyboards extensively to plan intricate shooting sequences in his films.

As important as the storyboard is in serving as a production guide, it can serve an even more important function in the planning stages of a project. For the visually minded, storyboards are a vital technique for generating ideas and clarifying possible directions for a video production. In that sense, the storyboard is not a mere illustration of the written script but an alternative tool for getting your creative thoughts down on paper.

SCRIPTWRITING AND STORYBOARD ASSIGNMENT

For this assignment, you are to throw your hat into the media ring and devise a 30-second political ad for use in an upcoming primary or general election. You can choose any likely candidate for a congressional, state, or local contest, but be ready to do some research about the person you plan to support. One alternative would be to create an issue-oriented spot related to a ballot initiative or—if the next election is really distant—a spot that urges citizens to take sides on a social or environmental issue that has generated controversy in your community. In the latter case, create the spot for a concerned citizens group in lieu of a political campaign organization.

Because the assignment requires a broad range of talents and interests, you may want to work together in teams. There are three parts to be completed:

1. A typed script for the 30-second advertisement, using live-TV format.
2. A complete storyboard including sketches of each shot—probably six to nine—with accompanying directions for video, audio, and special effects.
3. A brief statement explaining the strategy behind your ad.

Here are a few rules to keep in mind when you create your political spot. Like all rules they can be broken, but only if there is a good reason. Think in visual terms. Television is predominantly a visual medium. Therefore, try to incorporate images with motion or visual appeal. Use close-ups of people and your candidate.

Keep the script simple. Concentrate on one major reason to elect your candidate or support your cause and build your script around this. Use simple words, phrases, and concepts. Limit the number of performers appearing in your spot. The more people included in a scene, the wider the camera shot and consequently the less intimate the scene. If your candidate is a relative newcomer with little name recognition, be sure to mention his or her name at the start and the end of the ad.

ADDITIONAL READINGS AND VIDEOTAPES

Packaging the President: A History and Criticism of Presidential Campaign Advertising by Kathleen Hall Jamieson (Oxford University Press, New York, 1984). Jamieson provides a scholarly chronicle of eight presidential election contests from Eisenhower-Stevenson to Reagan-Carter on the basis of political campaign advertising, divining what the operation of the ad campaign implies about the candidates and the electorate at each four year interval.

The Responsive Chord by Tony Schwartz (Anchor Press/Doubleday, Garden City, NY, 1973). The "Daisy" spot is just a small part of this book in which Schwartz lays out his communication philosophy. "A listener or viewer brings far more information to the communication event than a communicator can put into his program, commercial, or message," writes Schwartz. "The communicator's problem" he continues, "[is to] evoke the stored information."

The Spot: The Rise of Political Advertising on Television by Edwin Diamond and Stephen Bates (MIT Press, Cambridge, MA, 1988). Diamond and Bates document the rise of TV political spots from the first Eisenhower ads through the 1984 Reagan-Mondale contest. For each election they provide scripts and freeze frames of the most memorable spots.

The 30-Second President, produced by Bill Moyers (PBS Video, Washington, DC, 1984). By comparison to books I have recommended, this 1-hour installment in *A Walk Through the Twentieth Century with Bill Moyers* just scratches the surface. But only videotape can show you exactly what some classic political spots look like. In addition, the documentary includes fascinating interviews with Rosser Reeves and Tony Schwartz.

8
Situation Comedies

When the TV comedienne Lucille Ball died of heart failure in April 1989, there was no funeral. The star of "I Love Lucy" had specified in her will that no services were to be held. But at the urging of Lucy's children, thousands of fans across the country observed a moment of silence the following Monday at 9:00 P.M. sharp, the time millions of Americans had tuned in regularly throughout the 1950s to watch Lucy become enmeshed in and then disentangle herself from yet another harebrained dilemma.

The notion of paying last respects to a television star by commemorating her spot in the prime time schedule is odd indeed. But it is just one indication of the enduring impact sitcoms have on American TV audiences. On February 28, 1983, an estimated 125 million Americans tuned in for the last episode of "M*A*S*H." As a senior editor of *Harper's* rhetorically asked his readers: "What defines the seventies better than 'All in the Family'? Or the eighties better than 'The Cosby Show'?" To his mind, the situation comedy is as peculiar to the American character as the short story and the sermon. In some cases it mixes the purposes of both. For all these reasons, including our intensive exposure to sitcom programming, the sitcom genre makes an ideal starting point for a discussion of dramatic writing for television.

CHARACTERIZATION, SETTING, AND PLOT

Good sitcom writers are experts, of course, at generating laughter. But the best sitcom scripts are built on a solid dramatic core. Beyond the punch lines and slapstick antics, the writer must create an engaging story as a vehicle for comedy. In 22 minutes of air time, divided into two acts by a commercial break, the writer must reveal through words and action how an attractive and interesting group of characters, placed in a distinctive locale, has been tested by a series of obstacles in pursuit of an initially elusive goal. Thus, like a playwright, the sitcom writer must deal with the fundamental components of drama: characterization, setting, and plot.

Despite all the memorable sitcom episodes we've seen, however, we should not forget that on one level sitcoms are an industrial product. They are created by a production team filling a slot in the network's prime-time schedule. For economic and organizational reasons, many of their characteristics are unchanged from script to script and series to series. Foremost among those repetitive elements is the setting. Sitcom producers limit the settings for each series to a few standard locations. Because the earliest sitcoms revolved around families or married couples, the most familiar locale was the living room or the kitchen with an occasional excursion to Dad's place of work. All that changed, however, when writers and producers started creating new types of sitcom "families." The ensemble cast of "The Mary Tyler Moore Show" played out its conflicts in the newsroom, the studio, and Mr. Grant's office as well as Mary's bachelor apartment. And, of course, the men and women of MASH unit 4077 broke new ground, trading insults and heartbreak in the operating room, the recovery ward, the mess tent, Colonel Potter's office, and "The Swamp." Shot in motion picture style, "M*A*S*H" cameras even moved outdoors to reveal exteriors of the military compound and the Korean countryside. Ultimately, exceptions such as "M*A*S*H" only serve to highlight the rule. Sitcoms are usually performed on the same basic stage from week to week, shot with studio cameras live on tape.

In "M*A*S*H," the true-to-life settings added a sense of verisimilitude to the sitcom that sharpened the bite of each satirical jest. In most other sitcoms, however, the setting is chosen because it facilitates the development of story ideas. Ricky Ricardo's night club opened the door for multiple plots involving Lucy's desire to break into show business. Laverne and Shirley were revived by a move from blue-collar Milwaukee to trend-setting L.A.

Most critical may be the opportunity a setting provides to bring diverse characters into contact with one another. Bob Newhart's success as a stand-up comic was based on his deadpan reactions to extraordinary people engaged in extraordinary events. In both his long-running sitcoms he was placed in settings where he would become inextricably involved in other people's problems, in the 1970s as a clinical psychologist in urbane Chicago and in the 1980s as the owner-operator of a historic New England inn. The setting for his second series, as Newhart has described, occurred to him while visiting an inn in the Pacific Northwest. There he could not help but notice what a diverse range of people passed through the inn's lobby. The barroom locale for "Cheers" inspired by a Boston taproom, is another setting waiting for a story to develop. No longer situated in the home, these series are sometimes classified as "arena" sitcoms. "Taxi," whose oddball characters sit in a garage waiting for driving assignments, is another memorable "arena" sitcom.

As central as an unchanging setting may be to our notion of a situation comedy, the term may well be a misnomer for the best examples of the genre. As screenwriter Stewart Bronfeld has pointed out, these programs are not as dependent on their settings as they are on their characters. Bronfeld suggests that sitcoms should actually be called "charcoms," that is, character comedies, because their drama and humor arise not so much from the particular situation in which the actors and actresses find themselves but from the clash of their unique but appealing personalities.

The variety and depth of character development in such classic sitcoms as "The Mary Tyler Moore Show" and "All in the Family" were so great that the producers generated numerous spinoffs based on supporting characters. From "All in the Family" came "The Jeffersons," "Maude," and "Archie's Place." From "The Mary Tyler Moore Show" came "Rhoda," "Phyllis," and even the hour-long dramatic series "The Lou Grant Show."

Television critic Jane Feuer has observed that the use of seven main characters, around whom the plot could revolve in any one episode of "The Lou Grant Show," evolved naturally from the ensemble format of the "The Mary Tyler Moore Show." And, ultimately, the ensemble cast shaped the structure of the most successful dramatic programs of the 1980s: "Hill Street Blues," "St. Elsewhere," and "L.A. Law." All were longer and more expensive to produce, but, like sitcoms, each relied on a "family" of characters attached to a "home" setting, whether that be a precinct station, hospital, or suite of offices.

No matter how much viewers may appreciate a sitcom's unique setting and characters, every episode must include a third component to hold the audience's attention. That often elusive element of drama is plot. What exactly is plot? At the most rudimentary level, it is a sequence of events that are causally related. The notion bears a strong resemblance to the concept of mental scripts that we discussed in regard to news value in Chapter 5. A script could be described as a logical sequence of events, but it scarcely generates a full-blown plot. A plot develops only when the normal sequence of events is interrupted by an unlikely or unpredictable action. As in the restaurant script, there must be an anomaly that draws in the audience. The characters sit down, order, then leave. Only when the audience asks "Why?" do we begin to engage them in a story. What the dramatist is free to do—and in fact must do—is create a mechanism to generate and a motivation to power such unexpected events. Unlike the journalist, the dramatist can tinker with reality, altering settings to generate unexpected events and adjusting character to motivate human conflicts. Indeed, conflict is an essential ingredient in creating a dramatic plot.

Creating a compelling drama, however, requires more energy and imagination than simply thinking up an acceptable conflict. For one thing, the management of conflict takes an extremely sensitive touch. The primary conflict is always preceded and followed by numerous premonitions, rumblings, and aftershocks. There is not so much a single conflict as a series of conflicts and challenges, advances and setbacks. From the point of view of the hero in a drama or sitcom, conflicts are treated as if they are problems to be solved. But initially heroes almost always fail to resolve their major problem, and so they find themselves in even worse predicaments than before.

As a sequence of events, the plot may actually be viewed as a series of unsuccessful attempts at resolving the conflict. Each failure actually increases dramatic tension until a climactic resolution takes place. Think of the adventures of Steven Spielberg's famous character, Indiana Jones. In the first film, *Raiders of the Lost Ark*, Jones meets constant conflicts and challenges: South American Indian booby traps, Nazi assassins, Middle-Eastern assassins, secret codes, snakes, Army trucks, U-boats, and so on, until the hand of God itself resolves the conflict by destroying Jones's enemies. Spielberg is unrelenting. The movie provides a cascade of conflicts designed to emotionally exhaust the audience. Not all plots need to be this emotionally charged, but we must avoid the novice writer's tendency to create a plot in which there is only a single conflict and an immediate resolution. The novice forgets that the plot is composed of numerous episodes and that often things have to get worse before they get better. Otherwise, the plot can barely sustain a single act.

Another vital point is the relationship between plot and character. A well-constructed plot is necessary but not sufficient to please an audience. What pulls us in, makes us interested in a drama or comedy, is the fact that the conflicts the audience witnesses are focused through characters the audience cares about. Bronfeld, ever mindful of the characters' role, reminds us that "what contributes drama to the plot is not the conflict itself, but rather what the character does or how he or she does it in response to that conflict." The spectacle in an Indiana Jones movie is fun, but ultimately the adventurer is more important than the adventure. The primary attraction of the sequel is the thought of the main character responding to a series of new conflicts. That is why the viewer tunes in weekly to watch "The Cosby Show" or "L.A. Law."

PLOT AND CHARACTER: A SITCOM EXAMPLE

As was noted, the intricate interrelationship between characterization, plot, and setting can only be fully illustrated by example. The description of "Newhart" on the next four pages is not an actual script but an extended synopsis along with two brief segments of dialogue, in short, enough to launch a meaningful discussion about the program's two-act dramatic structure.

This particular episode, "The Way We Thought We Were," aired in the program's first season. The ensemble cast then included Dick Louden (owner of the inn), Joanna Louden (his wife), George Uttley (the rustic handyman), Leslie Vanderkellen (a Dartmouth student who worked as a housekeeper) and Kirk Devane (the devious young owner of the Minute Man Cafe).

The plot centers on George and a former sweetheart, Eleanor. Much of the comic relief comes from Kirk's campaign to get Dick to contribute to a kids' hockey team named the "Eye-Gougers" and his amorous advances toward the upstanding and easily embarrassed Leslie.

"THE WAY WE THOUGHT WE WERE"

ACT ONE

FADE IN:

INT. STRATFORD INN DINING ROOM—BREAKFAST

Kirk, Leslie, Dick, and Joanna are seated at the table. Dick is trying to eat his breakfast while Kirk inveighs him to contribute a hundred dollars for peewee hockey jerseys. Then eyeing Leslie and unashamedly expressing his amorous feelings for her, Kirk asks wistfully whether that's Leslie's knee he's touching. He evokes a gruff "No!" from Dick who is sitting a chair away. When George, the handyman, enters, Leslie gives him her place at the table. Uncharacteristically George asks for a few days off. To everyone's surprise, George admits that he needs the time to entertain a high school sweetheart who's going to spend the weekend at the inn. George explains how the romance abruptly ended when Eleanor moved away.

GEORGE

Well, I was going to ask her to marry me. You know how it is sometimes. You mean to do something. And then you put it off. And before you know it, the person's moved.

JOANNA

How long's it been since you've seen her.

GEORGE

Thirty-one years.

JOANNA

And you haven't kept in touch all that time?

GEORGE

She moved so far away, there was no point.

DICK

Where'd she move?

GEORGE

Montpelier!

DICK

That's fifty-nine miles from here.

GEORGE

(*THE PARAGON OF PAROCHIALISM*) I know! I figured I'd never see her again.

INT. LOBBY — LATER THAT MORNING

Kirk enters an empty lobby and starts hammering the bell on the front desk. Dick, Joanna, and Leslie all come running. Irritated, Dick reminds Kirk that he's been told not to touch that bell. Kirk categorically denies that Dick ever told him that. He's come, however, to take extra orders for tee shirts. And for that he needs eveyone's size, especially Leslie's. Joanna and Leslie leave to attend to chores. George, dressed in his usual handyman overalls, enters the lobby and takes up a position at the door to wait for Eleanor. Kirk uses the occasion to get Dick to talk about old flames. Dick refuses, but then under Kirk's prodding breaks down, reminiscing about a tryst with Lorraine in the cornfield. Joanna reappears just in time to ask Dick whom he took to a cornfield. Dick dismisses the incident as a "stupid, meaningless night...that I've never forgotten." A moment later, a smartly-dressed, attractive middle-aged woman enters the lobby. Everyone stares, waiting for George to welcome his old sweetheart, but he doesn't recognize the woman. Finally, she has to introduce herself to her stunned host. Joanna takes Eleanor to her room, leaving George at the front desk with Dick to regain his bearings. A disheartened George tells Dick that what he liked about the old Eleanor was that she was so plain. He could talk to the old Eleanor, but he feared this "lady has heard everything I have to say." Dick tries to console George only to find how deeply disappointed he is. Asked what he wanted to happen this weekend, George responds, "I expected to fall in love again."

END OF ACT ONE

ACT TWO

INT. ELEANOR'S ROOM — CONTINUOUS ACTION

Joanna helps Eleanor get settled in her room. Eleanor explains how George had been sexy and dashing as a young man, always good at building things, including a ladder he used to reach her bedroom window, until her father found out. But now, says Eleanor, it seems as if George has grown "rough around the edges." As if to underscore her remark, George comes to get Eleanor for lunch or "tie on the feed bag," as he puts it. When George and Eleanor leave, Dick and Joanna compare notes. George is too rustic. Eleanor is too sophisticated. The romance appears dead.

INT. DICK'S OFFICE — NEXT DAY

Dick is at his desk typing, but notices George hanging around at the door...obviously waiting to discuss what to do about Eleanor.

DICK

So how's everything going with you and Eleanor?

GEORGE

How did you know that's what I wanted to talk to you about?

DICK

Shot in the dark. (PAUSE) Still a little...a little awkward between you two?

GEORGE

Awh Nawh. There's no awkwardness. We just can't think of anything to say to each other. (PAUSE) How am I going to get Eleanor back to being Eleanor?

DICK

I don't think you can, George.

GEORGE

Oh.

DICK

At least...at least not...not quickly.

GEORGE

Well, how much would you say I could get back?

DICK

It depends on how much you do.

GEORGE

What would you do?

Dick explains how he and Joanna once celebrated their anniversary by spending a night in the same hotel where they went on their honeymoon. Dick suggests that George take Eleanor to a favorite spot where they once spent a lot of time together. George says that would be hard to do since he sold his pick-up truck, but he does have another idea.

INT. SHOE STORE — LATER THAT DAY

George ushers a bewildered Eleanor into the shoe store. Ignoring the salesman, he directs Eleanor to sit down in a corner of the store. Still bewildered, Eleanor asks what's going on. An excited George reminds Eleanor that this shoe store used to be the Clover Cafe, and they're sitting at their old table. In a half-hearted way, Eleanor tries to fan whatever romantic sparks remain. She recalls George as a dashing young man who could make her laugh and her expectation that when she moved to Montpelier, George would come dashing after her. George is upset. He never realized that's what Eleanor wanted. "You mean the last thirty-one years have all been a misunderstanding?" he asks. Eleanor tries to console him. She reminds him that although neither one of them has married, both pretty much lived the lives they wanted to. George wishes for a second chance, but not Eleanor. "I think we both changed too much," she responds.

INT. STRATFORD INN LOBBY — SAME DAY

Kirk enters the lobby just as a guest comes down the stairs from his room. Kirk points at the bell on the front desk and urges the guest to ring it harder and harder. Dick, Joanna, and Leslie come running. All three glare at him. But Kirk points a finger at the guest. "He did it," Kirk rationalizes. Dick puts the bell behind the counter. Kirk has come to show the three of them a sample of the peewee hockey jersey. "Minute Man Cafe" is boldly embossed on three lines across the back while near the hem in tiny print it says "and the Stratford Inn." Dick's blood pressure rises. Kirk says he'll try to fix the design. George enters through the front door smartly dressed in a black tuxedo jacket and bow tie. Dick, Joanna, and Leslie are all taken aback. He has no idea where to take Eleanor on their last evening out, but thought she'd like his dressing up. He admits that the weekend hasn't gone well. Eleanor thinks he's changed. Eleanor comes down from her room dressed in a simple wool sweater and skirt. Despite the mismatch, it's obvious that each is delighted with how the other looks. "Now this is the Eleanor I remember!" he tells the others. Elated, George takes her arm to escort her out the door. "My chariot awaits you," he exclaims. Eleanor laughs heartily as she squeezes his arm and moves closer to him.

FADE OUT.

THE END

Plotting the Plot

No single sitcom episode can exemplify all the possible ways in which scriptwriters may exploit character and setting to generate a compelling plot. The introduction of a new character as a catalyst is just one technique to get the wheel of fate rolling. In an action-adventure series, the arrival of a stranger often forebodes danger or violence. In sitcoms, characters often show up at inopportune times with farcical and slapstick results.

In this episode of "Newhart," news that George's old flame is coming to the Stratford Inn generates expectations from the simple "What's she like?" to the more profound "What does this mean?" Half an hour later, we have experienced not just a reunion between two high school sweethearts, but four rolls of the dice, three of which turned out poorly. First was the awkward moment when they set eyes on each other after 31 years. Second was Eleanor's bittersweet recollections about a romance that ended when she moved to Montpelier. Third was George's attempt to revive old emotions by visiting old haunts. Only on the fourth try—when Eleanor laughs at George's chivalrous remark—do we regain some part of the romantic hope that infused the opening scene of act one.

Character and Action

It has often been said that a sitcom is a three-act play that begins with the second act. Because viewers are familiar with the main characters and settings in a weekly sitcom, the scriptwriter can jump ahead and begin the story almost immediately. There's no need for preliminary scenes that establish a character's personality, work routines, social relationships, family backgrounds or other motivating forces. But this doesn't mean that these forces haven't been well thought out. As the American novelist Henry James pointed out in his famous essay, "The Art of Fiction," the elements of character and action merge in any good novel. "What is character but the determination of incident? What is incident but the illustration of character?" So it is in drama. Character motivates action, and action reveals character.

For the scriptwriter, each character must have a real and complete personal history. Scriptwriters must know where characters were born and raised, what they were like as children, their schooling, their first jobs, their careers, their failures, and their successes. They must know what their characters think about the world, about themselves, about the actions of others. And, finally, they must know their characters' behavior—from their speech, movements, and gestures to how they react to diverse situations and people. Consider the implications for the "Mary Tyler Moore Show" if Mary Richards had been a divorcee—as first proposed by the show's creators—rather than a single "career woman."

In "Newhart," the conflict between characters generates the core of the drama. Eleanor dislikes George's rustic lifestyle. Her big city manners disappoint him. Each scene illustrates how far apart they are. Even more profound, however, are the internal conflicts. How much change will George and Eleanor accept in a person they once loved? How much will each change to accommodate the other? Of course, the audience is rooting for a breakthrough that will permit some semblance of a happy ending. The hoped for resolution appears possible only when George and Eleanor adjust their habits just enough to adjust their appearance. She dresses simple. He dresses dashing. The final scene reveals a measure of mutual concern that had been absent from their previous engagements.

Showing It

The last scene also illustrates an aspect of stagecraft that every scriptwriter knows. Show it, don't say it, the dramatic equivalent of action speaks louder than words. When George makes his entrance in black tie and tuxedo jacket, rather than overalls, checked shirt, and hunting cap, it knocks the wind out of the audience. The audio track records a collective sigh. The effect is redoubled when Eleanor appears neat and simple in a skirt and sweater. No one has to say that Eleanor and George have changed to suit the other. The audience can surmise as much from what they see. They're now ready to savor the couple's reactions. It should also go without saying that facial expressions and gestures can be as important as dialogue.

Like every other aspect of scriptwriting, there are no automatic rules about when to show and when to tell. But clearly the writer wants to put as much evidence before the audience as possible without having to say outright what they should believe or feel about a character or incident. Though Kirk is a secondary character in this episode, even a new viewer would soon come to the conclusion that Kirk is a schemer, a snoop, and sexually obsessed. The question is how does the audience know. Does anyone say Kirk is a schemer? Does anyone say he is a snoop? Did any one of the three woman characters say, "Kirk, you're sexually obsessed!"? In truth, no one did. But in the first act, when Kirk was pressing Dick for a hundred dollar contribution to Pee Wee hockey, the audience heard Kirk impatiently complain that he had looked for Dick in his bedroom and that he knew where Dick kept his checkbook. In the second act, when Kirk brings in an undersized tee-shirt for Leslie to try on, viewers can only infer the worst.

There is one type of telling that beginning scriptwriters must be especially conscious of. That's exposition. Exposition is the setting forth of facts or ideas, in short, a detailed explanation. In plays it is often necessary to set forth details about earlier events in the lives of major characters to help explain what motivates their current behavior. At the beginning of act two, Eleanor gives the audience a fairly large dose of exposition in her description of George as a young man. The verbal flashback is permitted, because it serves double duty. Given the disappointment of their first meeting, it needs to establish what Eleanor once found attractive about George and foreshadow what it would take to win her back. He was dashing. He could make her laugh. If this script had been written for a feature film instead of a sitcom, the budget may well have accommodated this visual flashback. Pictures of George climbing his ladder to Eleanor's bedroom window would have been used to reveal what George was like as a young man. But given the tighter financial constraints typical of sitcom production, the scriptwriter had no choice but to take the cheap way out. Joanna sits down on the bed, and Eleanor tells her the story of George Uttley's ladder, with as few words but as many laughs as possible.

Sitcom Dialogue

Ultimately, the bulk of the writing in a script is in the form of dialogue. Like every aspect of a good sitcom, it demands considerable attention. The dialogue must be infused with humor, and it must convey critical information that moves the story ahead. The trick is to incorporate both the jokes and the critical information in what passes for everyday conversation. Just by examining how dialogue from "The Way We Thought We Were" appears on the printed page, we can infer some of the rules involved. First, to make scripted dialogue sound like conversation, characters usually have very short speeches, and the speaking parts are swiftly alternated from character to character. The words they use are familiar and colloquial. Their sentences are simple and declarative. Incomplete sentences are permitted. Contractions are preferred. If the information is complicated, then the characters may explore it through a series of questions and answers. Rarely does a character wax philosophical. In most cases, long speeches bring the dramatic action to a resounding halt.

One last item: Some writers are tempted to capture every nuance of a character's speech by altering spelling to convey a special accent. Usually this isn't necessary. Sitcom actors need no prompting to remain in character week after week. Even if a new character is being introduced in a particular episode, the writer should not go overboard in specifying how this character is to be played. Producers, directors, and actors require some freedom to create their own interpretation. A more important test is whether the scripted words are consistent with the personality of the characters who speak them. If it makes no difference whether character A or character B delivers the lines, then the odds are that the dialogue is neither convincing nor essential.

SOURCES OF COMEDY

Our approach to "Newhart" has been so analytical that it is easy to forget that this sitcom was conceived first and foremost to entertain. That it provided painful insights into the pitfalls of romantic love only attests to the skill of the scriptwriters. But we should not forget that comedy relieved the emotional tension at every turn. George's literal-minded grasp of language led to humorous misunderstandings in every exchange. Moreover, the subplot involving Kirk's support for a Pee Wee hockey team was more than a device to ridicule Kirk's scheming personality. It got the episode off to a humorous start, diverted us as we anticipated Eleanor's dramatic first entrance, and cheered us after the shoe store disaster. Kirk's childish efforts to get Leslie into an undersized, tight-fitting tee shirt provided a humorous counterpoint to the serious problems that George and Eleanor were experiencing.

The reasons why people laugh in reaction to certain auditory and visual stimuli are not fully understood. As novelist and essayist Arthur Koestler explained in a treatise some years ago, our disposition to laugh may reflect some of the most primitive workings of the human brain. Humans can rarely outrun their natural enemies nor overpower them. As a result, our long-term survival has depended on our ability to recognize and respond instantaneously when something is amiss in the environment. We are on constant surveillance, unconsciously drawing comparisons between incoming sensory information and intricate memory traces stored in our brains. When the patterns match, we are relaxed. But the body is put on alert whenever major incongruities occur.

This natural response to novelty in the environment is known as an orienting response. Nature has guaranteed that we will shift our attention to any possible threat to our existence. In a world as diverse as ours, however, not every novelty is a threat. Koestler's laughter hypothesis is that society could not evolve without humans finding a harmless outlet for dissipating the excited emotional and physical state that accompanies powerful responses to novel stimuli. In a figurative way, civilization transformed the snarl into a sneer or a snicker. Eventually, the muscles of the face relaxed, the corners of the mouth turned up, and humankind learned to smile.

We should not forget, however, that underpinning our bemusement is an aggressive disposition that is at odds with our modern circumstances. That aggressiveness evidences itself in many forms of humor from the practical joke to the put down. In fact, part of our enjoyment of comedy may stem directly from an unconscious sense of relief that the other guy is the victim. That does not mean, however, that excessive verbal aggression in sitcoms should be tolerated. Certainly, the best sitcoms have more to offer than name calling, insults, and put downs.

The truly creative component of comedy comes from what Koestler calls bisociative thinking. According to Koestler, our normal routine is to engage in single-minded thinking in which all our thoughts about an idea or situation can be accounted for within a single frame of reference. Humor, however, can only arise when we are tricked into thinking in a double-minded fashion; that is, when we are forced to consider two frames of reference that unexpectedly intersect. In classic geometry, the intersection of two planes is a line. For Koestler that line "vibrate[s] simultaneously on two different wavelengths...not merely linked to one associative context, but bisociated with two."

This binary reality of comedy is apparent in many of its most common forms: role reversals, impersonations, misperceptions, imagined predicaments, double meanings, non sequiturs, and backhanded compliments all depend on credible but unexpected associations between two contexts. Reversing roles for comedic effect is as old—probably older—than the tale of the farmer and his wife changing jobs. In the "Newhart" episode we witnessed an analogous twist. Tragedy is narrowly averted only when George reverts to dashing and Eleanor returns to simple. The entire humorous conflict is precipitated, of course, by misperceptions about how each will appear after a lapse of 31 years.

The "Newhart" writers seem especially adept at incorporating non sequiturs into the dialogue. In one breath, Kirk is promoting Pee Wee hockey as good clean fun. In the next, he identifies the team as "The Eye-Gougers." Dick explains to Joanna that his first sexual encounter with a farmgirl named Lorraine was a "stupid, meaningless night...(SIGH)...that I'll never forget." Finally, literal-minded George is completely unfathomable. From his reaction to Eleanor's 59-mile move to Montpelier, "I thought I'd never see her again!" to his straight-faced observation, "There's no awkwardness...we just can't think of anything to say."

There are some forms of humor, however, that don't seem to work well in sitcom dialogue. Strictly literary forms such as puns and spoonerisms may put too much of a mental burden on the audience to work out the joke, especially when punch lines are delivered at rapid-fire pace. The human mind has a natural inclination to use contextual clues to block out double meanings. Words are like signposts that guide us down a single path until we arrive at the speaker's intended meaning. To figure out a pun, we often have to backtrack to the fork in the road where the two paths diverged. Thus, we almost never recognize a pun without conscious thought about it. Our attention must be shifted from the ongoing dialogue to our memory of what has just been said. When the double meaning is finally unraveled, we are just as likely to groan as laugh because of the mental effort we have expended.

We can always cite a handful of sitcom characters whose linguistic eccentricities helped define their personalities. Hawkeye Pierce was as skilled with the pun as he was with the scalpel. And Archie Bunker usually topped off his bombastic rhetoric with a timely malaprop. But wordplay—like the Reverend Spooner and Mrs. Malaprop—may endear itself chiefly to a certain literary sensitivity. For mass audiences, spoken humor seems more readily appreciated when it's based on the clash of meanings rather than incidental similarities between the sounds of words. Sitcom dialogue is successful as humor when the fractious conflict between meanings is vivid and effortlessly perceived.

COMEDY VERSUS TRAGEDY

The most common explanation of the difference between comedy and tragedy distinguishes the two dramatic forms by their endings. In comedies, the ending is happy. In tragedies, there is always a death. In light of our discussion of the underlying structure of drama, what should be clear by now is that no matter which ending—happy or tragic—both represent resolutions to conflicts that energized the plot. In that sense, sitcoms may be judged just like any other drama as being creative, inventive, or even brilliant. An interesting question, though, is whether sitcoms can ever be judged as enduring art. I think the answer is no. Koestler in his treatise on laughter makes a very telling point when discussing a humorous story that Sigmund Freud once used in an essay on the comic. The anecdote goes as follows:

> Chamfort tells a story of a Marquis at the court of Louis XIV who, on entering his wife's boudoir and finding her in the arms of a Bishop, walked calmly to the window and went through the motions of blessing the people in the street.
> "What are you doing?" cried the anguished wife.
> "Monseigneur is performing my functions," replied the Marquis, "so I am performing his."

Koestler points out how different the Marquis's response is from that of a tragic character faced with the same dilemma. His example is Shakespeare's Othello, who, believing his wife has been unfaithful, kills her, and then kills himself when he realizes that Iago has skillfully tricked him into mistaking the merest trifles as incontrovertible evidence of his wife's betrayal. As Koestler explains,

> In the tragedy the tension increases until the climax is reached: Othello strangles Desdemona; then it ebbs away in a gradual catharsis...In the Chamfort anecdote, too, the tension mounts as the story progresses, but it never reaches its expected climax. The ascending curve is brought to an abrupt end by the Marquis' unexpected reaction, which debunks our dramatic expectations; it comes like a bolt out of the blue, which, so to speak, decapitates the logical development of the situation.

Thus, the comic resolution of conflict, depending as it does on the intersection of two surface representations of reality, distracts the audience from the depth of emotion and feeling that the Marquis must feel at the moment of his discovery. Comic resolutions by their nature then are superficial. George and Eleanor change their clothes and improve their prospects for an evening. A wondrously romantic turnabout, but what about those 31 years? For comic resolutions to work, they cannot support very much inspection and in fact encourage the audience not to reflect on the unfortunate set of circumstances that brought the conflict to a climax. In the end, then, comic resolutions are quick fixes that forgive the characters for their flaws and permit us to disregard our own. The insights provided—from "Father Knows Best" to "The Cosby Show"—work only in the best of families and in the best of circumstances. Sitcoms rarely provide or provoke the intense scrutiny of a complex reality that characterizes our culture's most important works of art.

SCRIPTWRITING ASSIGNMENT

Write a two-minute dialogue sequence (approximately 250 words) for a currently aired prime-time situation comedy. The dialogue can treat any subject matter appropriate for the show, but writing part of an opening scene, which suggests the beginning of a conflict, generally produces the best results. The dialogue you write should be original and not a transcription of a program you have seen. It should incorporate the show's current settings, themes, and continuing characters. But don't try to include all of them. Two to four characters will suffice. If you do not have a favorite or familiar show, you may well benefit from choosing a program that airs daily in syndication. That will allow you to watch the program more than once before writing your script.

Pay careful attention to the example of three-camera script format presented in Chapter 2. Notice how the scene is set. After the FADE IN:, the "conditions of work" line specifies an interior (INT.) or exterior (EXT.) set, identifies where the action takes place (HARTLEY'S APARTMENT), and indicates the time of day (DAY or NIGHT). Two lines below the "conditions of work" are the "stage directions," which describe the action to be filmed or videotaped. For your script, set the scene as vividly and succinctly as possible. These "scene-setting" elements are important, because they establish the context in which the characters reveal themselves.

ADDITIONAL READINGS

Act of Creation by Arthur Koestler (Macmillan, New York, 1964). A remarkable achievement on the part of a distinguished writer to search out the psychological bases for humankind's appreciation of art and literature. It's a long book. However, Koestler engagingly begins his treatise with an investigation into the psychological basis for humor.

MTM: Quality Television, edited by Jane Feuer, Paul Kerr, and Tise Vahimagi (BFI Publications, London, 1984). As the title implies, these scholarly critics judge the "Mary Tyler Moore Show," "Lou Grant," and "Hill Street Blues" to be innovative, high quality television series. The essays they present explain why.

Successful Sitcom Writing by Jurgen Wolff (St. Martin's Press, New York, 1988). For people who dream about becoming a sitcom writer. Wolff gives an inside view of the craft and the business and then urges you to start writing.

Writing for Film and Television by Stewart Bronfeld (Simon & Schuster, New York, 1986). An excellent short introduction to dramatic scriptwriting. Bronfeld is very good at describing the interplay between character and plot and explaining the importance of conflict and motivation. His chapter on the writer and the camera provides a painless introduction to the technical details of dramatic scriptwriting.

9

Screen Adaptations

Each year when the Academy Awards® are announced, there are two "Oscars"® for best screenplay. One is for the best original screenplay. The other is for the best adaptation. Hollywood director Edward Dmytryk estimates that at least 80 percent of the scenarios written for theatrical film production are based on novels, short stories, plays, or other scripts. Dmytryk makes no apologies for this practice. Dmytryk himself directed 51 Hollywood films, but his most famous is the adaptation of Herman Wouk's wartime novel, *The Caine Mutiny*.

When millions of dollars are at stake, television is no different than film. Even though ABC more or less created the concept of the miniseries, its first, "Roots," was based on Alex Hailey's novel. Almost every successful miniseries since then has been inspired by a novel that has won an audience in print before its translation into video. In retrospect, the practice of adapting dramatic material from one medium to another should not surprise us.

It is a formidable task to create sympathetic and attractive characters engaged in a conflict that generates emotional impact. When network executives carve out huge blocks in their prime time schedule to insert special programming, they want some indication that the audience won't zap the channel control button. That a dramatic story attracted a few million readers in paperpack first eases the nerves of network executives as air time approaches.

Neither Hollywood norms nor audience ratings are reason enough, however, for us to focus on adaptations in this chapter. Our intent is more liberal minded. To highlight once more the strong bond between two forms of mass media, which are produced, for the most part, on opposite coasts of the country, we must ask again the popular question: Which is better, the movie or the book? By the end of this chapter, we'll see that there is no easy answer to that question. Nevertheless, the goal is to heighten our understanding of each medium by exploring how form shapes dramatic content when the printed page is translated into sight and sound.

In the discussion, we will analyze some adaptations in considerable depth. But the best way for you to master this subject is to write an adaptation yourself. It may seem like a formidable task at this point. But for your first effort you need not adapt a best-selling novel or commit yourself to writing the screenplay for a full-length feature film. A 15-minute script based on a short story will do. Besides, depending on how astutely you select your material for adaptation, you may end up collaborating with one of the world's greatest authors.

SELECTING MATERIAL FOR ADAPTATION

The truth is that writing for broadcasting almost always involves adaptation. When representatives from the American Heart Association ask us to write a radio PSA for an upcoming health fair, they're likely to provide a recent pamphlet on smoking and heart disease, a reprint from the *New England Journal of Medicine*, and a schedule of events. From these printed materials, we create the radio script. If it's a television PSA, we must visualize the presentation as well. In either case, the print material is composed of more "words" than we can ever use in the 30-second spot. We select those elements of the print material, however, that we can effectively fashion into a coherent and compelling radio or TV message.

In selecting a short story for adaptation, the challenge is essentially the same, although the judgments are more complex. In developing a PSA, we evaluate the available materials and seize on a small set of facts from which to create a theme and coherent structure. The short story, however, has its own integrity. If it's any good, it already has a coherent theme and structure. While an exceptional adaptation may well open up new dimensions in the original story, we will rarely satisfy our critics if the teleplay strays too far from the theme and structure of the original work. Thus, the choice of a short story represents a form of commitment to the author's intent and the integrity of the story. At least in the beginning it does. As with any rule in broadcast writing, we can break this one. But it must be a conscious act, not just an oversight.

The selection of a short story should be guided by a critical evaluation of the work as a piece of dramatic writing. Does it have sympathetic and attractive characters? Are their conflicts credible? Is the final and most serious conflict resolved in an emotionally satisfactory manner? And, most important, can these events be revealed through dialogue and action rather than interior monologue? The author of dramatic fiction can *tell* the story. The screenwriter must create a script that *shows* it. In what follows, we will look closely at a film adaptation of Stephen Crane's "The Blue Hotel." Be prepared for both subtle and major changes. The screenwriter may (1) cut, add, shorten, or embellish scenes, (2) eliminate, sharpen, combine, transform, or create characters, (3) alter settings, (4) disregard subplots, and (5) even censor portions of the original work too shocking for cinematic portrayal. All these changes are permissible if the screenwriter remains essentially faithful to the author's original intent.

"THE BLUE HOTEL"

By title alone, "The Blue Hotel" does not give the prospective screenwriter much to go on. The title refers not to characters nor conflict but to a setting, the Palace Hotel in Fort Romper, Nebraska. Crane's story is about a young Swede from New York who mistakes the fringes of the western frontier for the Wild West he has read about in dime novels. The outcome could be comic or tragic. In this case it is tragic. The tense and awkward Swede has a premonition that he will be killed, and he is.

The story first appeared in serial form in two issues of *Collier's Weekly*, dated November 26 and December 3, 1898. Interestingly, Crane divided "The Blue Hotel" into nine segments, each of which roughly delineates a scene. Six of those nine scenes take place at the Palace Hotel, and, perhaps more important, eight of the nine transpire within a single day and evening. Thus, the story unfolds within a limited spatial and chronological framework. To judge how adaptable that framework is to film presentation, we need to develop with some detail a narrative outline of those nine parts.

   I. The story opens with a description of the Palace Hotel and its enterprising owner, Pat Scully. Scully is meeting the morning train, entreating passengers, who have no doubt sighted the Palace—with its shocking light blue paint—to accept the civilized comfort that awaits them inside. "Scully performed the marvel of catching three men: "a shaky and quick-eyed Swede," "a tall bronzed cowboy," and "a little man from the East." Scully leads the men to the hotel where they enter a small parlor with an enormous stove. Scully calls on his son Johnnie, who's playing cards with an old farmer, to help the guests with their baggage while he attends to their needs to warm up, wash up, and partake of the noontime dinner. The Swede never relaxes. His observation that "some of these Western communities [are] very dangerous" leaves the others perplexed.
  II. After the meal, the men return to the front room where Johnnie takes up cards again with the old farmer. When the game ends in a quarrel, Johnnie invites the new guests to join him in a hand of high-five. The

cowboy suggests they play with partners. He joins Johnnie, and they encourage the Swede to team with the Easterner. The cowboy turns out to be what Crane calls a board-whacker." He and Johnnie are enthusiastic and lucky players. "The countenances of the Easterner and the Swede were miserable whenever the cowboy thundered down his aces and kings, while Johnnie, his eyes gleaming with joy, chuckled and chuckled." But Johnnie's demeanor suddenly shifts when the Swede inexplicably remarks, "I suppose there have been a good many men killed in this room." The others are incredulous. But the Swede pursues the point. Scully, who had missed the beginning of this conversation, now returns to find the Swede convinced that "these men are going to kill me." Scully accuses Johnnie of "troublin' this man," while the Swede resolves that he must pack up his baggage and leave. Scully threatens to "lather" his son for this. Johnnie protests his innocence.

III. Scully follows the Swede upstairs and tries to convince him Romper is a civilized place. To settle him down, Scully shows the Swede pictures of his children and finally offers him a drink from "a large yellow-brown whiskey bottle."

IV. Downstairs, Johnnie, the cowboy, and the Easterner discuss the Swede's strange behavior. The Easterner believes the Swede is scared, probably because he has read too many dime novels about the Wild West. Scully then returns downstairs with the Swede, who begins to talk "arrogantly, profanely, angrily." The Swede is presumably drunk.

V. "At six o'clock supper, the Swede fizzled like a fire-wheel." Afterward, the Swede insists on another game of high-five. Scully leaves to meet the 6:58 train. When he returns the "Swede has adopted the fashion of board-whacking." Suddenly the Swede accuses Johnnie of cheating, which leads to a challenge and a fight outdoors.

VI. The five men move outside into a raging blizzard where Scully referees the battle between the Swede and Johnnie. Scully is forced to restrain the cowboy who's yelling, "Kill him, Johnnie!" But the bigger Swede thrashes Johnnie. Unable to continue, Johnnie is taken inside where his mother and sisters nurse him. The Swede can be heard upstairs in his room.

VII. The Swede comes downstairs to check out. Scully refuses to let him pay anything. As the Swede leaves, he mocks the cowboy, yelling, "Kill him! Kill him! Kill him!"

VIII. The Swede finds a saloon where he continues to drink. He talks boisterously with the bartender and attracts the attention of four men at a nearby table when he describes how he pummeled Johnnie Scully. The Swede begins to talk to the men at the table: two prominent merchants, a district attorney, and a professional gambler, who is nonetheless a model citizen of Fort Romper. But when the men refuse to have a drink with the Swede, he grabs the gambler, who pulls a knife in self-defense and fatally stabs the foreigner. The gambler leaves the saloon, telling the bartender that he'll wait for the authorities at home. The bartender goes for help, leaving the Swede's corpse to lay there with "its eyes fixed upon a dreadful legend that dwelt atop of the cash-machine: 'This registers the amount of your purchase.'"

IX. "Months later, the cowboy was frying pork over the stove of a little ranch near the Dakota line, when there was quick thud of hoofs outside, and presently the Easterner entered with the letters and papers." The Easterner tells the cowboy that "the chap that killed the Swede has got three years." They both agree that it was a light sentence, but are struck with how unfortunate the killing was. The cowboy says the bartender could have prevented it if he had cracked a bottle over the head of the Swede in time. The Easterner, even more mindful of the ironies involved suggests that "a thousand things might have happened." But when the innocent cowboy asserts that the Swede might still be alive if he hadn't accused Johnnie of cheating, the Easterner calls him a fool. "Johnnie was cheating!" the Easterner explains "We, five of us, have collaborated in the murder of this Swede...and that unfortunate gambler... gets all the punishment." To the end, however, the cowboy remains blind to the complex reality the Easterner has described. As if to heighten the irony, Crane gives the cowboy the last word: "Well, I didn't do anythin', did I?"

If you have read "The Blue Hotel," this 1,100-word synopsis of the 11,000-word story should refresh your memory. But if your exposure to the "The Blue Hotel" has been limited to the teleplay adaptation by writer Harry Mark Petrakis and director Jan Kadar, you may still be scouring your memory for images of the saloon and the little ranch near the Dakota line. In a word, don't. In the screen adaptation of "The Blue Hotel," there is no saloon and there is no ranch. The Swede meets death—just as he predicted—in the front room of the Palace Hotel, and the story ends—as it began—at the Fort Romper train station. Section VII of the story tumbles headlong into section VIII with startling abruptness.

> The Swede comes downstairs to check out. Scully refuses to let him pay anything. The heady Swede taunts Scully, the cowboy, the Easterner, and even the badly beaten Johnnie and then turns to a traveler who enters the hotel just at that moment in search of a room for the night. The traveler tries his best to avoid contact with the boasting Swede, but when the offensive and offended Swede grabs him, the new guest pulls a knife and fatally stabs the Swede. The traveler tells Scully that he should notify the authorities. In the meantime, he'll await their questioning in his hotel room.

This sudden climax permits one further economy. The emotional impact of the killing requires an almost immediate denouement. Thus, the final scene takes place as the cowboy and the Easterner prepare to resume their train trip across the prairie the next morning.

> The Easterner and the cowboy arrive at the Fort Romper station, talking about the killing the night before. The cowboy remarks how the Swede might have been alive if he had only left the hotel 15 minutes earlier. The Easterner's perspective is broader. He relates how he saw Johnnie cheating, but said nothing about it. To him, they all share responsibility for the Swede's death. The cowboy responds, "Well I didn't do anything, did I?" The Easterner says maybe not. The two men gather their luggage to board the train.

Which is better, the book or the teleplay? Oddly, the screenwriter has reconfigured the story in what some may argue is a more perfect structure: collapsing into one 24-hour cycle, the beginning, middle, and end of a drama that is now neatly delineated by the arrival of three men and the departure of two at the Fort Romper train station. But what were the motives of the screenwriter? To heighten the impact of Crane's message by intensifying its elements? Or was this a cost-cutting move? To eliminate two new settings and four additional actors? Did the film have to meet time criteria—under an hour—for presentation on television?

On the other hand, how should we account for the rambling end to Crane's original story? Did *Collier's Weekly* pay Crane by the word? Did its readers expect some of the trappings of a Wild West story—the saloon and the ranch—even if dime novel fantasies were otherwise denigrated? Did Crane envision the entire story as a flashback to the ironic juxtaposition of the Swede's corpse and the cash-machine legend: "This registers the amount of your purchase"? These may be interesting questions, but they are only tangential to our focus. What we are concerned with is how the characteristics of the film medium prompted a broad range of changes in the original story, from cutting, condensing, lengthening, and inventing scenes to eliminating, combining, transforming, and creating characters. Only on one point would I question the screenwriter's faithfulness to the original. Why at the end of the film did the Easterner seem to acquiesce when the cowboy protested his innocence: "Well, I didn't do anythin', did I?" It is fair to ask whether the screenwriter was true to Crane's intent. But, otherwise, our focus should be on how the screenwriter envisioned the printed page as a projected image.

ELEMENTS OF ADAPTATION

Of all the elements of the original story, only dialogue retains its essential form in both the print and cinematic versions. As long as the original author has not burdened the characters with excessive exposition, the screenwriter can rely heavily on the original dialogue in the story. But putting dialogue aside for the moment, the screenwriter must recognize that whatever the author has told, the screenwriter must show. Description must be transformed into action, and philosophy, if imparted, must be communicated as allegory. Thus, realistic writers, such as Crane and Hemingway, who rely heavily on dialogue and action and seemingly say little about philosophy, appear ideally suited for adaptation.

But that doesn't mean that the screenwriter has an easy time of it. Many devices that work in print are ineffectual on the screen. For instance, Crane sets the scene for his story with a description of the hotel:

> The Palace Hotel at Fort Romper was painted a light blue, a shade that is on the legs of a kind of heron, causing the bird to declare its position against any background.

No matter that the film adaptation depicts a dark blue hotel (most likely for budgetary reasons). This is a static shot. The camera could have encompassed the few hundred feet from the train station to the hotel with a moving shot, but as every filmmaker eventually learns, the "motion" in motion pictures refers to action in the frame, not zooms, pans, tilts, or other movements of the camera. Thus, it's no surprise that the opening shot of the film focuses on the train station, taking its cue from the third paragraph of the story:

> One morning, when a snow-crusted engine dragged its long string of freight cars and its one passenger coach to the station, Scully performed the marvel of catching three men.

As the train trudges in, we see the credits supered on the screen. And when it pulls to a stop, we see the "eager little Irishman" with "a heavy fur cap squeezed tightly down on his head" scurrying along the wooden platform to corner the disembarking passengers.

One clear loss is Crane's colorful language. That Scully's fur cap "caused his two red ears to stick out stiffly, as if they were made of tin." Or even if the hotel had been painted light blue, that the color was "a shade that is on the legs of a kind of heron." Of course, if these statements were vital to Crane's message, they could be incorporated as dialogue. The fact is that film critic James Agee did exactly that in a screenplay he wrote for "The Blue Hotel" that was never filmed, but nevertheless published after his death.

>   EASTERNER
> (politely concealing his
> faint nausea)
> I've never seen the shade before,
> but once.
>
>   SCULLY
> (a little jealous, but
> very polite)
> And where might that be, may I
> ask?

EASTERNER
On the legs of a kind of heron;
one of the wading birds. It's a
very strange color; there's nothing
else quite like it in Nature. It
declares the bird's position against
any background.

But the question is to what effect? Perhaps if we want to establish the Easterner as a thoughtful, literary type. But otherwise it only slows our progress toward recognizing the Swede's inner anxiety and the conflict it begets. In the Petrakis teleplay, which was ultimately produced, the Easterner's character is revealed instead by his wool suit, his pipe, and his diction. Here, too, the screenwriter took some liberties. Crane described the Easterner as "a little silent man from the East, who didn't look it." In the film, he did.

Indeed, if conflict is to be built on character, it is not surprising that the primary goal in the opening sequences of the film is to reveal the distinctive personalities of the five main characters. The screenwriter seizes and exploits each opening Crane provides. When Scully and the three men arrive at the hotel, Scully's son Johnnie and the farmer are playing high-five and quarreling.

> With a loud flourish of words Scully destroyed the game of cards, and bustled his son upstairs with part of the baggage of the new guests. He himself conducted them to three basins of the coldest water in the world. The cowboy and the Easterner burnished themselves fiery red with this water, until it seemed to be some kind of metal polish. The Swede, however, merely dipped his fingers gingerly and with trepidation. It was notable that throughout this series of small ceremonies the three travelers were made to feel that Scully was very benevolent. He was conferring great favors on them. He handed the towel from one to another with an air of philanthropic impulse.

In its cinematic form, the handwashing ceremony is redolent with cues about character and setting. First, the water Scully offers his guests is warm, not cold, a point he boasts about, thereby reinforcing the notion that the Palace Hotel is at least an oasis from the rough frontier and that as proprietor Scully will make every effort to assure his guests' comfort. Second, there are three towels, but only one basin. The guests must take turns washing. Thus, the camera methodically studies the three men close-up through the mirror above the basin. The cowboy, to use Crane's words, "burnishes" himself with the water. But the Easterner is more refined. Scully hands each a towel and collects it as they finish. Finally, it is the Swede's turn. He dips "his fingers gingerly and with trepidation" as the audience looks on. Scully hands him a towel, which, when finished, the Swede thoughtlessly drops into the basin of gray soapy water. Scully grimaces, but says nothing. The gesture foreshadows the conflicts to come.

Within the film we can find many changes so subtle that it takes attentive reading to separate film from fiction. Crane describes two meals that day, dinner and supper. The screenwriter cuts out the dinner. On the other hand, the screenwriter invents other props and pieces of business. In the film version, young Johnnie eats jellybeans as he plays cards, a sign of his boyish vulnerability despite his tough talk. Scully's "yellow-brown whiskey bottle" is transformed into "Bombay gin" to enhance the dialogue. The front room of the Palace Hotel boasts a coin-operated music box. If it exists in Crane's story, it is silent. In the film it plays twice. As we watch the characters listen to the music, we can rehearse our thoughts about them. Similarly, the high-five game is embellished with bidding to emphasize the players' faces rather than their cards. And when the Swede is stabbed, the camera cuts swiftly from face to face to reveal astonishment, horror, and guilt.

WRITING THE TREATMENT

Describing a film adaptation is one thing. Writing it is another. Writer Ray Bradbury, whom director John Huston employed to write a film adaptation of *Moby-Dick*, describes a strategy of total immersion:

> I read the book nine times.... I made 35 outlines. I wrote two thousand pages trying to figure out what the book was all about...it took about nine months of stuffing my head—with Shakespeare and Conrad as well as Melville. Until one morning I got out of bed in London, I looked in the mirror and said, "I am Herman Melville."

Nine months, 35 outlines, 2,000 pages. Those are large numbers. But *Moby-Dick* is an enormous book. The important element here, however, is to read, outline, and write until you feel as if you were the story's author. At this point, though, the product is not a screenplay but rather an intermediate product called a treatment, a nontechnical, third-person narrative describing the content of a film.

The treatment is a peculiarly commercial document used to propose (in Hollywood terms "pitch") the making of a motion picture. For a full-length motion picture, the treatment may be a simple outline as short as two to seven pages (a short treatment) or a complete narrative, with character descriptions and representative dialogue, encompassing 75–200 pages (a full treatment). Basically it is a selling tool, used to convince people with money, power, or both that a film will reward their investment more than handsomely at the box office. Outside the commercial sphere, however, a treatment can be a thinking tool, helping the writer articulate a vision of the film unencumbered by the technical details formally addressed in a script. The example treatment reproduced next was written by a student adapting for the screen a classic O. Henry short story: "The Last Leaf."

The LAST LEAF

A Treatment for a Screenplay

by

James Bolen

Adapted from a Short Story by O. Henry

FADE IN:

Snow falls gently down on the icy rooftops of a quaint corner of Greenwich Village. Through the frosty window panes horses and carriages can be seen scurrying about like miniature toys on the street below. Slow dolly back from the window shot to the interior of a dingy, dimly lit hallway. Muffled voices grapple with the early winter stillness. SUE, a gray-eyed, dark-haired young artist, and a middle-aged DOCTOR, looking like Sigmund Freud with a stethoscope, talk quietly in the hallway. The doctor is dressed in a gray suit and has a prominent watch fob dangling from his vest. He is the image of purpose. Sue wears an artist's smock blackened with charcoal. The tone of the conversation brings to mind a funeral. "There can be no recovery without hope...I will do all I can, but there must be hope." Sue looks up at the doctor dismally, searching for a reply. They continue to converse about Sue's roommate JOHNSY, who is deathly ill with pneumonia. The doctor tells Sue that Johnsy probably will die unless she regains the will to live and decides to fight for life.

The doctor disappears into the darkness of the corridor, and Sue, distressed by the grim prognosis, shuffles sadly into the drawing room of the small apartment. The room is drab in itself,

2.

but comes to life among the assortment of brushes, palettes, and lively sketches which fill its every corner. Sue begins to cry. The art world is lonely enough without the loss of her best friend. With some difficulty she composes herself, and grabbing a sketchbook and pencil walks into the adjoining room. On the bed lies Johnsy, seemingly swallowed up by quilts and blankets. She is a thin, pallid girl with bountiful black hair and eyes like midnight. She breathes heavily, and with a certain sensitivity that might well lead to her untimely end. The earliest rays of twilight stream in through a singular window across from Johnsy's bed, casting the fragile contours of her face in a hazy half-light. The girl's labored breathing seems to scrape against the awful stillness. Sue sits down quietly beside the bed and eyes the sketchpad blankly. Summoning false cheer, she waits to speak no longer. "Johnny, it's Sue...how are you feeling today?" She is met at first by silence, then comes a shaky reply. "Only twelve left, Sue...now only eleven. The end is near, my friend." Sue fearfully demands an explanation, and Johnsy directs her attention out the window to a weather-worn ivy vine clinging alone to a brick wall just across the street.

Johnsy counts down the leaves as they are blown from the vine by the cold November wind. The leaves fall with an alarming regularity until only one remains, clinging valiantly to the vine. "When the last leaf falls, I too shall die," whispers Johnsy, much to the chagrin of her roommate. Sue quickly changes the subject, saying that she needs a model for her sketch. She tells Johnsy that she is going to get MR. BEHRMAN, a used-up old artist on the floor below. She hurries from the room, and the

3.

scene cuts to Johnsy's POV of the last leaf swaying precariously in the breeze.

Mr. Behrman, awakened by the knocking, opens the door and ushers Sue into his dimly lit dwelling. It seems more like a deserted museum than an apartment. Everything is so old. The silence here is even worse than upstairs. Behrman is an old man around sixty, his small body engulfed by a flowing white beard. He speaks loudly and rudely with a heavy German accent. His motions are slow and sad, as if every move gives him pain. Gin bottles abound, as do unfinished sketches and crumpled portraits barely begun. Behrman's room is like a place for everything forgotten. Sue asks the old man to pose for her sketch, and then almost involuntarily spills all the details of her dying roommate, the doctor's report, and most of all the leaf. Behrman, usually bitter and apathetic, seems very upset by Johnsy's condition, almost to the point of anger. Shades of true concern and tenderness can be seen through the mask of embittered rage and desperation forged by so many years of mediocrity and failure. "Ach! Dot poor lettle Miss Yohnsy. Eht shoot not be so."

Mr. Behrman agrees to pose for Sue and follows the young artist back upstairs. It is dark now, and they decide to sketch in Johnsy's room. As Sue draws the old man, Johnsy awakens from a light sleep and stares out the window into the cold darkness beyond. The light from the sketching lamp faintly illuminates the wall with the vine, and Johnsy can barely make out the outline of the last remaining leaf. "Sue, have you told Mr. Behrman about the leaf?" Sue stares helplessly down at her

4.

roommate and then at Mr. Behrman, who has gotten up and walked slowly over to the girl's bed. Johnsy's eyes close sleepily as Behrman strokes back her long dark hair in an act of comforting tenderness so long absent from the old man's soul. "Eht shoot not be so...." These words hang in the air as Behrman and Sue stare out the window at the lone surviving leaf, swaying dangerously in the increasing wind and rain of an approaching storm.

The next morning is alive and sunny. Sounds of scampering carriages and bustling crowds accompany the sunlight pouring in the window of Johnsy's room. Johnsy awakens bathed in sunlight, and looks over to Sue, who is sitting by the bed, staring intently out the window. "Perhaps you should take a look." Johnsy sits up weakly, and the camera follows the motion of her head upward to the brilliantly lit window. Her eyes open in surprise. The leaf is still there. Johnsy turns quickly to the smiling Sue. "It survived the storm...but how? I was sure it would fall...." Sue quiets Johnsy and tells her that she should rest. Johnsy, invigorated by the leaf's example, swears that she, like the leaf, will brave the storm and fight for life. The scene ends with Johnsy's hand clasping Sue's, with the sunlit window and the distant vine in the background.

Cut to the same window shot which opened the first scene. This time the town is sunlit and full of life. Sounds of children, bells and carriages fill the hallway in which the doctor and Sue are speaking. The doctor tells Sue that Johnsy has made an encouraging turnaround and will recover slowly with time. "Oh, by the way," mentions the doctor, "they found an old

                                                                5.

man last night soaking wet out in the storm. A Mr. Behrman, I
believe it was. I am going to check on him now, but I am afraid
there is little hope." Sue's eyes widen in disbelief. She
rushes downstairs to the old man's room. Behrman is lying
motionless on the bed. The sad, distant stare of the nearby
nurse says everything. The old man is gone. Sue slowly reaches
down to take his hand, only to find a small, used paintbrush held
tightly in his grasp. She stares questioningly at the brush,
then hurries from the room in the haste of realization.

She arrives quickly at the wall outside Johnsy's window, and
can see her roommate sleeping within. She examines the vine
sprawled across the woodwork and finally locates the last leaf
growing there. It is not a leaf at all, but a masterfully
rendered facsimile. Holding the brush beside the painted leaf,
she sees that the colors match exactly. "This is Behrman's
masterpiece..." she says to herself, cradling the small brush
gently against her chest.

Sue returns to Johnsy's room where Johnsy is sleeping
soundly. She places the brush along with the earlier sketch of
Behrman on the nightstand beside the bed. She stares down at
Johnsy, then out the window. The scene cuts to her POV of the
vine outside and slowly zooms in to the last leaf. Perhaps
Johnsy will never know.

                                                    FADE OUT.

                           THE END

FROM STORY IDEA TO TREATMENT

With the completion of a treatment, the writer moves on to what is called a master scene script. We will also (in the next chapter). But before jumping the next hurdle, it may help to elaborate this intellectual process in greater detail: to provide a plan of attack, a strategy for developing a story idea into a film treatment. Writing a screenplay calls for a very unromantic sense of discipline. Sure, writers like to overload themselves with ideas and emotions and then let the words spill onto paper. But writers are keenly aware that strict discipline must be imposed as step by step they refine a story idea into a treatment and finally a script.

Because screenwriters recognize that revising their words is cheaper than wasting hours on the set of a motion picture, they understand well why they must develop a well-defined vision of any teleplay or film they are proposing for production. They can't be vague. As a rule, they begin by reducing their story idea to a core concept or a dramatic premise and writing it as a one-sentence statement or what-if question. Thus, the premise of "The Blue Hotel" can be summed up with the question: "What if a European traveler comes to the western United States believing everything he's read about the Wild West?"

Next, the screenwriter should be able to summarize the bare structure of the story in a three or four sentence synopsis.

> A Swedish emigrant traveling across America has a sudden premonition that he will be killed by fellow travelers when he confuses the rough habitat of a small-town Nebraskan hotel for a frontier outpost in the Wild West. Emboldened by drink, he picks a fight and pummels the son of the hotel's owner. As a result, the Swede decides to leave, only to be stabbed to death at the town saloon by a local gambler whom the Swede physically provokes.

In actuality, these semantic exercises challenge the screenwriter. Retelling the story in such concise terms tests the screenwriter's mastery of its essential dramatic structure. We should not be surprised, however, if different writers derive different premises from the same story or highlight different events in their synopses. In the case of "The Blue Hotel," a synopsis of the teleplay calls for a slight variation in the last sentence: "As a result, the Swede decides to leave, only to be stabbed to death by a newly arrived guest whom the Swede physically provokes." As we have seen, however, the change in the synopsis is the consequence of a multifaceted examination of the original work.

A logical next step in preparing the treatment is to draw up a list of characters and a list of scenes as described in the original short story. As you draw up these lists, you may be surprised to see how an offhand phrase in the story may string out the drama if the screenwriter slavishly conforms to the structure of the original. Consider this paragraph in the first segment of Crane's story:

170 *Chapter 9 Screen Adaptations*

Later, at dinner, he spoke a little, addressing his conversation entirely to Scully. He volunteered that he had come from New York, where for ten years he had worked as a tailor. These facts seemed to strike Scully as fascinating, and afterward he volunteered that he had lived at Romper for fourteen years. The Swede asked about the crops and the price of labor. He seemed barely to listen to Scully's extended replies. His eyes continued to rove from man to man.

Two words, "at dinner," call for a change in setting for a conversation that can be portrayed anywhere the Swede and Scully might talk. Furthermore, the information revealed is not so important as the Swede's anxious behavior, which can be emphasized whenever the Swede appears on camera.

Thus, you can chip away at the story writer's original structure, cutting out extraneous scenes and secondary characters until a bare bones outline of the film's structure is left. With this outline of what happens, what happens next, and so on, you are ready to write your treatment. In fact, you would do well to let the story spill out onto the paper from beginning to end with all the emotional intensity you can muster. Then set it aside for a few days. When you return to your treatment, think about its impact on potential readers. Have you visualized the story to the extent that you have created concrete scenes? Have you fleshed out the characters and the details of the plot? Do the characters act in a manner consistent with their revealed motivations? Does the story evoke laughter or sorrow? Is it clear? Revise accordingly. The overall purpose of writing a treatment is to block out the adaptation in enough detail that its flaws can be uncovered and corrected. Revise until correct.

SCRIPTWRITING ASSIGNMENT

Select a short story that you would enjoy adapting as a teleplay. Study the story's settings, characters, and plot, review the sample treatment in this chapter, and then write a three to six page treatment for the screen. For the most part, tell the story in present-tense narrative form, emphasizing dramatic action and its visual portrayal. You may include some dialogue. Your goal is to attract and sustain the reader's interest from beginning to end. The story line should be clear and uncluttered, the characters compelling.

Except for an opening FADE IN:, the capitalization of the names of new characters on first mention, and a closing FADE OUT., technical directions are minimal. One additional convention is to provide a very brief descriptive phrase that epitomizes each new character's appearance or bearing. This phrase, called a "dominant impression," usually follows the character's capitalized name. Otherwise, the format for a treatment is nearly identical to any other type of fictional prose: normal paragraphing, down style, and double spaced.

ADDITIONAL READINGS

The Blue Hotel, directed by Jan Kadar (Perspective Films, Chicago, 1974) is now distributed on videocassette by Monterey Home Video. The short story by Stephen Crane is available in *Complete Short Stories and Sketches* (Doubleday, Garden City, NY, 1963). James Agee's feature-length motion picture script was never shot but was recently republished in *Agee On Film II: Five Film Scripts* (Grosset & Dunlap, New York, 1988), which also includes an adaptation of another Crane short story, "The Bride Comes to Yellow Sky."

"The Last Leaf" in *Collected Stories of O. Henry* by O. Henry (Avenel Books, New York, 1979). This story runs only seven pages. Compare it with the sample treatment in this chapter.

On Screen Writing by Edward Dmytryk (Focal Press, Boston, 1985). Dmytryk has a long list of screen credits, and this book is clearly grounded in his experience. What makes it especially interesting for our purposes is its extensive coverage of adaptations.

Writing for the Media: Film, Television, Video, and Radio by Paul Max Rubinstein and Martin Maloney (Prentice Hall, Englewood Cliffs, NJ, 1988). Once you pick it up, it's hard to put down because its range of topics is so vast. It has a long chapter devoted to treatments, both fiction and nonfiction, that should help you with yours.

10
Master Scene Scripts

Novelist and screenwriter William Goldman tells a revealing story about his first venture in scriptwriting. In the mid-1960s, actor Cliff Robertson came to him with a short story,"Flowers for Algernon," that Robertson thought would make a good movie. Goldman then was a young, but experienced author. He had published five novels. But when he began to write, he suddenly realized that he knew nothing about the proper format for a screenplay. Working late in New York City, he dashed out to an all-night bookstore in Times Square to find a book that could explain the proper format. Goldman says he bought a book but found the rules too restrictive for his creative style. Instead he invented his own format. He then submitted the script to Robertson, who promptly fired him because of the bizarre format and hired someone else. Robertson apparently made the right decision. When the film appeared in 1968, it was titled *Charly*. Robertson starred in the title role and won the Oscar that year for best performance by an actor.

In this chapter, you will be introduced to the script format that Goldman found so onerous. You will need it to complete a final scriptwriting assignment that calls for you to develop your treatment into a full-fledged teleplay. The best way to do this is to illustrate the process by discussing other adaptations. In particular, we'll deal with dialogue and dramatic structure and finish with some reflections on broadcast violence.

MASTER SCENE FORMAT

The script format Goldman found too cumbersome is almost universally accepted. It's known as master scene format. Beginning on page 175, you'll find a four-page example, the opening scenes for an adaptation of "The Last Leaf," written by the same student who submitted the treatment in the last chapter. Glance over it briefly now. After some preliminary remarks, you'll be ready to study it in detail.

The single-column structure should remind you immediately of the three-camera format used in studio television production. For example, both highlight the "conditions of work" in all capital letters. But, in truth, the three-camera format for television is at best a simplified version of the master scene format. As we have seen in Chapter 8, dialogue is usually the predominant element in sitcom production. Thus, the director's primary focus is on arranging the three or more studio cameras to follow the dialogue: camera 1 on the speaker, camera 2 on the listener, camera 3 on the scene and so on. The director can then intercut the pictures in a manner that best clarifies and intensifies the dramatic impact of the situation.

An ambitious teleplay or screenplay, however, often advances without dialogue. The goal is to show rather than tell. Master scene script format—devised originally for film—supports a liberated creative environment. The camera moves from location to location, constrained only by the budget. A much higher proportion of the scenes are shot at exterior locations, and the script format must accommodate detailed descriptions of diverse settings and actions. Importantly, editing as an element of production is now separated in time from the filming process. The shots must fit together, but the script envisions the movements of a single camera, which must be stopped and moved to a new position (or angle) before filming is resumed.

Another unique characteristic of the master scene script format is that it is only an intermediate script form. It's the form in which the writer most emphatically describes his or her vision of the film before directors, photographers, producers and actors take over. As the film goes into production, any or all of them may want to cut scenes because they are too expensive, add specific shot notations that reflect their vision of the film, or change dialogue to suit the actor or actress selected for the part.

Another defining characteristic of the format is the tradition of numbering scenes. Like the little used custom of numbering lines in a radio drama script, this tradition is quickly falling out of fashion. But it is a reminder that at some point in the production process scenes must be easily identified to determine budgets and shooting schedules. When a screenplay or teleplay is actually filmed, scenes must be sorted into a rough geographic order so that cast and crew can shoot all the scenes at one location at one time. If a film about the Wright brothers' historic flight at Kitty Hawk, North Carolina, begins and ends at their bicycle shop in Dayton, Ohio, there's no reason for the production company to set up shop twice in Dayton (or whatever location represents Dayton). It's much more economical to shoot all the Dayton scenes

"THE LAST LEAF"

FADE IN:

1   INT. HALLWAY OUTSIDE SUE AND JOHNSY'S APARTMENT - DAY

DOLLY BACK SLOWLY from the second story window shot showing horses and carriages moving on the snow-covered streets below. Continue to DOLLY BACK from the window and down the hall past the door to the apartment, stopping as SUE, a grey-eyed, dark-haired young artist, and the DOCTOR, looking like Sigmund Freud with a stethoscope, emerge quietly from within. Snow falls silently beyond the window behind them. The hall is eerie and dimly lit. Muffled tones penetrate the stillness.

                    SUE
               (grasping, shaken)
          There must be something you can
          do. Surely with all your
          medicines...

                    DOCTOR
               (firmly)
          Medicine can heal the body, but
          there is little it can do for
          the mind.

                    SUE
          What are you talking about? She
          has the flu. Have you never
          treated anyone with the flu
          before?

                    DOCTOR
          It's true that your roommate has
          the flu, but that is not her
          greatest ailment.

                    SUE
          What does that mean?

                    DOCTOR
               (slightly puzzled)
          It's as if she doesn't want to
          live.

                    SUE
          What?

                                        (CONTINUED)

1   CONTINUED:

                    DOCTOR
          Johnsy has given up hope. She
          refuses to fight the sickness.
          I will do what I can, but there
          can be no recovery without hope.

                    SUE
               (concerned)
          I don't understand. Poor Johnsy.

                    DOCTOR
          She is very sick, and her chances
          are slim from the illness alone,
          but without the will to live she
          has no chance at all.

                    SUE
          But with rest and medication,
          surely...

                    DOCTOR
          I offer little hope for any
          patient who is already counting
          carriages in her funeral
          procession.

                    SUE
               (desperately)
          Then what can I do? I feel so
          helpless.

                    DOCTOR
          You must convince her to fight
          the illness. If you can heal
          her mind, then perhaps I can
          heal her body.
               (putting the
                stethoscope in
                his bag)
          Talk to her. Convince her she
          must live. Until she believes
          this, there is little I can do
          for her.

                    SUE
               (preoccupied)
          I... see.

                                    (CONTINUED)

3.

1   CONTINUED (2):

        The doctor walks down the hall and stops in front of
        the window. He turns back to Sue as she is closing
        the door.

                              DOCTOR
                    Sue...

                              SUE
                    Yes?

                              DOCTOR
                        (with warm purpose)
                    I don't suppose a prayer would
                    hurt.

2   INT. DRAWING ROOM OF THE APARTMENT - DAY

        Sue closes the door to the hallway and walks into the
        drawing room. She pulls down the shade and lights an
        old candle that casts ghostly, nightmarish shadows
        about the room. She puts on a smock and hesitantly
        begins to sketch, surrounded by brushes, canvases and
        the like. After a few seconds she drops the sketchpad
        and begins to cry.

                              SUE
                        (frustrated)
                    It's not fair! Why Johnsy?
                    She's never hurt anyone...
                    I'm so afraid of losing her.
                        (breaking down)
                    Oh God... I'm so afraid of
                    being alone.

        Sue slumps over, cradling her face in her hands. She
        is now crying out of control. DOLLY BACK to reveal
        her all alone at the drawing desk, accompanied only
        by the phantoms and ghostly shadows that dance wildly
        about the room.

                                                    DISSOLVE TO:

3   INT. JOHNSY'S ROOM - DAY

        JOHNSY, barely making a ripple under the blankets,
        lies quietly, looking out the window. Sue enters
        cautiously, obviously distraught. The room is silent
        and dark except for the light straining in through
        the window. Sue approaches the bed slowly.

                                                    (CONTINUED)

3   CONTINUED:
                         SUE
               Johnsy, how are you feeling?

                         JOHNSY
                    (weakly, after a
                     delay)
               Only twelve left... now only
               eleven.

                         SUE
               What's that? Johnsy... what are
               you talking about?

                         JOHNSY
               You mean you haven't seen the
               vine? Oh, you must see it, Sue!
               It all depends on the vine, you
               know.

                         SUE
               What vine? What do you mean?

                         JOHNSY
               I'm talking about that vine...
                    (motioning toward
                     the window)
               my vine.

     Sue walks around to the window and looks out. Her
     P.O.V. reveals a withered ivy vine growing on a
     crumbling brick wall across the alley. A CLOSE UP
     of the vine with its leaves being blown away by the
     wind is momentarily linked with Johnsy softly
     counting OFF SCREEN.

                         JOHNSY (O.S.)
               Ten... now just nine... there...
               another. Only eight left now.
               It won't be long.

                         SUE
               I don't understand.

                         JOHNSY
                    (consumed)
               Seven...

                         SUE
               Tell me! Tell me what you're
               counting.

                                             (CONTINUED)

consecutively no matter when they might occur in the film. In fact, the production-ready shooting script for a motion picture may designate the order of filming shot by shot, taking into account the possibility that some sets will be partially disassembled to achieve exactly the angle or composition the director and photographer have decided upon. One-hour TV dramatic shows may cost more than a million dollars an episode. Budgets for feature films may be counted in tens of millions of dollars. But in neither case need the money be wasted because no one looked ahead in the script to see that later scenes would require a similar setting.

BASIC RULES

To lay out rules and provide examples for every contingency that might arise in master scene script format would take a book as long as this one. There are typing services in Hollywood that reformat incorrect scripts. There are specially developed word-processing programs as well. But the most important elements can be summarized in a few paragraphs.

As the name implies, the master scene script format conceives of the film as a series of major scenes. Every scene begins with a "scene heading" that specifies an outdoor (EXT.) or indoor (INT.) setting, names the location, and designates the time of day. The scene heading can also include, if succinctly described, the camera angle and what is shown. For example:

```
EXT. KITTY HAWK - DAY - LONG SHOT - SAND DUNES
```

More commonly, however, the writer will stick to revealing just the three traditional conditions of work, integrating specific shot information into the next format element, the "stage direction."

Stage directions tell everything about the scene the writer envisions except the actual dialogue. The stage directions describe the location of the set, the action, the characters, their activities, and any technical details including camera movements and sound cues. They can be quite extensive and are written in down style to make them more readable. As a matter of form, most of the stage directions come immediately after the scene heading, but they can start up again after the dialogue has begun. They can even interrupt the dialogue of a character to describe some action or activity that suddenly commences or synchronously occurs.

Dialogue is presented within a narrow column down the center of the page. It, too, is in down style, although the "character cue" that identifies the speaker is in all capitals. Short descriptions of the character's actions or manner of speaking, known as "personal directions," can be set off in parentheses just after the character cue or even between lines of dialogue. Personal directions should be no more than 20 typewritten characters wide and extend for no more than four lines. They must also relate only to the character speaking. If longer, or meant to describe the actions of another character, they must begin like a stage direction at the left margin, even if they interrupt the speaker's lines. As a rule this interruption is noted with a new character cue followed by "(CONT'D)" in parentheses.

The final element in the scene is the "scene close," a brief technical designation in all capitals describing the transition from one scene to the next. Usually it will be CUT TO:, DISSOLVE TO:, or MATCH CUT TO:. The CUT TO: designates an instantaneous switch from one shot to the next. Because it is the most common transition, it need not be designated on the script. The DISSOLVE TO: indicates a fading out of the present scene as the new scene fades in. By convention it generates a sense of passing time or designates a major change in location. A MATCH CUT TO: indicates that some element in the last frame of the last shot of the scene will reappear in exactly the same position in the first frame of the new scene. It's a nifty visual trick. A splotch of green paint might be matched in the "The Last Leaf" from the brick wall to Behrman's brush. One other scene close is the final FADE OUT., which designates the end of a screenplay or the end of an act in a teleplay.

The various margins and line spacings in the master scene script can be reduced to a few essentials. Each individual component (scene headings, scene descriptions, scene endings, and speaking parts including character cues and personal directions) is typed using single spacing within components and double spacing between them. Triple spacing can be used between scenes. Starting from the left side of the paper, the margins and tabs should be set as follows. The left margin is set one and one-quarter inches from the edge for scene numbers, followed by tab settings at one and three-quarter inches for scene headings and descriptions, three inches for dialogue, three and three-quarters inches for personal directions, four and one-quarter inches for character cues, six and one-quarter inches for scene endings, and seven and one-quarter inches for page numbers.

To account for every eventuality in an original teleplay or screenplay is simply impossible. Try your best to interpolate from "The Last Leaf" script segment reproduced in this chapter. For more detailed examples, consult the books I have listed as references at the end of Chapter 9 and this chapter.

ADAPTING DIALOGUE

It is axiomatic in screenwriting that the more time a writer devotes to the treatment the faster the actual scriptwriting will proceed. It would seem, in fact, that much of the narrative description from the treatment can be plugged in directly as stage directions. Thus, one major task in writing the master scene script is to flesh out the visual descriptions with speaking parts, a task that on first glance may appear extremely easy if your famous coauthor has already provided a substantial amount of dialogue in the print version. Even here, however, you are bound to recognize that dialogue that is effortless to read is not always effortless to speak. Furthermore, when adapted to the screen, it may appear interminably long.

To give you an example of the economies that may be required, here is a section of dialogue from a Sherlock Holmes mystery, "The Stockbroker's Clerk," and the equivalent passage in a radio drama adaptation written for the BBC. It occurs at the beginning of the story. Holmes is working on a case that requires him to travel to Birmingham. He has come to Watson's home to invite him along. Watson enthusiastically accepts. When Holmes asks if Watson can abandon his medical practice temporarily, the doctor assures him that a colleague next door will fill in. Delighted that Watson has accepted his invitation, Holmes then makes a surprising observation about Watson's health.

> "Ha! Nothing could be better!" said Holmes, leaning back in his chair and looking keenly at me from under his half-closed lids. "I perceive that you have been unwell lately. Summer colds are always a little trying."
> "I was confined to the house by a severe chill for three days last week. I thought, however, that I had cast off every trace of it."
> "So you have. You look remarkably robust."
> "How, then, did you know of it?"
> "My dear fellow, you know my methods."
> "You deduced it, then?"
> "Certainly."
> "And from what?"
> "From your slippers."
> I glanced down at the new patent leathers which I was wearing. "How on earth——?" I began, but Holmes answered my question before it was asked.
> "Your slippers are new," he said. "You could not have had them more than a few weeks. The soles which you are at this moment presenting to me are slightly scorched. For a moment I thought they might have got wet and been burned in the drying. But near the instep is a small circular wafer of paper with the shopman's hieroglyphics upon it. Damp would of course have removed this. You had then been sitting with your feet outstretched to the fire, which a man would hardly do even in so wet a June as this if he were in his full health."
> Like all Holmes's reasoning the thing seemed simplicity itself when it was once explained. He read the thought upon my features, and his smile had a tinge of bitterness.

In the radio drama script, the question about who will tend Watson's practice is skipped over entirely. Greater economy is achieved instead by linking Watson's health to his readiness to take the train trip to Birmingham.

> HOLMES: You're quite sure you're fit to travel?
> WATSON: Fit? I told you I've never felt better.
> HOLMES: But you've not been too well lately I see.
> WATSON: Now how on earth——?
> HOLMES: Your slippers of course.
> WATSON: Slippers?
> HOLMES: They're quite obviously new. Not more than a few weeks old in fact. I noticed the soles when you were sitting opposite me there. They're

scorched. For a moment I thought you must have
gotten them wet and dried them too vigorously.
But near the instep there's a little wafer of
paper with a shopman's hieroglyphics on it. Damp
would have had that off. Obviously you've been
sitting with your feet stretched out to the fire.
And a man would hardly sit so long in front of a
fire in June if he were in his full health.

WATSON: (*CHUCKLES*) Right as usual.

Of course, on Saturday, June 15, 1889, the date that Sherlock Holmes scholars and literary sleuths have deduced that this fictional conversation must have taken place, the vocabulary and cadences of British speech may have been more like the original than the adaptation. But it's a moot point. The goal is to keep the audience interested and the story advancing. The syntax of the printed dialogue has been simplified and the sentences shortened to make it sound even more like a natural conversation. Yet the writer has achieved this effect without any fatal loss of the substance or the flavor of the print version.

DRAMATIC STRUCTURE

No matter how attractive the characters in your story, how contemporary the theme, or witty the dialogue, it's likely that the treatment will have some structural problems that need to be ironed out in your master scene script. William Goldman argues that the success of a motion picture as an entertainment depends most of all on its structure, a linear structure he has described as a series of surprises waiting to be detonated. While not every script need set off those explosions in as rapid fire order as an Indiana Jones or James Bond adventure, Goldman is right that American audiences become restless when the pace of the narrative begins to drag, when the emotional payoff for their undivided attention barely registers a blip on their internal heart-monitoring mechanisms. Of course, that could be the sort of story it is. But unless the writer saw opportunities to make its portrayal on the screen as emotionally compelling as it was in print, then we have to ask why an adaptation was contemplated in the first place.

To get the structure of an adaptation correct, the writer needs a strategy for analyzing the story in its original form. Most writers for the screen probably do this intuitively, that is, they do a rough mental accounting something like this: Does this story have enough explosive scenes to justify the emotionally neutral ones when the charges are set? To answer this question, the writer must identify those surprising scenes and then decide which minor ones in the narrative are essential to their development. Obviously this takes more deliberation than simply dividing the story into a traditional beginning, middle, and end. It requires intensive analysis.

The strategy I suggest is adapted from a print journalist who has won Pulitzer prizes for his feature coverage of real-life events. Jon Franklin has achieved his success by shunning traditional journalistic forms, relating factual events through dramatic formats. Franklin is certainly a maverick in the newspaper business, but, fortunately for us, it has forced him to give a great deal of thought to the elements of drama in a factual world. For Franklin, it comes down to this: At the heart of every drama is a conflict that must be made explicit to the audience very early in the game. The endpoint is assuredly the resolution of that conflict, but along the way suspense is created by revealing a series of major complications. It's hard to believe that Franklin is describing the structure of a feature news story. It sounds like plot development. But, it's a strategy that has won him the Pulitzer prize on two occasions. More than that, it's a strategy that's so straightforward that it's accessible to any writer even if he or she has no experience writing fictional prose. By way of example, I will try to apply it to a teleplay that is most likely available on videotape in your college or university library.

Richard Wright's short story, "The Man Who Was Almost a Man," provides the literary basis for this adaptation. The teleplay, retitled, *Almos' a Man*, conforms very closely to Wright's original narrative about a black teenage farm worker in the Deep South during the late 1930s. The producers describe the teleplay as follows:

> Like many teenagers today, David is struggling for a new identity—as a man. David's parents protectively deprive him of independence, yet he persuades his mother to give him part of his earnings for a used handgun. While practicing with it, he accidentally kills a mule. The boy confesses, is demeaned by his father, and bondaged by the landowner to work twenty-five months to pay for the animal. Then, in the moving climax, he retrieves his gun and hops aboard a passing train, filled with notions of a new life.

On the surface, this is a fairly complete synopsis, although don't mistakenly assume that this teleplay has anything to do with David's 25 months of bondage. He jumps that passing freight train less than 24 hours after he kills the mule. That climactic act is ingeniously foreshadowed, incidentally, by the sounding of a distant train whistle in two earlier scenes. What this synopsis does leave out, however, is a well-articulated description of the conflict that motivates David's actions and three essential complications—in addition to David's killing the mule—that heighten suspense yet skillfully direct events towards a seemingly unavoidable conclusion.

First, the conflict: "Almos' a Man" is not only the story of a 17-year-old boy, who wants to be independent from his parents, but one who recognizes how powerless are the black men who toil in the fields with him. The conflict is between David's dreams of a fully empowered adulthood and the sharecropper reality that threatens to envelope him. While Wright's short story opens with David walking home in the evening already fixed on the idea that getting a gun is the only way he could show the physically bigger fieldhands that he isn't scared of them, screenwriter Leslie Lee's teleplay opens with David behind a wooden plow, ineptly scratching the dry earth as the mule Jenny jerks him along. Two older fieldhands berate him for not doing the job right and making their jobs worse. David feels nothing but contempt for these uneducated fieldhands, who will never rise above such menial work. To be ridiculed by them means that he is even more powerless than they are. Owning a gun would change all that.

The three essential complications that are not mentioned in the synopsis, but create dramatic highpoints on the screen, involve David's lying: first to his mother, next to Mr. Hawkins, the landowner, then to his father. In the first case, David's mother gives him the money to buy the handgun only after she's convinced that it would be a good idea for her husband to have one. She instructs David to buy the gun and then bring it to her. We see David the next evening giving the storeowner $2 for the used pistol and follow him as he carries the weapon home, holding it up as if to fire it at every bend in the road. The scene shifts to David asleep in his room late that night. His mother quietly tries to wake him—to retrieve the gun. David tells her he's hidden it in the yard and will give it to her in the morning. She leaves. David lifts his pillow. We see the gun. The effect is ominous: heightened suspense and foreboding about an accident that is waiting to happen. Predictably, it does. Next morning when David hitches up Jenny, takes her out to the field, pulls out the gun, and kills her with a wild shot.

The audience's sense of dread is activated yet again when David makes up a story to explain Jenny's death. As the two old fieldhands bury Jenny, Mr. Hawkins has David repeat the story before his parents and a crowd of onlookers.

> "...She started snortin n kickin her heels. Ah tried to hol her, but she pulled erway, rearin n goin in. Then when the point of the plow was stickin up in the air, she swung erroun n twisted herself back on it.... She stuck herself n started t bleed. N fo Ah could do anything, she wuz dead."

David's mother bursts the fiction with a simple question: "David, whut yuh do wid the gun?" When the crowd hears the truth, they begin to laugh. David is humiliated, and Mr. Hawkins passes judgment. David will have to work off the $50 debt for the dead mule.

The audience's sense of foreboding is activated for the final time (actually in the continuation of the same scene) when David's father asks him what he did with the gun. David says he threw it in the creek. His father orders him to retrieve it the next morning and return it to the store. But something is amiss. We watched the shooting, but never saw David relinquish the gun. From what we have witnessed we can only conclude that David is lying. We develop our first inkling that David's desire for adult power far outweighs whatever remorse he may feel about foolishly killing Jenny. Thus, we are scarcely surprised to see him rise early the next morning, recover the gun where he buried it, and test it once more. This time he masters the weapon. We hear the train whistle for the third time, beckoning a young man who has acquired his first taste of power. David runs to the tracks, chases down the train, and jumps aboard.

In structural terms, then, we might summarize the adaptation in terms of six essential scenes. The first one—showing David cursing the mule and (under his breath) the fieldhands who scold him for doing a poor job of plowing the field—reveals the conflict. Four more scenes—David's lying to his mother about hiding the gun, accidentally shooting Jenny, lying about how Jenny died, and lying about what he did with the gun—provide the succeeding complications. Together they prepare us for the climax and resolution in the final scene: David's hopping the train on his way to a new life.

PROBLEM STORIES

Not every short story, however, is amenable to adaptation. A good example is the film adaptation of Shirley Jackson's "The Lottery," which has been screened, it seems, in almost every high school English class in America. When the story first appeared in print, in the June 26, 1948, issue of the *New Yorker*, this troubling tale describing in meticulous detail how the residents of a small New England village drew lots each spring to select one among them to be killed, provoked an intense, emotional reaction from the magazine's readership. The shock ending—the townspeople gathering around wife and mother Tessie Hutchinson to stone her to death—hit a raw nerve among a public only three years removed from the horrors of World War II.

As the furor abated, other artists from other media were drawn to this provocative essay on human evil. The story was adapted as a radio show, a one-act play, a television drama, an opera, and even a ballet. Thus, not surprisingly, in 1969, when almost all Americans had become perplexed and frustrated by the eruption of violence in their own society, *Encyclopaedia Britannica* released an educational film meant to be a faithful adaptation of the original story. The nine-page story translated into a 17-minute film. But, it is my opinion that the film only works in conjunction with the story. That is, the cinematic version intrigues the audience only to the extent that they're interested in how the film is going to portray the story's shock ending. What will it look like to see the townspeople stone Tessie Hutchinson? How will the director maintain decorum in a film produced for a schoolroom audience?

The screenwriter faces two immediate structural problems. First, how are we supposed to reveal the conflict that motivates the dramatic action if the purpose of the lottery itself must be hidden from the audience to assure the shock effect of the surprise ending? Second, how is the audience supposed to identify and relate to the central characters in the film? In the case of Tessie Hutchinson, in particular, how are we to develop sympathy for this whining woman whose protestations about the conduct of the lottery are not understandable until the townfolk cast their first stones?

To some extent, of course, these problems are solved by the brevity of the film. Sixteen minutes may not be too long to wait to understand what's going on. But it's evident that without a clear exposition of the conflict at the beginning, a faithful portrayal of the events as they slowly unfold in the print version could result in a tedious series of shots on the screen. Thus, the film version relies on a cinematic trick to enliven the opening segment, a montage of unrelated shots and conversations: quick cuts from children playing in the village square to a pickup truck approaching to two men to two women to a shopkeeper to little girls to men walking toward the square to more boys playing. The action within the frames and the quick transitions from shot to shot are meant to mentally arouse the audience, even if the meaning is unclear. The narrative begins unfolding in earnest only when Mr. Summers, followed by the postmaster Mr. Graves, appears in the village square with the black wooden box from which each head of family will draw a folded piece of paper.

It is interesting to note by comparison that this purely cinematic effect cannot be emulated on the stage. Accordingly, playwright Brainerd Duffield, in his one-act adaptation of "The Lottery," has chosen to dramatize the conflict by inventing a new character, Mr. Summers' sister, Belva. She contests her brother's and the whole town's participation in the annual rite as the first act begins. The device solves both of the structural problems. It makes explicit to the audience the existence of a motivating conflict and it identifies two focal characters worthy of their attention. To do this, however, Duffield must create a major new character—a step that appears to betray Jackson's unadorned text. But it attests to my basic argument that the structure of the original story is one that resists adaptation to the screen.

One last comment based on a critique from another source. Fred Marcus, in his book, *Short Story/Short Film*, presents a much more comprehensive comparison of Larry Yust's film and Shirley Jackson's short story that is well worth reading. Marcus finds the film—despite its fidelity to plot, characters, and dialogue—flawed in regard to its pacing and its tone. One item he finds especially curious is a disclaimer at the beginning of the film, a printed message superimposed across the screen: "The following is fiction." Marcus suggests that the producers included this statement, because they feared the film might otherwise be censored owing to the powerful emotional reactions it could evoke. He is dismayed, nevertheless, because the warning potentially undercuts the apparent reality of the film's images. The audience might fail to suspend its disbelief.

I would counter, however, that the message is unnecessary for those viewers who already know the story. Rather, it serves to influence viewers unfamiliar with the text, warning them that this is no ordinary film. As such, it puts the members of the audience on alert for a sensational or sinister surprise and gives them a reason for paying close attention to the seemingly humdrum events depicted in the first 16 minutes of the film. Just one minute of the film remains when Joe Summers announces, "It's Tessie." It takes yet another half minute until the surprise is detonated as promised. Only then does the audience realize why Tessie and they had reason to fear the impending explosion.

A NOTE ON BROADCAST VIOLENCE

It would be hard to conclude any discussion of "The Lottery" without ultimately confronting the topic of violence in literature and the mass media. Stoning a person to death doesn't usually fall within the norms of everyday activity. But like the adoption of Dr. Guillotine's famous device, in an earlier era and a different place, this method of communal killing was construed in a more favorable light. Stoning had the positive virtue of alleviating the guilt of any single person who must act as executioner when, in fact, society as a whole has decided to take a human life. Thus, our shock at the ending of "The Lottery" may stem from our unfamiliarity with the form as well as the fact of the killing.

By contrast, it is intriguing to note that we have accepted without notable distress other forms of violence in at least two adaptations we have discussed. How should we respond to David's shooting the mule Jenny in "Almos' a Man?" Or don't animals count? And what about "The Blue Hotel?" Is violence so natural a component of the western genre that we should overlook the grueling fistfight between Johnny and the Swede and the stabbing death that follows? What responsibility does the broadcast writer have to censor violence on the screen? What responsibility does society have to censor the broadcast writer?

Freedom of speech is such an inviolate concept in our society that we always grow edgy when anyone raises the possibility of government interference in broadcast programming. As a result, the policy debate that has raged on and off for the past three decades has always placed a double burden on those who assert that violence on television promotes antisocial behavior. First, they must demonstrate a causal link. Second, they must show that the social impact is deleterious enough that censorship is warranted. It would be a mistake to think that the television industry always puts profits above public interest. Every network has a standards and practices department that censors objectionable programming material, including excessive violence. But the industry's strategy has been to deny the causal link—often advancing a possible cathartic impact as a positive effect of viewing violence—so the second question, which carries with it the implicit threat of government interference, need never arise.

Quite simply, as the evidence for a causal link has accumulated, the industry position has become less and less tenable. Long-term studies of children's media habits and peer ratings have confirmed the positive relationship between heavy television viewing and aggressive behavior, while laboratory experiments have demonstrated the mechanisms by which viewing and violence are linked. The most obvious mechanism is social modeling. Viewers witness a behavior on television that appears appropriate to situations and environments in which they later find themselves. For children, at least, an important variable is whether the behavior is rewarded or punished in the televised portrayal. Rewards or lack of punishment can make the behavior appear justified or simply acceptable. Another key is whether viewers ultimately find themselves in circumstances that facilitate the modeled behavior. As you might imagine, the mechanisms of social modeling can be exploited to promote prosocial as well as antisocial behavior.

Another less obvious mechanism is excitation-transfer. Viewing exciting fare on television can energize the body or the mind physiologically. Though a relatively short-term effect, once aroused, individuals may exhibit their excess energy by engaging more enthusiastically in their next activity. It may well be that writers exploit precisely this physiological mechanism in constructing a plot. Plot complications, though uniformly negative, still heighten the audience's arousal, thereby making the drama's climax and resolution all the more emotional when it finally occurs. Depending on the amount of excitement generated by the complications, tragedies appear more dreadful and happy endings more joyful.

An especially instructive experiment in the research literature on television and violence was devised by mass communication researcher Dolf Zillmann in the early 1970s. Zillmann divided his university student participants into three groups. One group saw a violent aggressive film, a second saw an erotic but nonviolent film, and the third saw a nonviolent and nonerotic nature documentary. Immediately afterward the viewers were put into circumstances that they thought constituted another experiment. They were to mete out punishments to a person who had just verbally provoked them.

The results of the experiment showed that the male students who saw the violent film exhibited more aggressive behavior than those who saw the nature documentary. But, surprisingly, those who saw the erotic film registered the most aggressive behavior of all three groups. Apparently, the sexual content had been more stimulating than the violent content, and thus the participants who saw the erotic film carried more residual arousal into their next activity. Interestingly, the fact that sexual material is as effective at generating audience arousal as violence has led some public policy experts to conclude that any effort to reduce violence on television will probably be compensated by an increase in erotic content. I will leave it to you to identify current examples of this phenomenon in prime-time programming.

Similarly, I will leave it to you to decide what levels of violence (and sexual activity) are appropriate in your scripts. But clearly there are choices to be made. About the time I began writing this book, I began reflecting on why the film adaptations I had been showing my class that year included so many key violent scenes. In addition, to *The Blue Hotel*, *Almos' a Man*, and *The Lottery*, I had screened an adaptation of Flannery O'Connor's short story, "The Displaced Person." It too included a violent climax as the workers on a Southern farm conspire to kill a Polish immigrant who threatened their jobs. He is smashed under the wheels of a tractor. When the students realized what was about to occur, many looked away from the screen.

The one exception was a film adaptation of Doris Betts' "The Ugliest Pilgrim." Entitled *Violet*, this short dramatic film had won an Academy Award. Violet was a young woman from the mountains of North Carolina whose face was disfigured by a scar from a flying axe head or exploding carburetor, depending on whether you read the story or saw the film. She was the follower of a television evangelist whose mammoth church was headquartered in Oklahoma.

The film begins as Violet embarks on a pilgrimage by bus, hoping that the faith healer can erase the scar from her cheek. On the bus, she meets two soldiers returning to camp in Arkansas. One seems to fall in love with her and asks her to come with him. But Violet will not be deterred from her destination. The soldier swears that he will be there to meet her at the bus station when Violet passes through on her return trip.

Violet travels overnight to Oklahoma, but meets only disappointment. The church is impersonal, the television preacher is gone. She speaks instead with a handsome assistant who tells her that she must live with her disfigurement. Violet rejects his counsel, matching his quotes from Scripture verse for verse. By virtue of his authority, however, the young pastor prevails. Defeated, Violet boards the bus determined to return directly home. Still scarred, she barely summons up enough courage to look out the window at the bus station where the soldier said he would wait for her. Not seeing him, though, she feels safe to disembark for the rest stop. Suddenly, he appears. Violet tries to run away and reboard the bus. But then, "Praise God!" he catches her.

This is clearly a gentle story. A chase, but no violence. We see Violet once dressed in a full slip sitting up in her hotel room bed, but there's no sexual activity on screen. The adaptation like all the others includes a conflict, complications, and a climax, but in this case the resolution is achieved, not through violence, but through personal growth. The main character changes and matures before our eyes. Thus, while some stories with immutable characters like the Swede and Johnny in "The Blue Hotel" move inexorably toward a violent clash, others involve us so closely in the development and growth of a character that our emotions are fully engaged as we personally empathize with each defeat and victory.

A test case for further discussion might be the portrayal of David in *Almos' a Man*. No screenwriter reading Richard Wright's story could possibly overlook the cinematic opportunities that arise when David accidentally shoots Mr. Hawkins' mule. Indeed, the most durable images of the teleplay may be the tragicomic shots in which we watch David chasing the fatally wounded Jenny across the clay-hardened field and then share his anguish when he discovers the bullet hole and tries to stop the oozing blood with handfuls of dirt. And yet the structure of the story does not absolutely demand this scene. We could see David fire the gun and then dissolve to the two old fieldhands burying Jenny while David tells his made-up story. Certainly an emotional moment would be lost. But it would be only one of many if the screenwriter has succeeded in totally involving us in David's struggle for adulthood.

SCRIPTWRITING ASSIGNMENT

Prepare a master scene script based on the short story treatment you have already written. Write the entire teleplay from opening FADE IN: to closing FADE OUT. While the prospect of writing an entire teleplay may be initially overwhelming, once you write a substantial portion of the script you will find yourself eager to complete it. As a rule, each page of the script should translate into approximately a minute of screen time. The script for a 15-minute teleplay should run approximately 15 pages.

Use the script segment from the adaptation of "The Last Leaf" as a guide for master scene format. The explanations in the text should help you lay out elements of the script on the page. Consult additional references if specific questions arise. First check the screenwriting texts by Bronfeld or Rubinstein and Maloney (noted at the end of Chapter 9) for appropriate examples. If you still have a problem, consult the format guide compiled by Cole and Haag listed as an additional reading at the end of this chapter.

ADDITIONAL READINGS

Almos' a Man, directed by Stan Lathan (Learning in Focus, 1976) is adapted from "The Man Who Was Almost a Man" in *Eight Men* by Richard Wright (Thunder's Mouth Press, New York, 1988). The film is now distributed by Monterey Home Video.

The Complete Guide to Standard Script Formats: Part I, The Screenplay by Hillis R. Cole, Jr. and Judith H. Haag. (CMC Publishing, North Hollywood, CA, 1988). This is for future reference. If you're serious about writing screenplays, you'll buy a format guide like this one and keep it next to your word processor or typewriter.

Adventures in the Screen Trade: A Personal View of Hollywood and Screenwriting by William Goldman (Warner Books, New York, 1983). Aside from the anecdotes about Hollywood stars and directors, there's an interesting section in which Goldman presents a short screenplay he's adapted from an early short story of his, "The Haircut." Goldman includes five critiques of the script from various Hollywood colleagues who work in the movie business, including director George Roy Hill, who proves that no one is immune to criticism. There's also a very good half-hour interview of Goldman, with clips from the films he wrote, as part of the series *Word Into Image: Writers on Screenwriting*, produced by Freida Lee Mock (American Film Foundation, 1981).

The Lottery, directed by Larry Yust (Encyclopaedia Britannica Educational Corp., Chicago, 1970) is adapted, of course, from "The Lottery" by Shirley Jackson (Popular Library, New York, 1949). An interesting contrast is an adaptation for the stage by Brainerd Duffield in *American One-Act Plays*, edited by Paul Kozelka (Pocket Books, New York, 1961).

Milestones in Mass Communication Research: Media Effects by Shearon Lowery and Melvin L. DeFleur (Longman, New York, 1988). Lowery and DeFleur provide a good overview in the final chapters on the controversy over media violence, which involves communication researchers, network television executives, federal agencies, and ad hoc governmental commissions.

Short Story/Short Film by Fred Marcus (Prentice Hall, Englewood Cliffs, NJ, 1977). Aside from *The Lottery*, Marcus provides critical assessments of 14 other short films (30 minutes or less) that have been adapted from famous short stories.

Violet, directed by Shelley Levinson (American Film Institute, Los Angeles, 1983) is adapted from "The Ugliest Pilgrim" in *Beasts of the Southern Wild and Other Stories* by Doris Betts (Harper & Row, New York, 1973).

Writing for Story by Jon Franklin (Atheneum, New York, 1986). Franklin's approach to analyzing the dramatic elements in nonfiction stories is both feasible and fascinating.

11

Epilogue

In the foreword to his booklength critique of television culture, *Amusing Ourselves to Death*, communication theorist Neil Postman contrasts the twin nightmares of George Orwell's *1984* and Aldous Huxley's *Brave New World*. Of the two visions for a totalitarian society, Postman argues that Orwell's vision of Big Brother controlling a future society is the less probable scenario. Rather, says Postman, western society is moving down the path Huxley predicted. People are controlled not by inflicting pain but by inflicting pleasure. Human preoccupation with sensory stimulation and pleasurable feelings is trivializing human culture.

Postman's particular focus is the role that television plays in the unfolding of this "brave new world." Television is portrayed as diabolically suited to providing the pleasurable, but trivial environments of which Huxley warned. According to Postman, as humans cozy up to the pastel colors of the phosphorescent screen, they lose the desire to process information at the depth that traditional print media demand. Without conscious effort, society may well yield to the superficial pleasures of picture watching, in short, become addicted to this effortless way of "knowing" and "experiencing" the world.

Yet, ironically, this ability to effortlessly know and experience the world has had some surprising repercussions on Big Brother as of late. Americans and West Europeans have watched with astonishment as the totalitarian governments of Eastern Europe self-destructed under public pressure. But, as remarkable as those glimpses of a reformed Eastern Europe have been to us, what we must accept as even more remarkable is the impact that video portrayals of the West and its material wealth must have had on the East Europeans themselves. Video representations of the West permitted East Europeans to effortlessly transcend their borders. In the end, pictures of a "better" society demolished what westerners came to believe was an implacable Leninist-Stalinist social order.

In the face of such a positive social result, can Postman possibly argue that television is all bad? Is this liberating spirit it has helped unleash in Eastern Europe just an interlude? Will television culture, inevitably, lead to a zombie-like civilization, with humans, West and East, meeting their pleasures with pictures from the tube? Probably not. But Postman does raise a serious problem that every liberally educated person must confront: What are the social consequences of a technology that can offer pleasure without mandating some form of physical or mental effort in return?

To Huxley it was obvious that human technology would one day be able to simulate intense pleasure with a physically-benign drug for the brain. In his novel, which takes place in the sixth or seventh century A.F. (After Ford), he called this drug *soma*. Postman argues that slickly produced video programming, among other artificial environments, is leading us down a similar path, creating pleasure through simulated experience, generating emotion, but not intelligence. Hence, the title of his book, *Amusing Ourselves to Death*.

On this score, the broadcast writer has a responsibility to study more fully the process of communication and the consumers of mass media programming to understand their motivations for tuning in. That, of course, has been a goal of this book: to give insights into the process of communication and consider the needs of the audience as we discuss the creation of nonfiction and fiction scripts. If you have learned your lessons well, you have probably developed an intuitive idea of how communication works in the area of broadcast programming. To respond to Postman's concerns, it is well worth our time to better articulate a theory of broadcast communication that faces up to his charges of television as a social threat.

Many theorists have developed models of human communication, but it is the nature of a model to simplify a complex process, so every model is incomplete. Very often the best we can do is to adapt a promising model that focuses on dimensions of the communication process that most centrally concern us. In Chapter 1, I introduced information theory, because it provided many insights into the symbolic nature of language and the mental bond that exists between writers and their audiences. By this point, it should be clear that shared experiences between the source and the destination are key factors in the successful use of not only speech but voice tones, music, sound effects, sketches, photographs, moving pictures, animation, and human gestures as signaling devices in a communication system.

As a starting point, then, we must acknowledge that broadcast communication operates on multiple levels. Between the transmitter and receiver we usually assume the existence of no more than two physical channels: audio and video. But at the destination, those signals may be further divided. The human brain may, in fact, process visual objects apart from visual movement, music and voice tones apart from verbal information, and linguistic structure apart from semantic meaning. The exact distinctions are still part guesswork and the subject of intense research and debate. But even so, we must assume that the brain simultaneously processes sensory inputs at multiple levels, producing a coherent picture, meaning, or emotion only at the nexus we refer to as consciousness.

What this model of information processing does not explain, however, is why we engage in such mental activities as reading, listening, or viewing. Why can the creators of programming anticipate the attention of mass audiences? In short, what motivates the audience?

Personality theorist Abraham Maslow has outlined a hierarchy of human needs that has gained wide acceptance as a model of human motivation. At the base of his pyramid are fundamental physiological needs such as food, shelter, and safety. At the next level are affiliation needs such as love, affection, and belonging. They are followed in turn by esteem needs such as self-respect, self-confidence, trust, and recognition. Finally, this pyramid is crowned with what Maslow labels self-actualization needs, the individual's desire to participate in creative endeavors and enriching experiences.

Not surprisingly, given the broad range of messages the mass media carry and the variety of social situations in which we respond to those messages, people's motives for paying attention would seem to cut across the entire range of Maslow's hierarchy. And yet, Maslow, in his focus on individual personality, may have overlooked a motive that is seemingly trivial but profoundly important in human information processing: the brain's physiological need for novel and exciting sensory inputs, in a word, its need for stimulation. We could make an argument that those stimulation needs do, in fact, represent a material counterpart to Maslow's spiritual notion of self-actualization, but it is not clear that Maslow would accept such a connection.

Nevertheless, starting in the 1950s, experimental psychologists began accumulating evidence from both animal and human studies in support of an exploratory-curiosity-manipulatory drive. The distinguished Canadian psychologist Donald Hebb was especially impressed by experimental studies of electrical impulses in the brains of cats that revealed the existence of what's known as the reticular activation system. In layman's language, psychologists had classically conceived of the brain as something like a giant switchboard. The brain routed sensory inputs to the appropriate portion of the cerebral cortex, where signals were generated to guide the correct behavioral response.

It turned out in the laboratory, however, that this single pathway was not sufficient to activate a response. All sensory signals had to be routed simultaneously through a diffuse portion of the brain stem known as the reticular formation to keep the entire brain energized. If experimenters stimulated the cortex with sensory inputs, but cut the pathways to the reticular activation system, then their laboratory animals would exhibit brain wave patterns characteristic of deep sleep. To Hebb and others came the realization that sensory inputs are required not only to guide behavior but to keep the mind wakeful, alert, responsive and vigilant. Neuroscientists have since established that there are a variety of such activation systems in the brain.

Hebb's personal realization of this phenomenon was reinforced after a series of sensory deprivation experiments in the early 1950s involving college students. The students were invited to participate in a study during spring break in which they would be paid $20 a day plus room and board "to do nothing, see nothing, hear or touch very little, for 24 hours a day." That $20 would be equivalent to $100 today. Despite the high pay, the students became increasingly unhappy. Few could endure more than two or three days. Cloistered in windowless, white rooms, wearing white gowns, lying on soft white mattresses, they developed a need for stimulation of almost any kind. The students made repeated requests for the experimenters to play recordings of nursery rhymes and old stock market reports. They looked forward to periodic testing, but paradoxically they found the tests fatiguing and performed poorly when confronted with problem-solving tasks. Their brains couldn't work when cut off from sensory stimulation. The result was desolation.

Soon after Hebb summed up his thoughts on arousal and the need for sensory stimulation by providing examples from everyday life, a life, incidentally, in which print media held more sway than television:

> When you stop to think of it, it is nothing short of extraordinary what trouble people will go to in order to get into more trouble at the bridge table, or on the golf course; and the fascination of the murder story, or thriller, and the newspaper accounts of real-life adventure or tragedy is no less extraordinary. This taste for excitement *must* not be forgotten when we are dealing with human motivation. It appears that, up to a point, threat and puzzle have a positive motivating value, beyond that point negative value.

Like the Greeks, Hebb realized that all good things come in moderation. Sensory stimulation increased mental alertness, interest, and positive emotion only up to a point. Sensory overload could cause uncertainty, anxiety, and emotional disturbance that humans would most certainly avoid.

Intuitively, we recognize that in many spheres of human activity there exists an indefinite crossover point from pleasurable surprise to stark panic. Broadcast programming, because it is a guest in the living room, rarely generates panic, but after 60 years of practice, first the radio industry and then television has become expert in maximizing surprise in order to win our attention. That, it seems to me is the crucial turning point in deciding if radio and television are to make positive social contributions. If program content becomes secondary to exploiting the audience's need for stimulation, then, as

Postman argues, those who continue to watch or listen may well end up brain dead.

    This book was written, however, with a much more optimistic outlook: that by examining the techniques of broadcast writing as we learn them, we are less likely as consumers to be impressed by sensational talk and superficial images. In addition, we are prepared to expend the mental effort necessary to question current production and demand broadcast programming as extraordinary as the technology that communicates it.

Credits

Figure on page 4 adapted with permission from *The Mathematical Theory of Communication* by Claude Shannon and Warren Weaver, University of Illinois Press. Copyright © 1949 by the Board of Trustees of the University of Illinois.

"Fairy Tale Case Book" on pages 5–6 courtesy of Glenn Mitchell.

Excerpt on page 9 from Edward R Murrow's radio report from Buchenwald courtesy of Edward R Murrow, *In Search of Light: The Broadcasts of Edward R Murrow 1938–1961*, © Alfred A. Knopf, Inc.

Excerpt on pages 10–11 from *The Elements of Style*, Third Edition, by William Strunk and E.B. White. Copyright © 1979 by Macmillan Publishing Company. Reprinted with permission of Macmillan Company, Inc.

Speech on pages 14–15 courtesy of Gary Mauney.

Speech on page 15 courtesy of Charles Kurault.

"Harvey" radio commercial on pages 24–25 courtesy of Elliott-Goulding-Greybar Productions, Inc.

"Hunger" radio story on pages 27, 91, and 92 courtesy of David Venable.

David Price political spot script on page 30 and freeze frames on pages 129–131 courtesy of Saul Shorr & Associates, Inc.

"Bulimia" radio PSA on page 47 courtesy of Sudi J. Dannenberg.

"Register," "Quick," and "Star Trek II" scripts on pages 50 and 55–56 courtesy of the U.S. Selective Service System, Washington, D.C.

"Slapstick" PSA script on page 52 courtesy of the Will Rogers Institute, White Plains, New York.

"Poverty" PSA script courtesy of the United States Catholic Conference, Washington, D.C.

"Message Development Guidelines" on page 56 reprinted from *Making PSAs Work: A Handbook for Health Communication Professionals* by the National Institutes of Health. Courtesy of the Office of Cancer Communications, National Cancer Institute.

Credits

Interview on pages 66–68 © 1988 "All Things Considered," October 19, 1988. Used with permission of National Public Radio.

James Challenger interview on pages 71–72 and 74–75 copyright © August 6, 1984, U.S. News & World Report. Used with permission.

"News is a Kind of Mystery to Me," lyrics on page 79 from *Nixon in China* courtesy Miss Alice Goodman (librettist) and John Adams (composer). Copyright © 1987 by John Adams. Used by permission of Hendon Music, Inc., Sole agent.

"Hunger" wire story on pages 89–90 courtesy of the Associated Press.

"San Francisco Hi-Rise Fire" story script and freeze frames on pages 102–109 and pages 112–113 courtesy of KRON-TV, San Francisco.

Memorandum of Dave McLean on page 114 courtesy of KRON-TV, San Francisco.

Eisenhower political spot on page 122 courtesy of the Political Commercials Archive at the University of Oklahoma.

Sketch of congressman on page 133 and story board drawings on page 134 courtesy of David Haynes.

"Newhart" script on pages 143–146 courtesy of MTM Enterprises, Inc.

Quotations on page 152 from *The Act of Creation* by Arthur Koestler; Copyright © 1964 by Arthur Koestler.

Excerpts on pages 161 and 170 from Stephen Crane's "The Blue Hotel" reprinted from *The Works of Stephen Crane, Volume X*, edited by Wilson Follet (New York: Alred A. Knopf, 1963).

Dialogue on pages 161–162 from James Agee's screenplay of "The Blue Hotel" is reprinted from *Agee on Film*, Volume II, © 1960, 1988 by the James Agee Trust. Reprinted with permission of Grosset & Dunlap.

Quotation on page 163 reprinted from *Strategic Advertizing Campaigns* by Don E. Schultz and Dennis G. Martin, (Crain Books, 1979).

Treatment and script excerpt from "The Last Leaf" on pages 164–168 and 175–178 courtesy of James Bolen.

Excerpt on page 181 from "The Stockbroker's Clerk" by Sir Arthur Conan Doyle reprinted from *The Illustrated Sherlock Holmes Treasury*, Copyright © 1984 by Crown Publishers, Inc. Used with permission.

Radio drama script on pages 181–182 of "The Stockbroker's Clerk" courtesy of Michael Hardwick and the British Broadcasting Corporation.

Quotation on page 184 from Richard Wright's "The Man Who Was Almost a Man" reprinted from the book *Eight Men* by Richard Wright. Copyright © 1940, 1961 by Richard Wright, Copyright © 1987 by the Estate of Richard Wright.

Index

A

ABC, 155
Abelson, Robert, 80
Abstract language, 12
Academy Awards, 155, 189
Active voice, 11–12
Actualities (recorded responses), 63, 64, 65, 68, 69, 70, 71, 118
Adams, John, 79
Advertising. *See* Commercials
Agee, James, 161, 171
Agnew, Spiro, 125
Ailes, Roger, 121, 126
"All in the Family", 139, 141, 151
"All Things Considered," 66, 69
Almos' a Man (Lathan), 183–85, 187, 188, 189
Amusing Ourselves to Death (Postman), 193–94
Anchors, news, 19–21, 28, 31–32, 83, 110–11, 113
AP (Associated Press), 83, 89, 94
Apollonius, 52

"Archie's Place," 141
Aristotle, 119
Armstrong, Louis, 13
Audience
  broadcast professionals as, 19
  knowledge shared by, 5–6, 9
  motivation of, 195
  new information presented to, 10
  physiological arousal of, 188
  and radio format, 48
  spontaneity appreciated by, 77
  targeted by commercials, 44
  targeted by public service announcements, 46–49
Audio, *See also* Sound
  coordinated with video, 99–110, 113
  inputs, 21, 28
  mixing, 21, 28, 31, 45
  sources, 21, 25, 27, 31, 34
Audiotape
  cartridges, 21, 27
  cassettes, 21, 27, 48, 116
  editing of, 63, 65, 78, 100, 118
  transcription from, 71

B

Baker, Howard, 83, 85
Ball, Lucille, 51, 139
Barnard, Doug, 29, 31, 132
Bates, Stephen, 125, 126, 127
BBC, 181
Betts, Doris, 189
"The Blue Hotel" (Crane), 157–63, 169–70, 187
Bolen, James, 164
Boorstin, Daniel, 76
Bradbury, Ray, 163
Brave New World (Huxley), 193
Bremmer, Arthur, 96
B-roll, 101, 111, 117, 119
Bronfeld, Stewart, 141, 142, 190
Bush, George, 83, 97, 121, 125, 126–27

C

Cable television, 3
The Caine Mutiny (Wouk), 155
Cameras, *See also* Shots
  in interviews, 65
  and master scene format, 174
  movements of, 135, 161, 174
  remote, 28
  and storyboard instructions, 135–36
  surveillance, 96, 99
  in television news, 28
  and three-camera format, 28, 34–35, 39, 153, 174
Carson, Johnny, 62
Cartridges, audio, 21, 27
CBS, 14, 94, 96
Censorship, 187
Chancellor, John, 83
Characterization
  in drama, 140, 147, 156
  in screen adaptations, 156–57, 162
  in situation comedies, 140, 141, 142, 147
Charly, 173
"Cheers," 141
Chromakey shots, 31, 120
Cinema. *See* Film
Close-up shots, 29, 31, 65, 100, 101, 135

Cloze procedure, 9, 17
Codes, in communication systems, 4, 7–10, 11, 43
Comedy, *see also* Situation comedies
  and equivocation, 8–9
  and parodies, 54
  psychology of, 150
  in public service announcements, 54, 56
  radio, 45
  and satire, 6, 140
Commercials, *See also* Persuasion; Propaganda
  effectiveness of, 42
  and live TV format, 28–31
  and memory traces, 43–44
  music in, 44
  persuasive strategies of, 43–44
  political, 28–31
  psychology of, 42–43
  radio, 3, 45
  and script formats, 26, 28–31
  slice-of-life, 52
  and sound effects, 45
  and target audience, 44
  and testimonials, 51, 63
  and time measurement, 43
  unique selling propositions in, 122–23
  and visual reinforcement of claims, 123
Communication systems
  channels of, 4–5, 8, 195
  codes in, 4, 7–10, 11, 43
  destinations in, 4–5, 7, 8, 9, 194, 195
  and development of mass media, 2
  equivocation in, 8–9
  information content in, 7–8
  messages in, 4–5, 7–9, 11, 17, 43, 124
  multiple levels of operation in, 195
  noise in, 4, 5, 8
  predictability in, 7–10, 17
  redundancy in, 8–9, 11, 17
  Shannon's theory of, 4–8, 124
  shared experience as key factor in, 194
  signals in, 4–5, 7–9, 11, 43, 124, 194
Compact discs, 21
Computers, 11, 28, 29, 80, 81
Concrete language, 12

Conditions of work, 35, 153, 174
Conflict, dramatic, 141–42, 156, 162, 183, 185–86
Conrad, Joseph, 163
Control rooms, 21, 28
Conversational style, 13, 86, 149
"The Cosby Show," 139, 140, 142, 152
Crane, Stephen, 157, 160, 161, 162, 163, 171
Credibility
  of news reporting, 85, 86, 98
  of political commercials, 128
Cremer, Charles F. 120
Culture
  impact of television on, 193–94
  and information theory, 17
cummings, e. e., 10

D

Democracy, 41, 76, 124
Design, compositional, 11, 73, 76
Destination, in communication systems, 4–5, 7, 8, 9, 194, 195
Dialogue
  in master scene scripts, 175, 176, 181–82
  in radio drama, 26
  in screen adaptations, 160–61
  and script formats, 26, 35
  in situation comedies, 35, 149, 174
Diamond, Edwin, 125, 126, 127
Directors
  of political commercials, 29
  and script formats, 21, 26, 28, 29, 31, 32, 34
  of television drama, 34
  of television news, 19–21, 28, 32, 70
Disc jockeys, 46, 48, 58, 83
Dissolves, 29, 35, 176
Dmytryk, Edward, 155
Documentaries
  compared to news stories, 114–15
  editing of 63, 115–16, 118
  and interviews, 116–19
  and mental scripts, 115
  and motivational psychology, 42
  political commercials as, 128
  producers of, 115
  and public service announcements, 52
  radio, 45, 114, 116–19
  video, 114–16, 119
  writing of, 114, 115, 116–17
Dollying, 135
Donahue, Phil, 61–62, 78
Drama
  characterization in, 140, 147, 156
  conflict in, 142, 156, 162, 183, 185–86
  directors' function in, 34
  and importance of print media, 3
  plot in, 140
  and political commercials, 128
  problem resolution in, 142, 156, 183, 185
  and public service announcements, 52, 54
  radio, 22–26, 54, 78, 174, 181
  and script formats, 22–26, 34
  setting in, 140
  showing versus telling in, 148, 157
  television, 3, 34
Duffield, Brainard, 186, 191

E

Economics, of advertising, 41–42, 58
Editing
  of audiotape, 63, 65, 100, 118
  and condensation of information, 70
  copyediting, 89
  of documentaries, 63, 115–16, 118
  of interviews, 63, 64–65, 70, 73, 77
  and jump cuts, 65, 101, 110
  and master scene format, 174
  and montage, 29, 97, 110, 124, 128, 186
  of videotape, 31, 63, 65, 100, 110–11, 115–16
Eisenhower, Dwight D., 122–23, 126
Electronic news gathering (ENG), 31, 120
Elements of Style (Strunk and White), 10–15
Elliott, Bob, 22
Entropy, 17
Epstein, Edward, 99

Equivocation, 8–9
Eroticism, 188
Establishing shots, 100, 101
Ethics, 57, 98
"Evening Magazine," 62
Exposition, 148

F

Fades, 35, 176
Fairy tales, 5–6
"Father Knows Best," 152
Features, radio, 70–73, 76, 78
Feinstein, Dianne, 126
Feuer, Jane, 141
Fiction, 2–3, 11, 28, 147, 194
Film
  dependent on print media, 2–3, 155–56
  and flow of ideas between media, 3
  and television news, 28
"Flowers for Algernon" (Keyes), 173
Franklin, Jon, 183
Freberg, Stan, 45
Freedom of speech, 187
Freeze frames, 101, 132
Freud, Sigmund, 43, 152
Full screen, 29
Function words, 9–10

G

Gallup, George, 126
Game shows, 3
Given-new contract, 75
Glenn, John, 125
Goldman, William, 173, 174, 182
Goldwater, Barry, 124–25, 127
Goodman, Alice, 79
Goulding, Ray, 22
Graphics, 21, 28, 29, 31, 98, 120. *See also* Storyboards
Greeley, Horace, 76

H

Haag, Judith H., 190
Hailey, Alex, 155
"The Haircut" (Goldman), 190

Hayakawa, S. I., 12
Hebb, Donald, 195–96
Heilbroner, Robert, 41
Hemingway, Ernest, 161
Henry, O., 163, 171
Hill, George Roy, 190
"Hill Street Blues," 141, 153
Hinckley, John, 96
Hitchcock, Alfred, 136
How to Lie with Statistics (Huff), 56–57
Humor. *See* Comedy
Huston, John, 163
Huxley, Aldous, 193, 194

I

"I Love Lucy," 139
Industrial revolution, 41
Information, *see also* Communication systems
  and audiotape editing, 65
  condensation of, 70
  and content words, 10
  fictional versus factual, 81
  and given-new contract, 75
  measurement of, 7–8
  and memory traces, 43–44, 150
  and mental scripts, 80–81, 94
  multiple levels of, 195
  and persuasive strategies, 42, 44
  pictorial, 97–99, 100
  from public relations departments, 71
  and writing for radio, 45
Interference, in communication systems, 5
Intersubjectivity, 69
Interviews
  and actualities (recorded responses), 63
  and documentaries, 116–19
  editing of, 63, 64–65, 70, 73, 77
  and information gathering, 63, 70, 75, 76
  and information selection, 70, 71
  literary, 77
  and news reporting, 62–63, 65–70
  as pseudo-events, 76–77
  radio, 63, 64, 65–70, 71, 72, 73, 116–19

Interviews, *continued*
  scripted feature, 73, 75–76
  spontaneity of, 77
  structure of, 73, 75–76
  and talk shows, 61–62, 77
  techniques of, 68–69, 71, 72–73, 75–76
  television, 61–62, 64, 65
  time measurement of, 68, 69, 72, 77
  and transcripts, 64, 65–69, 71–72, 118
  verbatim, 62, 63, 64, 70–73, 75, 76–77

J

Jackson, Shirley, 185–86, 191
James, Henry, 147
Jamieson, Kathleen, 126
"The Jeffersons," 141
Johnson, Lyndon B., 123–25, 127
Journalism. *See* News reporting
Joyce, James, 10
Jump cuts, 65, 101, 110

K

Kadar, Jan, 159, 171
Kennedy, John F., 124
Kennedy, Robert, 96
Koestler, Arthur, 150, 152
Kome, Hal, 43
Koppel, Ted, 62
Kozelka, Paul, 191
KRON memorandum, 114
Krulwich, Robert, 78
Kuralt, Charles, 14–16

L

"L.A. Law," 141, 142
Language, *See also* Communication systems; Writing
  abstract, 12
  and active/passive voice, 11–12
  and communication process, 4–5, 7–10
  and computers, 80
  concrete, 12
  content words in, 9–10
  function words in, 9–10
  and importance of print media, 1–3
  and mental scripts, 80
  redundancy in, 8–9
  shared experience enabled by, 194
  and syntax, 9–10, 11–12
Lasswell, Harold, 3
"The Last Leaf" (O. Henry), 163, 164–68, 171, 174, 176, 177–80, 190
Lathan, Stan, 190
Leads, news, 83–85, 93
Lee, Leslie, 184
Levinson, Shelley, 191
Linguistics, 6, 8–10, 11–12, 75
Literature
  Pound's definition of, 82
  and print media, 2–3
  and verbatim interviews, 77
Live-TV format, 28–32, 128, 135
"The Lottery" (Jackson), 185–87, 191
The Lottery (Yust), 185–86 191
"Lou Grant," 141, 153

M

McGinnis, Joe, 121
McLuhan, Marshall, 45
"McNeil-Lehrer News Hour," 62
Maloney, Martin, 190
Marcus, Fred, 186
"The Mary Tyler Moore Show," 140, 141, 147, 153
"M*A*S*H," 3, 139, 140, 151
Maslow, Abraham, 195
Mass media. *See* Communication systems; Film; Newspapers; Radio; Television
Master scene scripts
  and camera movements, 174
  character cues in, 175
  and conditions of work, 174
  dialogue in, 175, 176, 181
  and dramatic structure, 182, 185
  and editing, 174
  as intermediate format, 174
  margins in, 175
  scene closes in, 176
  scene headings in, 175
  scene numbering in, 174–75
  showing versus telling in, 174

Master scene scripts, *continued*
  stage directions in, 175
  and treatments, 169, 176
  typing style of, 175–76
"Maude," 141
Melville, Herman, 163
Memory traces, 43–44, 150
Messages, in communication systems, 4–5, 7–9, 11, 17, 43, 124
Microphones, 21, 32, 116
Milk, Harvey, 84
Miniseries, 155
Mitchell, Glenn, 5–6, 13, 54
Moby-Dick (Melville), 163
Montage, 29, 97, 110, 123, 128, 186
Morse code, 8
Moscone, George, 80, 84, 126
The Moviegoer (Percy), 61
Movies. *See* Film
Moyers, Bill, 122, 123, 125
Murrow, Edward R., 9–10, 45
Music, 3, 21
  in commercials, 44
  in public service announcements, 46, 52, 54
  in radio drama, 23, 25

N

National Public Radio, 5, 66, 70, 78, 116
NBC, 83, 94, 99
"Newhart," 140, 142–52
"Bob Newhart Show," 34, 36–38
News from Nowhere (Epstein), 99
Newspapers, 2–3, 11, 20, 71, 76, 85, 86, 95
News reporting
  abnormality as focus of, 82, 83, 84
  anchors in, 19–21, 28, 31–32, 83, 110–11, 113
  and attribution of sources, 85–86
  compared to documentaries, 114–15
  and condensation of information, 70
  conversational style in, 13, 86
  and copyediting, 89
  credibility of, 85, 86, 98
  and directors, 19–21, 28, 32, 70
  and five Ws, 79, 82, 83
  and flow of ideas between media, 3
  and information gathering, 82, 85
  and intersubjectivity, 69
  and interviews, 62–63, 65–70
  and leads, 83–85, 93
  and mental scripts, 80–82, 94, 115
  and narrative description of pictures, 96–98, 100–110, 113, 115
  and objectivity, 62–63, 69, 81
  and pseudo-events, 76–77
  and public relations departments, 71, 76
  radio, 3, 26–27, 83, 85, 93
  and readers, 82–83
  and reporter packages, 110–11, 113
  and reuse of video footage, 110–11
  and sports, 3
  television, 3, 19–21, 28, 31–34, 45, 70, 96–114
  timeliness of, 32, 86
  and time measurement, 70
  typing style in, 87–89
  and weather reports, 3, 95
"Nightline," 62
1984 (Orwell), 193
Nixon in China (Adams), 79
Nixon, Richard, 79, 121, 125
Noise, in communication systems, 4, 5, 8
Nonfiction, 3, 11, 70, 116, 191, 194
Nonprofit organizations, 41, 46, 58

O

Objectivity, in news reporting, 62–63, 69, 81
O'Connor, Flannery, 188
Opinion polls, 126–27
Orwell, George, 16, 193
Outcue (OUT-Q), 32

P

Panoramic shots, 135, 161
Parodies, 54
Passive voice, 11–12
Peirce, Charles, 6
Percy, Walker, 61–62, 69

Persuasion
  effectiveness of, 42
  and ethics, 57
  and memory traces, 43–44
  psychology of, 42–43
  and sleeper effect, 44
  and source credibility, 43–44
  strategies of, 43–44, 46–47, 51
  and testimonials, 51
  use of statistics in, 57
Petrakis, Harry Mark, 159, 162
"Phyllis," 141
Plot
  as conflict, 141–42
  in drama, 140
  and mental scripts, 141
  as problem resolution, 142, 148, 151–52
  showing versus telling, 148
  in situation comedies, 140, 141–42, 147
Political commercials
  and argument spots, 125, 126, 127
  and attack spots, 125, 127
  and Bush's presidential campaign, 125, 126–27
  credibility of, 128
  and deep sell technique, 124
  and documentary format 128
  and dramatization, 128
  and Eisenhower's presidential campaign, 122–23, 126
  and focus groups, 126
  and identification spots, 125–26, 127
  and Johnson's presidential campaign, 123–25, 127
  and live-TV format, 28–31
  and narration of video shots, 132
  and Nixon's presidential campaign, 121, 125
  and opinion polls, 126–27
  and personal-vision spots, 125, 127, 128
  production values in, 123
  script formats in, 28–31, 128
  and slice-of-life format, 128
  and testimonials, 128, 132
  time measurement of, 29
  unique selling propositions in, 122–23

Polls, opinion, 126–27
Postman, Neil, 193–94
Pound, Ezra, 82
Precis, 32
Predictability, in communication systems, 7–10, 17
Price, David, 29, 128–32
Print media, 1–3, 10, 13, 155–56, 193, 196. *See also* Newspapers
Producers
  of documentaries, 115
  and script formats, 21
  of television news, 19–21
Production techniques
  and audio mixing, 21, 28, 31, 45
  and audiotape editing, 63, 65, 78
  and computer-generated graphics, 28, 29, 98
  and montage, 29, 97
  radio, 21, 78
  and situation comedies, 34–35
  television, 28, 34–35, 65, 70
  and three-camera format, 34–35
  and video mixing, 21, 28, 31, 45, 98
  and videotape editing, 31, 63, 65, 100, 110, 115–16
Program directors, 47
Promotion, radio, 46
Pronunciation, 89
Propaganda, 42, 57
Psychology
  of comedy, 150
  and mental scripts, 80–81, 93, 141
  of motivation, 195
  of persuasion, 42–43
  and reactions to televised violence, 187–88
  and sensory stimulation, 195–96
Public relations departments, 71, 76
Public service announcements
  broadcasters' approval of, 46, 47
  and documentary style, 52
  dramatization of, 46, 52, 54
  guidelines for, 51, 54, 56
  humor in, 54, 56
  matched to station format, 48
  music in, 45, 52, 54
  and nonprofit organizations, 46, 58
  persuasive strategies of, 46–47, 51

Public service announcements, *continued*
  and screen adaptations, 156
  and script formats, 48
  slice of life, 52, 56, 63
  and sound effects, 51, 52, 54, 58
  and straight readers, 49, 54
  target audience of, 46–49, 56
  and testimonials, 51, 56
  timeliness of, 48
  time measurement of, 46, 48, 49, 54
Pulitzer prize, 183

Q

Quayle, Dan, 65–70, 73

R

Radio, *see also* Audio
  actualities (recorded responses) in, 63–65, 68, 69, 70, 71, 118
  audience involvement in, 45
  audience linked to format of, 48
  BBC, 181
  comedy, 45
  commercials, 3, 45
  creative possibilities of, 45
  dependent on print media, 2–3
  documentaries, 45, 114, 116–19
  drama, 22–26, 54, 78, 174, 181
  features, 70–73, 76, 78
  and flow of ideas between media, 3
  as hot medium, 45
  interviews, 63, 64, 65–70, 71, 72, 73, 116–19
  National Public Radio, 5, 66, 70, 78, 116
  news, 3, 26–27, 83, 85, 87, 93
  production techniques for, 21, 78
  promotion, 46
  and script formats, 22–27, 87–89, 93
  as source of sensory stimulation, 196
  syndicated features in, 5
  television's impact on programming of, 48
Raiders of the Lost Ark (Spielberg), 142
Reagan, Ronald, 83–85, 96

Redundancy, in communication systems, 8–9, 11, 17
Reel-to-reel tape, 21, 48
Reeves, Rosser, 122–23, 126, 138
Regan, Donald, 84
Repetition, 13
The Responsive Chord (Schwartz), 124, 137
Rhetoric, 41, 119
"Rhoda," 141
Robertson, Cliff, 173
Rorschach test, 124
Rubinstein, Paul Max, 171, 190

S

"St. Elsewhere," 141
Satire, 6, 140
Saussure, Ferdinand de, 6
Schank, Roger, 80
Schwartz, Tony, 123–24, 127
Screen adaptations
  characterization in, 156–57, 162
  conflict in, 156, 162, 183, 185–86
  dialogue in, 160–61
  and dramatic structure, 182, 185
  faithfulness of, 156–57, 160
  and modification of original story, 157, 159–60, 163, 170
  print media as source of, 155–56
  and public service announcements, 156
  setting in, 157, 162
  showing versus telling in, 157, 161
  and synposes, 169, 183–84
  and treatments, 163, 169–70
Script examples, radio
  commercial, 24–25
  interview feature, 74–75
  news, 27, 91, 92
  public service announcements, 47, 50, 52, 53, 55–56
Script examples, television
  news, 33, 112–13
  political commercials, 30
  situation comedy, 36–38
  teleplay, 177–80
  treatment, 164–68

Script formats
  alternate, 35, 39
  and compositional design, 11
  and conditions of work, 35, 153, 174
  and dialogue, 28, 35
  directors' handling of, 21, 26, 28, 29, 31, 32, 34
  line lengths in, 25, 26, 32, 35, 48
  and live television, 28–32, 128, 135
  margins in, 25, 28, 35, 48, 87, 93
  and political commercials, 28–31, 128
  producers' handling of, 21
  and public service announcements, 48
  and radio drama, 22–26
  and radio news, 26–27, 87, 93
  and situation comedies, 34–35
  split-page, 28, 31–34
  tape-live, 35, 39
  and television drama, 34
  and television news, 28, 31, 34
  three-camera, 28, 34–35, 39, 153, 174
  and time measurement, 11, 25, 26, 28, 32, 48
  and typing style, 23, 26, 35, 87–89, 93
Script psychology, 80–82, 94, 115, 141
Segues, 26
The Selling of the President (McGinnis), 121
Semiotics, 6–7, 17
Setting
  in drama, 140
  and master scene format, 174
  in screen adaptations, 157, 162
  in situation comedies, 140–41, 147
Shakespeare, William, 152, 163
Shannon, Claude, 4–8, 11, 124
Short Story/Short Film (Marcus), 186, 191
Shots
  B-roll, 101, 111
  chromakey, 31, 120
  close-up, 29, 31, 65, 100, 101, 135
  cutaway, 65
  Dolly, 135
  establishing, 100, 101
  freeze-frame, 101
  long, 100, 135
  and master scene format, 174
  medium, 135
  panoramic (pan), 135, 161
  in political commercials, 28
  reuse of, 110–11
  stand-up, 110
  talking-head, 64
  in television news, 28, 31, 64
  tilt, 135, 161
  and videotape editing, 65
  wide-angle, 100
  zoom, 100, 135, 161
Signals, in communication systems, 4–5, 7–9, 11, 43, 124, 194
Sirhan, Sirhan, 96
Situation comedies, 3, 34, 139
  arena type, 141
  characterization in, 140, 141, 142, 147
  conflict in, 141–42
  dialogue in, 35, 149, 174
  exposition in, 148
  and mental scripts, 141
  plot in, 140, 141–42, 147
  problem resolution in, 142, 148, 151–52
  setting in, 140–41, 147
  showing versus telling in, 148
  sources of humor in, 150–51
  and three-camera format, 174
Slice-of-life commercials, 52, 128
Slides, 28
Slow motion, 97
Soap operas, 3
Sound, *see also* Audio
  background, 51, 64, 65, 69
  bites, 20, 27, 32, 52, 63, 70, 71, 73, 111, 118, 119
  effects, 21, 23, 25, 32, 45, 51, 52, 54
  on tape (SOT), 31–32, 111
Spelling, 8, 9
Spielberg, Steven, 136, 142
Spinoffs, 141
Sports, 3
The Spot (Diamond and Bates), 125, 137
Spots. *See* Commercials
Station managers, 46, 47, 48

Statistics, 57
Storyboards
 applications of, 136
 camera movements for, 134–36
 graphic design of, 132–34
Strunk, William, 10–15, 76
Supers (superimpositions), 113
Syndication, 3, 5
Syntax, 9–12 *passim*

T

Talking heads, 64
Talk shows, 3, 61–62, 77
"Taxi," 141
Technology
 and development of mass media, 2
 as nexus of communication process, 4, 7
 and stimulation of pleasure, 194
 and transition from film to video, 31
Teleprompters, 29, 31
Television, *see also* Video
 ABC, 155
 cable, 3
 CBS, 14, 94, 96
 and computer-generated graphics, 28, 29, 98
 and coordination of audio and video, 99–100, 113
 cultural consequences of, 193–94
 dependent on print media, 2–3, 155–56
 drama, 3, 34
 and flow of ideas between media, 3
 interviews, 61–62, 64, 65
 live, 28–32, 128
 and narration of video shots, 96–98, 100–110, 113, 115, 132
 NBC, 83, 94, 99
 news, 3, 19–21, 28, 31–34, 45, 70, 96–114
 production techniques for, 28, 34–35, 65, 70
 radio formats affected by, 48
 and reuse of video footage, 110–11
 and script formats, 28–35

 as social benefit, 194, 196, 197
 as social threat, 193–94
 as source of sensory stimulation, 194, 196
Testimonials, 51, 63, 128, 132
Thompson, John, 51
Three-camera format, 28, 34–35, 39, 153, 174
Timeliness
 of news reporting, 32, 86
 of public announcements, 48
Time measurement
 of commercials, 43
 of interviews, 68, 69, 72, 77
 of public service announcements, 46, 48, 49, 54
 and script formats, 11, 25, 26, 29, 32, 48
 of television news, 70
 and time cues, 113
"Today" show, 62
"The Tonight Show," 62
Total running time (TRT), 32, 111
Total story time (TST), 32, 111
Totenberg, Nina, 66–70, 73
Tragedy, 151–52, 157
Transcripts, 64, 65–69, 71–72, 118
Translations, 64
Treatments, 163, 169–70, 176
Twain, Mark, 17

U

"The Ugliest Pilgrim" (Betts), 189, 191
UNIX, 11
UPI (United Press International), 83, 93

V

Video, *see also* Television; Videotape
 coordinated with audio, 99–110, 113
 and freeze frames, 101
 informational value of, 97–99
 inputs, 21, 28
 mixing, 21, 28, 31, 45, 98
 narrative description of, 96–98, 100–110, 113, 115, 132

Video, *continued*
  and reuse of footage, 110–11
  and slow motion, 97
  sources, 23, 28, 29, 34, 98
Videotape, 9
  editing of, 31, 63, 65, 100, 110–11, 115–16
  in political commercials, 29, 31
  with sound on tape (SOT), 31–32
  in television news, 28, 31–32
  with voice-over (VTR/VO), 32, 120
Violence, televised
  and action-adventure series, 147
  aggressiveness caused by, 187
  and excitation-transfer theory, 188
  and social modelling, 187–88
Violet (Levinson), 189, 191
Voice-over, 29, 31, 32, 64, 110–11, 113, 115, 119–20

W

Wallace, George, 96
Wallace, Mike, 96–97
Walters, Barbara, 62
Weather reports, 3, 95
White, Dan, 84, 126
White, E. B., 10, 76
Winfrey, Oprah, 62

Wire services, 83, 89, 93
Wouk, Herman, 155
Wright, Richard, 183, 189
Writer's workbench, 11
Writing, *see also* Communication systems; Language; Script formats
  and active/passive voice, 11–12
  adjusted to conventions, 71
  and compositional design, 11, 73, 76
  concision in, 14–17
  and conversational style, 13
  and creative possibilities of radio, 45
  and documentaries, 114, 115, 116–17
  and importance of print media, 1–3
  and narration of video, 115
  news, 89–93, 113
  nonfiction, 116
  precision in, 17
  Strunk's rules for, 10–17, 76
  and time constraints, 11

Y

Yust, Larry, 186, 191

Z

Zillmann, Dolf, 188
Zoom shots, 100, 135, 161